West of Independence

by

Matthew Deane

Printed in the United States of America

First Edition, 2013

This book is a work of creative nonfiction. I have done my best to recreate events, places, dates, and conversations from my memories of personal experiences. In order to maintain their anonymity I have changed the names of certain individuals. Any inaccuracies are not intentional or malicious. Feel free to write your own book if you think that my memory is in need of correction. -Matthew Deane

matthew.deane@frogsdontweartights.com

www.frogsdontweartights.com

About the author

In 2011, a chapter from Matthew Deane's first book, West Of

Independence, won the Non-Fiction prize in the Seacoast Writers

Association contest. His essays have been published on various

writing websites, as well as on his blog,

www.frogsdontweartights.com. Matthew now lives in the mountain

town of Oakley, Utah with his wife and three children.

For Jared, with thanks to Elizabeth and the kids

And where would this book be without my

New Hampshire Writers Group?

Answer: In poorly written *shards*.

Chapter 1: October 2009

Mom's driving would frighten the devil himself into buckling his seat belt. Her high-speed tailgating, sudden lane changes, Tourettes-like shouting, and uber-sighing combine to create a riding nightmare for anyone unwitting enough to fall passenger-prey to her offer of a ride.

But Mom had been the only person available to run the three of us to the airport in Manchester that morning. When we arrived, I was for once eager to board a plane and hit some turbulence.

By nightfall, my suitcase slid down the silver chute and onto the conveyor belt of the baggage claim in Kansas City. I hoisted the big black bag, and then carried it over to the space behind a row of empty seats. My apprehension mounted as I knelt down and pulled at the zipper. I glanced around before flipping the case open and pushing aside my clothes to check on Jared's remote control truck.

After verifying that it had made the plane trip without any damage, I felt a pressure valve within me give way, venting the worry that had plagued me since packing the truck into my suitcase the night before. I muttered a quiet thanks to no one in particular while putting everything back in place and zipping the case shut.

I sat on the floor and pulled out my cell phone. A few rings later Ella picked up.

"Well, we made it to Kansas City," I said wearily.

"I was wondering when you'd call, I can't believe it took you all day to fly from New Hampshire to Missouri."

"Our flight out of Manchester was delayed, so we missed our connection in Atlanta. We should be watching Free HBO in a crummy hotel outside of Wichita right now," I complained.

"Did your luggage make it to Kansas City with you?" Ella asked, familiar as she was with my travel history.

"Mine did. Connor didn't check any luggage, he only brought that little black backpack," I answered.

"What? That's it? But you guys are going to be on the road for a week!"

"But that's Connor," I replied.

"You'd better hope he brought some deodorant," my wife said with a chuckle.

"I'm nervous," I confessed.

"I know you are..."

"We've hardly said a word to each other all day," I worried.

"Give it time, I'm sure that once you hit the open road things will loosen up," Ella assured me.

"I hope so, but-"

"No buts!" Ella cut me off mid-whine. "This trip is not just about you," she reminded me.

"I know," I said, my voice loaded with doubt.

"Matthew, promise me that you won't force moments on this trip," she demanded softly.

"I promise," I said, injecting a measure of confidence into the reply.

"I love you," Ella said.

"I love you too," I said back.

I hung up and pocketed my phone, then made for the exit, wheeling my suitcase behind me.

I walked through the automatic doors and felt the chill of a mid-west October night on my skin. Connor was outside the baggage claim, leaning against the wall while he smoked a cigarette. The tiny backpack hung lightly on his shoulder. Watching him blow nicotine clouds into the darkness, I wondered what he had packed into that little bag, and if it included a change of clothes. I was sure there were cigarettes, chocolate, and maybe a pair of socks to hide his weed in, but I didn't bother to imagine that he might have also packed toothpaste, or as Ella had hoped for my sake, a stick of deodorant.

As I approached my younger brother I noticed that just beyond him, looking through the half open window of a parked car was Ziggy, his tongue hanging out of his mouth.

But it wasn't really Ziggy. Dead for twenty years and buried under a tree in Mom and Dad's garden, Ziggy had been Jared's dog. Dad had promised my little brother, thirteen years old at the time, that if he won his age group at the state gymnastics meet he could have a puppy. Jared won gold in every event, and held Dad to the promise he'd made. Ziggy was the runt of a wired-haired terrier litter, and Jared's choice on the spot.

"Connor, check it out, it's Ziggy!" I walked over to the car window and smiled at the happy dog, his little nub of a tail wagging with the desire to jump into my arms and play.

"And of course, Jared isn't here to see," Connor muttered before turning away, as if searching for our brother in the small crowd of people passing through the open doors with their luggage in tow.

I shifted my own backpack from one shoulder to the other, and looked around for a rental car shuttle.

A few minutes later the car carrying Ziggy's doppelganger drove away, leaving us at the curb with the memories dredged up by his scruffy, happy face. A tear surprised me, rolling down my cheek. I turned and wiped it away, the cold air stinging my eyes as I did.

"Well, maybe you can tell me what your brother was doing out in Independence, Missouri." My father never really offered a proper greeting when calling; he liked to jump right into the middle of the conversation he had prepared for prior to dialing your number.

"No, I have three brothers. Which one are you talking about?"

"Jared. Your mother was home alone this afternoon and the phone rang. The caller ID just said *Independence*, but she answered it anyway..." Dad paused, probably for effect.

I ignored the effect, too busy marveling at the fact that my parents never failed to mention the shortcomings of caller ID when relating a phone call experience. It was a wonder they answered the phone at all; you'd think that only cities, states, and non-English speakers ever called them.

"Did Jared tell her what he was doing out there?" I was annoyed at having to ask.

"It wasn't Jared that called, it was a nurse..." Another pause.

"What? Is he okay?" I pulled the car around into a u-turn and headed for my parent's house.

"He's still asleep, but they say that he's going to be okay. We don't really know anything more than that. We are waiting for someone from the hospital to call us back with more information. The nurse was just calling all of the numbers in Jared's cell phone, trying to find a family member. What great timing they have out in Missouri, calling when your mother was home alone. She was all worked up by the time I got back."

"I'll be right over," I said.

By the time I got to Mom and Dad's, the nurse had called again, this time with more information. Dad was hanging up the phone as I entered his office, an upstairs bedroom that had been mine almost twenty years before.

"Jared was found unconscious on the floor of a motel room. The nurse said that they had to pump his stomach, because he had taken some sleeping pills after drinking a whole bottle of liquor." Dad offered this information up like unreliable hearsay, an invisible wave of his hand dismissing what it suggested.

"He tried to kill himself..." It wasn't a question, and the words escaped my lips before their implications could be calculated.

"We don't know that," Dad snapped. The words alone were enough to convince me that my father was already in denial, but the tone of his voice when he said them left no room for doubt.

"Sleeping pills and booze? Do the math!" My response was sharp, frustration surging within me.

My father spoke his next words slowly and methodically, while glaring at me the way the emperor's tailor must have looked at the little boy who shouted "Naked!" "He is still sleeping; they haven't been able to talk to him yet, so we don't know what happened."

"Okay, then what now?" I asked, shifting conversational gears from reaction to action. Surely he and Mom would need a ride to the airport that evening.

"We need to wait and see what they find out when he wakes up," Mom said.

I turned to see her standing in the doorway.

"Shouldn't someone go out there?" I asked, straining to keep the disbelief out of my voice.

"I don't think we should jump on a plane until we can talk to him and figure out what's going on. I am worried about his car, or should I say *my* car, since I am a co-signer on the loan. I doubt the motel he was at is very nice, so the car might be stolen, broken in to, towed away, or who knows what else." Dad turned back to his computer, his participation in the conversation over.

"We'll know more when he wakes up," Mom repeated, as if Jared had taken a nap, not a bottle of sleeping pills.

9

My little brother wasn't the only one that needed to wake up.

Chapter 3: October 2009

At the car rental counter, I was greeted with a smiling hello from a young man no more than a year out of college. With him were three more young men, each a carbon copy of the other. I imagined them as members of some bizarre fraternity for car rental agents. Calling themselves the Renta-Renta-Ride house, they shared a large apartment, held keggers on weekends, and were doing their best to hold onto the good old days of campus life.

"I have a reservation for tonight," I said, swallowing my disdain for fraternities and returning the smile. I was feeling good; we would soon be making tracks, so why not spread a little sunshine of my own?

"Okay, if I could just see your license and credit card, we'll get you in a car and on your way. What brings you to Kansas City?" His question seemed harmless enough, and my purpose for being there made for a good story, so I opened up my wallet along with my mouth in a gesture of good will.

"We're finishing a road trip for with our brother. He was driving west to see the Grand Canyon last spring, but ran out of money in Independence and tried to kill himself. We decided we would help him finish the trip, and so here we are. The car has unlimited mileage, right?" I slid my license and credit card across the counter.

"Yes, unlimited mileage, but if you are taking the car across state lines, I need to charge you an additional fee," he said, clicking and clacking away at his keyboard.

My head began to ache.

"Let's see… that will add another hundred and forty-nine dollars. Did you want navigation as well?" The smile had turned, at least in my mind, into a sneer. I felt stupid for having cast my pearls so carelessly before Renta-Renta swine.

"So, just for driving across a line or two on a map, I have to pay another hundred and fifty bucks? That's silly! I don't suppose there is any way you can just forget that I mentioned that we are driving to Arizona? Can't you help out a man on a mission?" I looked him square in the eyes with a pleading smile on my face, searching his soul for signs of empathy and praying that he had a little brother of his own that he loved very much.

"Sorry, there's nothing I can do for you. I have to charge you the fee." His eyes broke away from my desperate gaze.

I hated him.

"Ok, then I want to cancel my reservation, and I don't expect to pay any cancellation fees." I held out my hand as a silent request for my license and credit card. I was done speaking to him.

"Sure, no problem, here's your card and your license," he said with a smirk.

I tucked the credit card and my license into my wallet, and he returned to the vapid company of his fellow Renta-Renta frat boys.

"Here *are*," I muttered, correcting his use of the singular verb when referring to my card and license together.

"Good luck finding another agency that will rent you a car at this time of night, let alone one that won't charge you more," he said over his shoulder.

I turned and walked away, making a mental note to be more guarded about the purpose for our trip in the days to come. The wheels of my suitcase clicked along the tiled floor, sounding to me like the *tisk, tisk* clicking of a tongue.

"What's up?" Connor asked as I approached.

"Idiots! What's up is that they suck. They wanted to charge me another hundred and fifty bucks to leave the state." I looked around the lobby at the other rental agency signs, wondering which of them was my best bet for a good deal and a decent car. I chose the one that had the best color scheme and approached the counter.

This time around, I didn't mention the purpose of our trip, the Grand Canyon, or state lines. I declined navigation, insurance, and the pre-paid fill-up. Within minutes, I had a car key in my hand and was walking away from the counter. I led the way down an escalator and out into the sea of shiny cars in search of our alphanumeric spot, where our little economy chariot awaited. My spirits were higher than they had been several minutes ago; adventure with my brothers lay ahead on the open road. I was so eager to get driving that the sight of our rental, a little black toy car sitting on what looked to be over-inflated bike tires, didn't damper my spirits.

"Well," I said, popping the trunk and dropping my bag inside. "We won't be breaking any speed limits in this thing, will we? I'm glad we scheduled a week for this trip."

"This car's a little gay. We need a rainbow sticker on the bumper to make it complete," Connor said, lighting up another cigarette.

"Yes, a very appropriate chariot, isn't it, Jared?" I shouted happily into the night, the parking lot surrounding us void of life.

I looked over the roof of the car at Connor and said, "By the way, it's a two-hundred and fifty dollar cleaning fee if they find out that anyone smoked in the car, so you'll be paying it if they charge me." My tone was less than threatening. I didn't care about fees and fines and flight delays anymore because we were on our way.

"What the hell is wrong with them?" I wondered aloud, leaning back against the kitchen counter, my arms crossed over my chest.

"I don't know. I gave up trying to understand your parents a long time ago." A buzzer sounded, and Ella opened the oven door to slide a frozen pizza onto the middle rack.

I felt a wave of heat as she closed the door. I flinched as she set the timer, jabbing at the buttons as if they were in the middle of my father's chest.

"They were talking as if Jared were napping upstairs, and that they didn't want to disturb him. I thought Dad was going to jump out of his chair and hit me when I said that he must have tried to kill himself. They are in complete denial. Dad seems more worried about Jared's car being parked too long at a sleazy motel than he is about Jared lying in a hospital bed after having his stomach pumped!" I marveled.

"He's alone," Ella said.

"With no one to hold his hand, to hug him, or kiss him," I noted.

"Or tell him that they love him," Ella added.

"And Dad's worried about the car because he co-signed for it!"

Ella put a hand on my arm and squeezed. I looked up and saw tears in her eyes.

"Matthew, your little brother tried to kill himself! Why aren't your parents on a plane right now?" Her nails bit into my arm. I winced, but didn't move.

Ella released her grip, and I answered her as best as I could. "I don't know. All I know is that they are in total denial, and that they have been for years." I was unable to explain my parent's behavior because I didn't understand it myself.

I turned to get a glass out of the cupboard.

14

Ella tugged at my shoulder, spinning me back around to face her. "Matthew, you know that if this were one of our kids, I would already be there, because I would have left right after the first phone call, even before hearing about the pills."

"I know, I know, and I would be right there with you, believe me," I said, assuring her that the matter was already settled. Should we ever be confronted with such an awful situation there was no question as to our first course of action.

"Our kids have to know that we love them no matter what," she said, wiping her cheeks with the back of her hand.

Not knowing what more to say, I pulled Ella close to me and held her tight. I heard the laughter and squealing of our happy kids playing in the yard outside, and thought of Jared alone in a hospital bed.

Chapter 5: October 2009

"You have arrived," Maggie announced a second time.

"I don't think so, unless the Super Budget Motor Inn is in fact under a bridge! Get it right Maggie, we have driven this same stretch of road three times and there is no motel!"

"Calculating route," Maggie replied, her silicone voice maintaining an even tone.

Before the trip, I had downloaded an update to my GPS device, and it was becoming apparent to me that the update was not an improvement. This was not the trip I had envisioned. Flight delays, frat-boy rental car agents, and a geographically challenged GPS; the bad beginning to our quest was rapidly moving into the bad middle.

"What's the number again?" Connor asked, his gentle tone offering a measure of calm that stilled my sudden madness.

"15014." I slowed the car and scanned both sides of the road ahead, glancing up at the rear view mirror every couple of seconds to make sure no one was following behind us, honking, screaming, and waving middle digits at me for driving less than half the speed limit. Mom would have rammed our little car off the road and carried on her way had she been stuck behind us.

"Is that it?" Connor pointed at a sign set further back from the road than I would have placed it, had I wanted to advertise my motel to passing travelers.

"Super Budget Motor Inn. Yep, this is it. Great way to make your business noticeable," I said as I turned into the nondescript entrance. The crunch of gravel under our tiny tires invited us to the motel.

"Maybe that's the point. I bet most of their guests are not supposed to be here," Connor remarked.

Our headlights lit up the motel's office, a pink stucco cottage complete with blue neon sign advertising a drive-thru window around the side.

"Wow, look at that, you can drive up to the window and pay your bill. Lusty temptation brings them in, convenience keeps them coming back," I said.

We followed the curve of the parking lot to the right, driving past the office as we did. The woman inside looked up at us as we drove by, her face lit by the glow of late night television. We must not have been more captivating than whatever rerun she was watching, however, because she immediately returned to it.

The motel was to our left, just beyond a fenced-in area that turned out to be a pool, its dark cover in place for the coming winter. I turned the wheel and nosed the car forward, coming to a stop just a few feet away from the fence. The headlights shined through it, over the pool and into the motel's courtyard beyond. I left the car running as we surveyed the poorly lit parking lot. The U-shaped building had about fifty rooms, each one visible from our vantage point. Three large pickups, four sedans, and two minivans sat parked in the courtyard lot. Only one vehicle, a sedan, was without a companion; the rest seemed to have paired off. This place was proving to be the real deal, a no-tell-motel that charged by the hour, most of it paid in cash.

"I need a cigarette." Connor dug into his bag and pulled out a fresh pack.

The crackling sound of the cellophane conveyed his desperation. He produced a lighter from his pocket, and I rolled down all the windows. The cold air of Missouri in October filled the car. I turned the heat up as high as it would go. A flick of Connor's thumb brought a flame to life, and I watched my brother light his pleasure stick.

A good Mormon boy, I had never smoked a cigarette in my life. I doubted that it really was as calming to the nerves as movies made it appear to be. Connor had chain-smoked his way through summer, and had never calmed down enough for me to notice.

"Man, I didn't know it was going to be so damn cold already," I complained, rubbing my arms.

I turned around and dug my sweatshirt out of my backpack, pulling it over my head. I didn't want it to smell like cigarettes, but since everything in the car would soon be reeking of nicotine and tar, warmth won out over fresh scent. I settled into my seat and looked at the motel, my eyes moving from one door to the next. I was not sure what to say, so I said nothing.

Connor finished his first cigarette, and then used it to light another.

"So he did try to kill himself?" I asked, standing in Dad's office just as I had twenty-four hours earlier.

"It looks that way." Dad had a knack for admitting the truth, without actually admitting the truth.

"Did you talk to Jared directly?" I asked.

"No, your mother did. He called when I wasn't here."

"What exactly did he say?" I felt like a lawyer handling a hostile witness.

Dad sighed. "He was angry at himself for waking up. Then he cried and said he was sorry that he had done this to us, and that he wants to come home." It was a matter of fact statement.

"They aren't going to release him onto the street are they? He can't be alone, what if he tries again?" My question seemed absurd, but then the conversation itself was absurd. We should have been having it over the phone, with Dad pacing a hospital corridor on the other end of the line.

"No, they are going to send him to the mental health unit as soon as he is physically recovered. They will let us know when it happens."

"So, what next?" I asked, lobbing the question like an underhanded pitch into Dad's strike zone. It hung in mid-air over the plate. All Dad had to do was swing away, telling me that he and Mom were flying out to be with Jared that evening.

"Well, we wait for them to call with more information," he replied.

I could almost hear the bat hit the dirt as the crowd booed. Dad had walked away from an easy home run.

Connor flicked his third cigarette out into the night and cleared his throat. I rolled up the windows but left the heat on.

"I knew what he was going to do, and I didn't try to stop him." Connor held his hands up to the hot air blasting from the dashboard vents.

I held my breath and didn't respond. I knew that any words offered to alleviate his guilt would be of little value to Connor, because the words had meant nothing when spoken to me many times by many friends over the past several months.

"He stopped at my apartment on his way out of town and gave me a bunch of his stuff. He said he wouldn't need it anymore. He told me he was going to see the Grand Canyon, and then he played a song that he had made while messing around on his computer. He called it 'Final Cliff Jump.'"

"I've heard it," I sighed, the meaning behind the title becoming clear to me for the first time.

The song began to play inside my head.

"It starts on a high note and drops down through the scales really fast, like something falling off a cliff in a cartoon," Connor continued. "Jared stood there grinning during that part, pointing at the speakers and nodding his head, like I was supposed to understand what it meant, and then be happy for him."

"Final Cliff Jump" played on in my mind.

"So he never said anything specific about trying to kill himself at the Grand Canyon?" I was careful to keep my tone clear of accusation.

"No, he just kept grinning at me and nodding. I looked away and ignored him, acting as if I didn't get it. He had told me so many times before that he wanted to die, that he was going to kill himself. Back when Brittany and I were getting divorced, I was in a really bad place.

He suggested that we do it together," Connor confessed, reaching for his lighter.

I rolled down the windows once his cigarette was lit. "I knew that he wanted to die," I said. "We talked about it when he started to lose sight in one eye a couple of years ago. He told Ella and me that he hoped it was a brain tumor that would kill him. We didn't take him too seriously, and played along. The three of us started planning our funerals, talking about what we wanted done with our remains. We told him that when we died, we wanted our kids to spend their inheritance on trips around the world, scattering our ashes in faraway places. He loved the idea."

A window in the motel went dark. I thought of my little brother sitting alone on the edge of a tired mattress, the yellow light of the parking lot filtering in through threadbare curtains. A bottle of sleeping pills stood on the nightstand, keeping company with a bottle of cheap liquor. On a little table nearby lay the whole of his life's fortune, sorted into rows of quarters, nickels, and dimes.

I wondered if it had occurred to Jared that his family wouldn't be scattering his ashes around the world with only twenty-four dollars and forty-four cents to cover the cost.

Chapter 8: March 2009

"I am on a plane tonight," Becky declared.

I winced, then covered the receiver with my hand and hoped that my older sister hadn't heard my facial muscles contorting in absolute distress.

"She wants to jump on a plane to Independence tonight," I whispered to Ella.

My wife shook her head in disbelief as she worked the iron over one of my favorite shirts. Steam rose around her like a little cloud of frustration.

I decided I would worry about burn marks later.

I shrugged my shoulders and removed my hand from the receiver. "Let's not jump ahead of Mom and Dad on this; he is their son and they should take the lead." I couldn't believe I was using Mom and Dad's role as parents for an excuse to keep Becky from running to Independence.

While my parents reaction to Jared's attempt at suicide was less than inspiring and provided for me no confidence in their willingness to parent, Mom and Dad were a much safer bet than Becky. Becky was the last person Jared would want to see.

"Matthew, they haven't done a thing other than to wait by the phone for some nurse to call and tell them what is going on out there! I say that if they won't go, we should." In the aftershock of Becky's offer to rush to Jared's side, I had forgotten that I was on a three-way call; our sister Sarah was also on the line.

"I know, but Mom and Dad are in denial," I said.

"No kidding," Sarah scoffed.

"Once the shock wears off, they'll go," I assured my sisters, hoping they would back off and allow Mom and Dad figure it out.

"I just can't stop thinking about Jared. He's alone in that hospital room, sad, scared, and waiting for someone to walk through the door. It should be Mom and Dad, but if they don't go soon, it's going to be us," Becky declared.

"I agree," I said.

"If one of my boys is ever hurt, sick, or heaven forbid, has tried to kill himself, nothing could keep me from running to his side," Becky added.

Delivered with the fury of what I perceived to be false conviction, Becky's words stirred up a hatred for her that I had held at arm's length for years. I felt no remorse as I considered embracing it.

Chapter 9: October 2009

"He sent me a text that night," Connor said, breaking up my mind's image of Jared with his miserable fortune laid out before him.

I sat still and listened as Connor continued.

"I just replied like nothing was wrong, and texted back some stupid shit about my friends. I know now that his text was a sort of warning, like I was supposed to try to talk him out of it. Instead, I made him feel like I was done with him, and that he was justified in doing it. I had new friends and a new life, while he was just my annoying drunk brother..." Connor paused, his guilt mixing with the smell of cigarettes inside the car.

After a moment he continued. "I had a feeling that he was going to do it that night, but I told myself there was nothing I could do. He didn't tell me where he was, and I didn't bother asking. Even if I had known he was here, what was I going to do? So I acted like nothing was wrong and went to a movie with some friends. But I knew that he was out there somewhere, about to kill himself." Connor looked out his window and wiped his nose with the back of his hand.

"Man that's heavy. I can't imagine what that must have been like. But you're right, there was nothing you could do, you didn't know where he was." My response sounded weak, but honest. Connor needed to hear it from someone other than himself so that someday he might start believing it.

"I know that people think I did nothing to stop him. They don't know shit," Connor said angrily.

"You're right, people do think that, and to be honest, I did too for a while. But I didn't know shit. Forget about what anyone else thinks. They weren't there, and they can't possibly..." My words trailed off, not because I was lying to him, but because I didn't know what more to say. I wanted to comfort Connor, to relieve him of the guilt he was carrying, but that was impossible, and I knew it.

Chapter 10: March 2009

After promising to connect with them for an update the following afternoon, I forced a polite goodbye to Becky and Sarah. I hung up the phone and sat staring at the floor. Ella had finished her ironing and was downstairs monitoring the kid's homework, leaving me alone to contemplate my family's long and dramatic history.

Twenty years earlier, the revelation by my older brother Harrison that he was gay had settled over our family like a hurricane front. Mom and Dad led the way, bent on restoring order to their fold. They boiled and raged, pointing fingers of righteous indignation and blame at the English teacher that had mentored Harrison through summer school when he failed to graduate with the rest of his senior class.

Mr. Beckler was indeed effeminate and quite possibly gay, but he was one of my favorite teachers. Although I had enrolled in as many of his English classes as my guidance counselor would allow, I hadn't felt any pressure from Mr. Beckler to experiment with my sexuality. If he had been trying to recruit young impressionable high school boys over to the gay team, he was in need of some training, because he was a piss-poor recruiter.

Harrison moved out of the house, stacking his hundreds of books into a shady pay-by-the-week motel room near the factory where he worked nights as a security guard. I visited him at the motel a couple of times, and while he never let me inside, I could see his posters of half-naked male models hanging on the walls.

It was hard for me to accept that my older brother was gay, and so I didn't. While I loved him for so many reasons, I also hated Harrison for causing so much confusion in my life. I was incapable of seeing his lifestyle as anything other than a bad choice, his failure to find love and comfort with girls driving him to decide that he must be gay. It disrupted my parent's lives, and since I had blindly followed my parents into the black and white fog of unyielding religious beliefs, it disrupted my life as well. I felt committed to my parents and all that they had taught us growing up in the Mormon religion. Harrison had decided to be gay, and therefore was subject to harsh judgments, condemnation, and a life full of misery. He would never be truly happy, and would risk the dangers of a promiscuous and unnatural life, namely AIDS and a horrible death.

And Harrison's earthly life wasn't the only life at risk. My big brother was endangering his eternal soul, and along with it the eternal nature of our family. Without him we could not be an Eternal Family, a blessing promised to the obedient and faithful.

I didn't want to believe this, and secretly hoped that God would have some small measure of mercy for my brother, if not for his sake, then for mine.

Over time, Mom and Dad adjusted to Harrison's lifestyle in the only way they knew how; with distance, both physical and emotional. They had long been planning to move the family up to New Hampshire, and when they did Harrison stayed in his little motel room, three hours away in Connecticut. He soon became my parent's seldom-mentioned oldest child.

Geography became the perfect and reasonable excuse for Harrison's name disappearing from family conversation. He was welcome in Mom and Dad's home should he ever choose to visit, but they made it clear that none of his boyfriends were ever allowed to so much as cast a shadow on their front door.

Harrison and I exchanged a few letters over the following year, and I even met up with him a couple of times while in Connecticut visiting friends, but before long we had little left in common to talk about. Although I had a desire to maintain a relationship with him, my own life was taking shape; before long I had served a two year Mormon mission to Paraguay, married Ella, and moved to Seattle. It was easy for us to drift apart, and so we did.

It was not long after the drifting that Jared came to live with Ella and me in Seattle.

Chapter 11: October 2009

Tired of sitting, I climbed out of the car for a stretch. Connor followed suit. We stood in front of the little black rental car, the smoke of Connor's cigarette swirling overhead. I sniffed at the wafting white cloud; it smelled like so many car rides and conversations with Jared. He loved his 'cigs' as he called them, usually in a southern drawl as one hung from the corner of his mouth.

I felt a sudden urge to light one myself, filling my lungs with its dangerous warmth.

"Jeez, look at this place, so cheap, sleazy, and lonely; it looks like desperation in brick and mortar form. No wonder Jared chose this as the place to try and end it all," I whispered.

Connor said nothing, standing very still and very quiet. I was sure that I could hear the crackle of tiny red fire as he took a long pull on his cigarette.

"I can't stop thinking about him here, feeling so lonely and sorry for himself, believing that no one loved him. It plays over and over again in my mind, like a movie that I can't switch off. He takes another big swig of booze, sets the bottle down on the nightstand, and stares at the bottle of sleeping pills. Finally, he picks it up, tears away the plastic wrapper, and twists off the lid. He dumps the whole bottle into his hand and holds the pills in his palm like a man holding a handful of diamonds, knowing that they are going to change his life forever." I stopped and looked over at Connor. He had finished his smoke, and was standing with his hands crammed deep into his back pockets, his mournful gaze fixed on the motel.

Connor nodded his head, as if to give me the okay to continue.

So I did. "He must have been happy at that moment, which I know sounds so wrong, because it was absolute sadness that drove him to try and kill himself, but in those few minutes, he must have felt relieved, like the end of his loneliness was close. It is the saddest thing I have ever imagined, Jared sitting alone in a dingy motel room, swallowing pills and drinking a whole bottle of liquor, hoping his life will soon be over. As unhappy as I have been at times, I cannot imagine the pain he was feeling. I think that is why I am not mad at him."

And just like that I was done, at least for the moment. The two of us stood there together, staring at the Super Budget Motor Inn.

I really needed a cigarette, and thought that maybe I would steal one from Connor later on.

Chapter 12: December 1994

Jared had been enrolled at a Mormon junior college in Idaho before coming to Seattle. An aspiring artist, my little brother had a hard time being told what to paint, draw, or sculpt, and being graded on the results. This frustration, along with a string of professors that he felt knew very little about art, led him to believe that a true artist had little or no need for higher education. He announced that he was dropping out to pursue a career as an artist on his own.

This caused a great amount of stress for my parents. Out of their four high school graduates, not one had stayed in college for more than a couple of semesters at a time. Between the four of us we might have had enough credits for a degree, but as Dad had explained to us in condescending detail, universities didn't pool sibling credits in order to award sibling degrees. Adding to their frustration was the fact that we had each been awarded educational grants by the large corporate machine that employed our father. We had essentially turned our backs on a free education.

As he often did when it came to difficulties with any of my three brothers, Dad called me to talk about Jared's future. He and Mom didn't want Jared coming home. They worried that his attitude about higher education would adversely affect the younger siblings, putting in danger Mom and Dad's chances of someday becoming parents of a college graduate.

"We'll take him," I offered with Ella's approval, but without a thought to the fact that we lived in a one-bedroom apartment that was little bigger than a custom van.

I was looking forward to the distraction that Jared was sure to provide. Our young marriage was suffering through growing pains, and fighting was as much a part of our life as anything else we did together. Though she never said as much, I was sure that Ella was thinking the same thing I was, which was that having Jared around would allow us little time alone to spend arguing. His company would make our situation more tolerable, perhaps even happy.

Jared arrived the following week and took up residence in our dining/living/family room. Our futon, the first of several furniture-bought-with-a-credit-card mistakes became his bed. He quickly found a part-time job at the local convenience store, opting to work the night shift so that Ella and I could have some time alone.

Weeks passed, and though it was tight quarters, no one complained. Jared slept while we were at work, and woke up to eat dinner and spend some time with us before walking to work. I was employed cleaning carpets at the time, and Jared would abandon sleep a couple of days a week to work with me and make some extra cash. We drove around Seattle together in a big van with a colorful carpet cleaning super hero painted on the sides.

The job sucked. Cleaning dirt, food, sewage, and various bodily fluids from stranger's carpets was gross, but the time spent working with Jared became something to look forward to each week. We made a habit of raiding the customer's kitchens for food, turning their stereos up too loud, and riding the carpet buffer across their living rooms. We dreamed aloud of being free and happy, living as we pleased someday, un-tethered by the worries of the average jerk. I hoped to become a published writer, and Jared a successful artist, but we gave little thought to the effort and heartache required to achieve such elusive aspirations.

To dwell on the hows was too depressing anyway. I had little hope or talent with which to materialize my own dream, while Jared was sure to succeed due to the raw creative genius that seemed to course through his veins and flow out his fingertips as he drew or painted.

We spent Christmas together that year, the three of us unwrapping gifts beneath a shabby little tree. There wasn't a lot of money to spend on presents, but it didn't matter. We gave Jared a pillow, an alarm clock, and a foam pad for the futon, and he gave us some candy and a pile of impulse items that he'd bought at the convenience store. After presents we ate a humble Christmas dinner and watched movies until Jared had to go to work. It was a simple but happy day.

Chapter 13: October 2009

It was getting colder. I pumped my arms and walked around to force some blood into my limbs. I heard a door slam, and looked across the parking lot to see a woman standing outside the motel office. A light bulb flickered on above her head, and I could see her looking over at us, her posture laced with suspicion.

Connor looked at the woman and heaved a smoke-filled sigh into the darkness. I watched the flash of flame as the woman lit her own cigarette. A moment later she blew her own smoke and began to walk in our direction.

"Hi there," she offered on approach. Her posture had abandoned any sign of suspicion, as if the glowing tip of Connor's cancer stick signaled peace and fraternity.

"Hello," I replied.

"You guys looking for a room tonight?" She folded one arm across her stomach to support the other at the elbow, her cigarette held high.

"No, thank-you, we just came to take a look," I replied.

"You gonna be here long? I can't have you hanging out in the parking lot," she told us.

"No, we're just about to leave. Say, how long have you worked here?" I asked, unsure as to where I would go with any answer that she gave me.

"I don't know, eight months maybe…" Ash from her lofty cigarette fell into the darkness.

"Do you remember a man being found unconscious on the floor in one of the rooms here back in March? Somebody called 911 and an ambulance took him to the hospital. He had tried to kill himself," I queried.

She puffed, as if thinking, then said, "No, I don't remember, but maybe I wasn't working here yet. I just started a few weeks ago." The suspicion returned to her posture.

"So, you don't remember that happening back in March?" I pushed, wondering why she had dropped the eight months down to a few weeks.

"No, I don't, sorry." She flicked her cigarette into the dark, then turned and walked back towards the office.

"Thanks," I muttered, wondering at her denial.

Finding a man unconscious from a suicide attempt where you work is the kind of story you'd tell over and over again for several days to anyone who would listen. It wasn't something you would likely forget.

Unless that kind of thing happens all the time where you work, I thought.

One final scan of the lonely motel told me that it was entirely possible. I looked over at Connor, and without speaking we both knew that it was time to leave the motel. We got in the car and I started the engine. Warm air blasted across my chilled cheeks.

I put the car in reverse and backed away from the fence. This time the crunching of gravel under our tires signaled a Godspeed, the true start of our quest. The sound put a lump in my throat.

We made for the interstate. The moment our tires hit the onramp, Connor leaned forward and dropped his head into his hands. His shoulders began to shake as the sound of his sobs filled the front seat. I reached out and placed a firm hand on his trembling back as we merged onto the highway, heading west of Independence.

Chapter 14: January 1995

"Is Jared gay?" Our friend Jessica's question more than caught me off guard. It struck away my powers of speech and thought.

My mouth hung open and wordless in reply, my eyes wide and unfocused. After an awkward moment, I managed to pry the lid of my brain open, and let slip the first thought to escape.

"No, he just dresses well." I blurted.

"But you don't think he's gay?" Jessica pressed.

"No, he's not gay, my older brother Harrison is," I offered, as though it were both an excuse and a compromise.

There could be no more amount of gay in my life. Harrison had already laid claim to the one gay spot allotted our family.

"And that means Jared can't be gay? Do you really believe that? I would think that one gay brother increases the odds, wouldn't you?" With her first question Jessica had pressed the knife between my ribs. Her second question twisted it.

"I would know if he were gay, he would tell me. He's my brother." The look in my eyes closed the door on any further discussion, and Jessica dropped the subject.

That night, in the darkness of our bedroom, I asked Ella what she thought of Jessica's line of questioning.

"Would it matter if Jared were gay?" She countered, avoiding a direct answer while quietly laying the burden of any response to Jessica's question at my feet. I had been hoping for reassurance from her that Jared was straight.

I didn't answer her question that night, and in time the topic was pushed aside by the worries of life.

Several days later I returned home after a long day of dirty carpets to find Jared and Ella sitting together, tears in their eyes and tissues in their hands. The closing credits to a movie rolled up the TV screen. I took a few steps across the room and picked up the video case sitting

33

on top of it. The movie was called "Shadowlands" and starred Debora Winger and Anthony Hopkins.

"Matthew, you have got to watch this movie." This came from Ella, a runny-nose sound to her voice.

"Why? You don't look very happy after having watched it."

"No, Matthew, she's right. You should watch it," Jared said.

"Isn't this movie about C.S. Lewis, the guy that wrote 'The Chronicles of Narnia?' Doesn't he die at the end? No thanks, I don't want to watch a sad movie about death," I laughed.

"Don't laugh! Yes it's sad, but it's also beautiful. And for your information he doesn't die, his wife does." Ella wiped her nose, dropping the tissue into a pile already on the floor.

"He finds the one true love that he always wanted, and they are so happy together. Then she gets sick and dies, and he is lost without her. I want to have love like that someday, to find someone I'd be lost without." The look on Jared's tear streaked face told me that to poke any more fun at the movie would be a mistake.

I dismissed Jared's usage of the term "someone." I was unwilling to entertain any more thoughts about him being gay, and was not about to ask him about it directly. I went to take a shower, and by the time I came out the movie and its case had been hidden away.

We continued to live, work, and play together, the three of us enjoying the limited freedom that comes from living on an hourly wage far away from the pressures of family.

Chapter 15: October 2009

"Shooting star, did you see it?"

Connor and I were leaned back in our seats, having pulled the car over to the side of the interstate just south of Wichita. I kept the engine running, the heat at full blast and the windows open while Connor smoked another cigarette.

"Yeah, and there's another," I said, looking up at the Kansas night sky.

We had driven south for a few hours, until my eyes felt as heavy as my spirit. While both of them needed a rest, a catnap could do nothing for the latter. The car shuddered as a truck blew past, causing cold air to billow in through the open windows. I pulled my arms inside my sweatshirt and hugged myself in an effort to keep my core temperature above freezing.

"This reminds me of all those road trips when we were kids. I remember how Dad would pull over on the side of the road, jump out and throw a sleeping bag on the ground beside the van to sleep for a couple of hours," Connor said, taking one last drag on his cigarette before flicking the butt out onto the prairie, my cue to man the four buttons that controlled the windows.

The change in climate was immediate, the heater vents no longer outpaced by the cold, rolling gusts of passing semis.

Connor's words were something to absorb, and I began to think about those family treks west.

Almost every summer when we were young, Dad would remove the bench seats from whatever van we were driving that year and build a wooden platform to fit in their place. Underneath the platform would go our luggage, and on top of it would go Mom and Dad's mattress. We kids would pile in, sitting, laying, and rolling around on the soft mattress as the miles passed beneath us. We would eat cheese sandwiches and drink milk that Mom kept in a big red and white cooler. There was never any air conditioning, so Mom would tape aluminum foil to the side windows to reflect away the sun and its heat, and open the front and rear windows to let the air flow over us. The hot desert wind would rush in, stirring up the pages of our books and blowing the girl's long hair in our faces.

After driving all day, with only a few quick potty breaks and perhaps a stop or two at historical markers along the highway, Dad would at last pull over to the side of the road for a rest. He would grab a sleeping bag and drop to the ground beside the van for a long nap. I would worry about my father out there on the ground. I feared his body being crushed by a passing truck, or wild animals tearing him from his dreams with their sharp claws and cutting fangs. I wouldn't sleep much at first, restless from the fear of losing him. Sometime after finally drifting off, I would wake to the creak of the driver side door opening, and then listen to the rustle of his sleeping bag as Dad crammed it into the space between the two front seats. The door would close with a click, and he would murmur something softly to my mother as she stirred. Only then would I feel safe again, and as he started the engine and merged the van back onto the highway I would fall back to sleep with a smile on my face. My dad was safe again, sitting behind the wheel where he belonged, driving the family forward.

On those road trips Dad would drink a sour grapefruit-flavored soda called "Squirt" that came in bright yellow cans. I would make a point of stealing a sip or two at some point during each trip. As I tasted the sweetened sour of Dad's soda, I imagined someday driving my own wife and kids across the country. I would drink Squirt, wear a Farrah Fawcett tee shirt with faded blue jeans, and block out the sun with big black sunglasses. My left hand would hold the wheel loosely, and I would bend my right arm up over my head, clasping the seat belt strap that hung from the doorframe above in my fingers. My wife would sit all pretty in the passenger seat, handing out crackers coated with squeeze cheese and bacon bits. I would listen to the kids sing along with John Denver and Olivia Newton John on the radio, then smile at their cheers when I pulled over at fireworks stands along the way.

"I could really go for some Squirt right now," I said, ending the memory on a high note.

"Some what? Is that a code word for sex?" Connor pointed out yet another shooting star.

36

"Well, I could use some sex with Ella right now, but no, Squirt is that soda Dad used to drink on road trips, don't you remember the yellow cans? I wonder if they still sell it out here. I am going to look every time we stop for gas, it's been years since I had some." I closed my eyes and thought of sleep, but the seat was uncomfortable. I needed to lie flat.

I needed a sleeping bag on the side of the road.

Chapter 16: March 1995

"I've decided that I want to go back to New Hampshire," Jared announced one night at dinner.

"What? Why?" I asked, a little too much desperation in my voice. Were Jared to leave, my marriage might crumble due to all the time Ella and I would have to spend together.

"I don't know, I just want to," Jared answered, a lack of conviction in his reply.

"Jared, if you think we don't want you here, forget it. We love having you here." Knowing Jared as well as she did, Ella's first reaction to his announcement was to assure him that he was welcome in our home, even if our home was a tiny one-bedroom apartment.

"I know. I love you guys, and I love it here. But I also know that you guys would never tell me that I'm in the way."

"You are not in the way. Let's just make that clear right now. You can stay as long as you want." My tone was firm, and I looked him in the eyes as I told him the truth.

"Ok, ok, I get it. I believe you. But I still want to go home. I miss Connor, all my stuff is there, and I just think it is time to go home." Jared wasn't crying, but his tone was climbing higher as if he were about to.

I didn't press him for more on his motivations for moving back to New Hampshire, and he didn't offer any further explanation. It hurt that he had mentioned our younger brother Connor as one of his main reasons for wanting to go home. Since our childhood, I had been a spectator to the relationship that Jared and Connor shared. They often seemed more like best friends than brothers. They knew and understood far more about each other than I ever would about any of my siblings. I had always felt left out in the cold watching them interact.

"When are you thinking of leaving?" I asked, swallowing the lump of jealousy that had lodged in my throat.

38

"As soon as I can," Jared said, wincing a bit as he did. The lump of jealousy dropped into my stomach with an acidic splash.

"You'll have to call Dad and ask him," I suggested, tossing into the air my last, best hope for keeping Jared with us.

"I already have," Jared said, his eyes avoiding mine. With that, hope landed like a dud grenade in the middle of the table.

Later that week, against my will, I drove Jared to the train station.

"It's cheaper than a one-way flight, and besides, I want to see the country from a train," he said, when I asked at a red light if he was sure he had thought through the idea of a weeklong journey by train.

In his lap sat our little cooler that Ella had filled with snacks and sodas. She made him promise to be careful, and reminded him to shout "Stranger! Danger!" if he felt threatened by someone he didn't know. I felt like we were sending our first born off to boot camp in the middle of a war, not knowing when or if we would see him again.

It was March, and the NCAA Sweet Sixteen tournament was in Seattle, bringing the downtown traffic to a slow crawl. I had not planned for the delay, and was doubtful that we would make it to Jared's train in time.

"Come on, people! It's the pedal on the right! Step on it!" I flung my emotions out the window towards my fellow drivers in the form of insults.

"Wow, did Mom teach you to drive?" Jared quipped.

I wasn't sure which urge was more powerful, to laugh or to cry. We were behind a string of cars that were slowly rolling through the green light up ahead. I watched the light turn yellow, and glanced at the dashboard clock; we were close, but we wouldn't make Jared's train if we stopped. As we approached the intersection, the light had already turned red. Cars were beginning to move across our path. I made a split-second decision and jumped on the gas.

Chapter 17: October 2009

"Shit, I think I just broke my leg!" I groaned, laughed, and then rolled onto my back, ten feet above Oklahoma.

"Idiot, how do you break a leg climbing up? I'm recording this by the way, so you're gonna have to edit out your swears before your kids can watch it," Connor warned.

"Yeah, I don't think they'll be allowed to see this one. Wouldn't want them to hear their father cussing as he moons the entire state of Oklahoma." I sat up and checked my leg for permanent damage. Finding none, I struggled to my feet atop the 'Welcome to Oklahoma' sign. I looked out across the rest area parking lot for police cars, dog walkers, and perverts. But for a few dark cars and a few idling semis, there were no signs of life.

"Move over to the middle of it, so I can get the whole sign in the picture," Connor said. I heard the whirring of the camera lens as he backed off on the zoom.

"You're doing fine, Oklahoma!" I shouted, unzipping my pants and yanking them, along with my boxers, down to my ankles. I spread my arms wide into the night sky and shouted the rest, "O-K-L-A-H-O-M-A, Oklahoma, OK!"

"What a loser!" Connor scoffed, but I could hear the smile in his voice. I pulled up my pants and jumped to the ground.

I had decided that since sleeping in the car was not going to work for me, we would keep driving until we felt it was time to stop and get a room. While standing naked on the 'Welcome to Oklahoma' sign served as a good indicator that the time to stop driving had arrived, it also made us laugh and got our blood pumping. I felt physically awake, my spirit lifting at the thrill of mischief.

My heart was still working hard and my mood remained light as we merged onto the empty highway once again. Connor grabbed my Ipod from the dock, searching for some road tunes.

"Put on something to keep us awake, something loud and energetic," I requested.

"Uh-huh," Connor said, acknowledging my request. He dropped the Ipod back into the dock, and the car was filled with the sounds of keyboards, guitars, and the Eighties. The unmistakable music of our youth threatened to blow the speakers as we cruised down the highway in our tiny black rental car, trying to match the singer's long high notes and jamming out the well-known but never tiresome riffs on our air guitars. I knew it was silly and cliché, but it didn't feel that way. We kept it up for miles, working our way through a long list of favorites.

When the playlist ended, Connor reclined his seat and settled in for a nap. The ability to sleep anywhere, at any time, was a skill that both my younger brothers had always possessed. On all of our many road trips as kids, outside on our trampoline, and while camping with our friends in high school, I had watched them drop to whatever disagreeable surface was available, falling asleep without too much trouble while I laid awake, uncomfortable and jealous of their deep breathing and unconscious state.

Connor had once slept in the bottom of our canoe for an entire day on a river, not even stirring when we ran some rapids. I was so worried he might be dead that I poked him hard with my paddle. It was like waking a sleeping bear by sticking a lit cherry bomb up his ass. Connor was so pissed off at me for waking him up that he thrashed around and nearly dumped us into the water.

I smiled at the memory, and at the realization that once more I had found myself awake with my little brothers at rest around me. Setting the cruise control at eighty-five, I sat up tall in the driver's seat and gripped the wheel, my hands at ten and two in order to ensure that I would not relax too much and risk falling asleep. The white center lines whipped past, disappearing into the darkness as the miles stacked up behind us.

Chapter 18: March 1995

We were going to get hit, I was sure of it. There was nowhere for us to go, the entrance to the train station parking lot was blocked by traffic. My only option was to jump the curb and drive over the sidewalk.

"Argh!" I growled, and put the gas pedal to the floor. We hit the curb at a good clip, and while the sound convinced me that both front tires had exploded, the impact convinced me that I had just cracked the frame of my little two-door hatchback beyond repair. I saw one of my passenger-side hubcaps roll ahead of us and disappear down the sidewalk out of sight. The car thumped down off the sidewalk and into the parking lot, and without hesitation I turned into the nearest empty space and brought the car to a halt between the lines.

"Whoa! What the heck Matthew! Mom really did teach you to drive, didn't she?" Jared's eyes were wide, his smile wider still.

"Relax, we made it in one piece didn't we?" I grinned.

"Maybe we did, but your car didn't. Did you hear that sound? I thought the tires had popped!" Jared swung his door open and jumped out to check his side of the vehicle.

"Did you see the hubcap fly off?" I asked with a laugh, still seated behind the wheel, the engine still running. The urgency that had sent us over the curb was gone.

"Yes, but I didn't see where it went, did you?" Jared asked.

"It went rolling down the sidewalk, I'll get it later. We'd better get you inside or you're going to miss your train," I warned.

"Oh man, now I feel bad! You didn't have to jump the sidewalk just to get me here on time. I'm sorry Matthew, I could have just waited an extra day to leave." Jared was scanning the parking lot, as if considering a search for my wayward hubcap.

"Kid, let's go, you need to make this train. I'll get my hubcap later." I was at the back of the car, pulling his luggage from the trunk.

"I'm sorry, Matthew," Jared repeated. He picked up a suitcase, but kept staring across the parking lot, as if expecting my hubcap to come rolling back like a boomerang.

"No big deal, I can get a four-pack of replacement hubcaps for twenty bucks at Fred Meyer. It's okay, really, I've done it before." I closed the trunk with a gentle push and a quiet click. I wanted to slam it, but didn't, because Jared would have taken it as a sign of anger, and it wasn't anger that I was feeling.

"No, it's not okay; you and Ella have been so nice to me and put up with me for so long, and now the last thing I do before I leave is break your car. I'm sorry." His back was to me, but I didn't have to see his face to know that he was holding back tears.

"Jared, I will be angry if you keep apologizing for nothing," I threatened.

"Ok, ok, I'm sorry..." he said, turning around.

"I know you are sorry Jared, but there is nothing to be sorry about. Now we have a cool story to tell about jumping the curb and losing a hubcap as we raced to get you to the train station on time." We stood facing each other, heavy baggage hanging from our hands. I wondered for a moment if he was hoping I would ask him to stay. Afraid that he would say no, I didn't dare.

We crossed the parking lot and entered the station. I walked him out to the platform, and we set his luggage down for the porter to tag and load.

"Ok kid, this is goodbye. Ella and I have loved having you here with us. It won't be the same without you sleeping in our living room. Take care of yourself, and be careful." I was playing so well my responsible big-brother role, but in truth I wanted to cry. He looked so fragile and innocent, my little brother about to board a train and ride alone across the country. I wanted to beg him to stay, to keep me company and to distract my marriage with his happiness.

"Matthew, thank-you for letting me live with you. Tell Ella that I love her, and that I'll give the cooler back when I see you again. I can't believe you let me sleep on your futon for so long. I'm sorry if I

43

was in the way of you two getting it on," Jared said, the last bit spoken from the corner of his mouth as if he were telling me a dirty secret. His eyes lit up, and he grinned at me.

"She knows, and she loves you too. Screw the cooler, we don't need it. We do need you to be safe though, so be careful and make sure you get on and off at the right stops. Ask someone if you aren't sure where to go or when to change trains." I stepped forward and wrapped my arms around him, patting him on the back and squeezing him hard.

"Thank-you Matthew. I love you," Jared said in my ear.

"I love you too," I replied. "You were never in the way, and you are welcome to come back any time. We will miss you...I will miss you..." I pressed him into me one more time, then let go and did my best to smile as he picked up his cooler and backpack.

Jared stepped up into the passenger car, then turned and waved from the steps. I waved back. Both of us made a big show of it, as if we were starring in our own black and white foreign film. I laughed, watching and waving as he disappeared into the train.

I turned and walked back through the station and out to the parking lot. I sat in my car and cried as I listened to the train pull away.

Chapter 19: October 2009

"Pack it deep!" Connor's sudden shout was like a sonic boom inside the little car. I startled out of my thousand-yard stare and into the moment. Adjusting my grip on the steering wheel and sitting up straight, I glanced up at the rear view mirror to check on Jared in the back seat, then the road behind us. Both were quiet.

"What are you talking about? What are you packing deep?" I asked, itching for some conversation. I had spent the past two hours with only my thoughts for company, and my thoughts were wearing thin on their welcome.

"Those ice cream signs. They started popping up in Kansas, and I've seen three since I woke up a minute ago. Does anyone in the Midwest eat anything other than ice cream?" Connor dug into his shirt pockets, pulling out a lighter and his cigarettes.

"Pack it deep? I didn't see that on any of those signs. Sounds kind of dirty if you ask me." I propped my knees against the wheel and reached down with both hands to zip up my sweatshirt, a weak defense against the cold air that would soon be rushing in as Connor smoked away slumber.

"That's the point, it's supposed to be dirty. Look at a road sign and try to make up a slogan based on the picture. It will usually end up being something dirty, because dirty is easier. His cigarette lit, I opened the windows.

"Damn, it's cold in Oklahoma!" I shouted out the window to no one. The frigid blast felt good; it flushed the stale atmosphere from the car and woke me up.

"Pack it deep!" I heard Connor bellow. I looked over to see him pointing at a huge sign up ahead. It was bathed in bright light from several bulbs mounted across its base. Pictured on the sign were a huge ice cream cone and a massive hamburger that did not look all that appetizing.

"Come into one of our many family-friendly locations and choke down a hot mealworm burger, then cleanse your assaulted palette with one of our world famous grease-cream cones!" I shouted. "Your colon never had it so good and deep as this!"

We passed the next hour or so watching for billboards that advertised products we felt needed new ad campaigns, and were rewarded with miles of laughter as we conjured up ridiculous slogans and irreverent uses for deodorant, jewelry, restaurants, cars, and hotels.

"It should be light soon," I noted as we passed through Oklahoma City.

"How far have we come?"

"A little more than three hundred and fifty miles," I replied, glancing at the GPS mounted on the windshield. I thought about adjusting the time on it by an hour to reflect the central time zone, but since we would be hitting another time zone in New Mexico I didn't bother.

"And we are still in Oklahoma? I forgot how huge these states are out here." Connor pulled out another cigarette.

"And flat," I said, rolling down the windows. "You can see so far that you feel like you're crawling, even when you're doing close to ninety miles an hour."

In the darkness, miles ahead of us, I could see the tiny flashing lights of a construction zone, proving my point. It took several minutes to reach the first blinking arrows, which indicated an impending split of the westbound lanes. When the time came I veered to the left, and we found ourselves speeding between parallel cement barriers. Our little car was so low to the ground that we couldn't see over them, and it seemed as though we were driving through a canyon of grey.

"It feels like we're in the Death Star trench!" Connor turned to shout so I could hear.

I smiled and looked dead ahead, watching as the cement blurred into the grey walls of Darth Vader's infamous death moon. The dark sky above, spotted with the bright twinkling of stars, added to the

46

effect. I imagined Tie Fighters above us, the whine of their ion engines threatening as they gave chase. My imagination sent them careening into the walls behind us, their large, flat wings spinning off into space, leaving the ball-shaped cockpits to plow into the bottom of the trench with explosive displays of good winning over evil.

"Matthew, trust your feelings, feel the force within you!" I heard Connor shout over the thunder of battle, which was in truth just the wind whistling through the open windows.

I reached up and turned off the GPS, a young Jedi-in-training turning off his targeting system. We sped through the trench for another mile or so, and as it ended I swerved over to the right lane as if I had just fired the kill shot into that tiny exhaust port and wanted nothing more than to get away as the Death Star disintegrated into flaming space dust.

"Did you hear, that?" I shouted.

"Hear what?" Connor asked.

"I swear I just heard Han Solo shouting 'Yahoo!'"

Chapter 20: Spring 1995

Just a few weeks after Jared left Seattle, we learned that Ella was pregnant, due in December. Had anyone been keeping a scorecard on our sex life (and yes, I was), they would have found it to be nothing short of a miracle that we had conceived. While Jared's presence had distracted us from our marriage troubles, it had not erased them.

December came too quickly for me, but then I wasn't the one carrying the extra weight of a growing child inside my belly. After many hours of painful labor, during which I marveled at the strength and elasticity of my petite wife, as well as the yielding properties of a baby's skull, our first-born entered our lives. We named him Noah, and I was humbled by his beautiful presence and frightened by his dependence upon us for everything.

Noah was a life ring thrown to us from the deck of God's Coast Guard Cutter. We were the unhappy, penniless, and clueless parents of a newborn boy, but in him we were given a future. He gave us a common purpose, and someone we could love together without any danger of being hurt or betrayed in return.

Eager to see their new grandson, our parents flew the three of us back East for Christmas. One evening during our visit, Ella's mom and dad, perhaps worried about the security and well being of their grandson, offered us room and board in their home under the condition that I return to college. We accepted on the spot, and within six weeks were driving back to New Hampshire, our tiny two-door hatchback loaded with our new baby and the bare essentials of life. A trip across the country in the bitter cold of February was not the most encouraging way to start a new and happier life of opportunity, but we could not afford to complain.

Living with the in-laws provided a new set of challenges to our relationship, but Noah was the best distraction we could have hoped for. He was neutral ground for everyone involved, the one thing upon which we could all agree. His well-being dictated the tone of my interactions with Ella's parents, while his chubby laughter and unconditional love for me filled in the pock-marks of self esteem with the confidence I so badly needed in those days. I was a young husband and father that knew nothing about being one or the other, let alone both at the same time. I was unsure of who I was, doubtful about what I was doing, and anxious about my future.

If my future seemed to me like an uncertain and frightening landscape, Jared's must have seemed to him like a bleak and dreadful wasteland.

Chapter 21: October 2009

As we neared the Texas border, the sun came up and my bladder neared its bursting point. Connor had been sleeping through the last stretches of highway that Oklahoma had to offer, and though I really had to pee, I had not wanted to pull over and risk waking him. He looked peaceful and at rest in the passenger seat, curled up as close to the fetal position as one could get while wearing a seatbelt in such a tiny car.

To sacrifice an hour or more of internal pressure and let him sleep a while longer as we sped across the open plains was no small gift that I could give to my little brother. I knew that much like myself, Connor had slept very little over the past several months, the level of physical comfort having nothing to do with it.

Cotton fields began to line the highway, the acres of white blossoms laying low to the ground like clumps of melting snow. I decided that when Connor woke up we would pull over to pick some cotton.

In the meantime I spied towering windmills dotting the plains in long white ranks, their blades turning lazily in the winds sweeping across the plains. In an instant Connor unwittingly became Sancho Panza to my Don Quixote, and together we gave chase to the savage titans that terrorized the land. I thought of Ella as my sweet Dulcinea back home. She had encouraged me to follow through on my quest, and I was lucky to have her.

"Are we in Texas yet?" Sancho was awake and wondering as to our progress.

"Almost. I have to piss like nobody's business," I said.

"Me too," Connor yawned.

"Ok, we'll stop at the border. I want some pictures of us at the welcome sign."

We passed the next few miles in silence, and I returned to chasing windmills. As we neared the border I smiled.

"Ever run through a cotton field before?"

"No, but let me guess, we're going to do it right now, aren't we?" Connor asked, looking out the window at the endless rows of cotton blossoms to our right.

"Yep," I answered, pulling over to the side of the highway. Leaving the engine running, I jumped out of the car and ran into the cotton field, laughing out loud like the carefree fool that I wanted to be. Connor followed close behind me, camera in hand to document the moment his older brother lost his mind.

"Take one of me picking some!" He handed me the camera and bent over to grab the nearest clump of soft white, looking back over his shoulder at the camera as he did. I snapped a shot of him looking like a kid caught with his hand in the cookie jar.

"Ok, now take one of me," I said, tossing him the camera.

I scooped up a couple of handfuls as he clicked off a couple of photos.

"Let's go, here comes the plantation owner!" I screamed, and sprinted for the car as if we were being chased.

Connor ran alongside me. I could see that he was holding the camera up, taking photos of me as we ran. Together we jumped in the car and I stomped on the gas, merging onto the empty highway as the little engine whined in high-pitched protest at what I was asking it to do.

"Damn! I was so excited that I forgot to piss!" I shouted.

"Look, another sign to climb on," Connor said, pointing ahead.

I pulled the car over and we climbed out once again. I ran for a gathering of bushes nearby and began to relieve my troubled bladder with a loud sigh.

"Knock it off, loser!" I said, turning away when I noticed Connor beside me, camera in hand.

"What, you don't want me to film you taking a piss?" he asked, feigning disbelief.

"Whatever," I chuckled, finishing my business and zipping up.

I walked over to the big brick sign that Connor had suggested as climbable. It was at least ten feet high. On the front there was a silhouette of Texas fashioned from what looked to be dark marble built into the façade. Within the state were etched a few of The Lone Star State's claims to fame, which included the Alamo, an oil well spraying black gold into the sky, and a ranch complete with a single longhorn steer and old windmill. Just above all of that were the words 'Welcome to Texas' in large black letters made of iron.

"Film me climbing it," Connor said, handing me the camera. I watched as he walked around the sign looking for handholds.

"Any luck?" I asked.

Connor replied by taking a running start towards the side of the sign, then launching himself into the air. His feet scrambled for purchase as his hands fumbled for a grip along the top edge. Gravity played well her part, yanking him back to the ground.

"Try again, from further away," I encouraged.

Connor took several long steps away from the sign, then turned at a sprint and made for the wall. He shouted, "Aw man, I'm not gonna make it!"

Sure enough, his fingers missed the top edge and he fell back to Earth.

"Again!" I shouted, my voice full of happy encouragement.

Connor rested a moment before giving it one last and grand effort. I watched in amazement as he clung to the top edge, and I held my breath as he struggled to pull himself up and onto the top of the sign.

"Yes!" I shouted as Connor climbed to his feet and stood atop the sign, his arms above him like an Olympic champion on the top of the medal podium.

It was a sweet moment of victory, and I snapped several photos of him up there with the big blue sky of Texas behind him.

Chapter 22: Summer 1996

Jared came out to the family a few months after Ella and I moved back to New Hampshire. The family's reaction made our response to Harrison's revelation that he was gay years earlier seem like a bar mitzvah in comparison.

In Harrison's case I had tried without success to pray away his gay. To realize that Jared's name would be joining Harrison's in my daily supplications to heaven was overwhelming. I was already tiring of my efforts to work out one brother's salvation. Jared's "decision" doubled my spiritual burden.

I was convinced that no man had ever been born gay. In my limited and religion-slanted understanding, homosexuality was a result of masturbation, choice, or sexual abuse, and regardless of the path taken to get there it was a sin as terrible as murder, rape, and child molestation. Punishment for the unrepentant homosexual was an eternity spent without the blessings of family and the loving influence of God.

I had been taught that families could be together forever, but only through obedience to the laws of heaven. In my mind's eye there hung a mirror in which our earthly family was reflected, dressed all in white, perfect, smiling, and happy, just as we would be one day in heaven. Harrison had pulled that mirror off the wall when he stepped out of the closet, but I had held onto a hope that he would someday repent, putting the mirror back in its proper place. Jared had stepped out of the closet with a hammer, shattering the mirror forever. I felt betrayed by the same brother whose peaceful presence in Seattle had unwittingly done much to preserve my marriage and bring the joys of fatherhood into my life.

Rather than repay him with that same peaceful support and calming influence, I stood in judgment of my little brother, telling him that I would do my best to thwart his efforts to damn himself.

Had I taken a step back and allowed the brotherly love that I felt for Jared guide my actions, I might have seen that to deny him my unconditional love and a measure of understanding was in fact a greater offense than that of his being gay. Instead, to my later great shame and regret, I succumbed to the pressure of my religion, my parents, and my own ignorance.

Dead armadillos and coyotes welcomed us into the Lone Star state. They were as common on the side of the road as the billboards advertising ice cream had been in Oklahoma.

"Have you noticed all the roadkill in this state?" I asked aloud, pointing at something dead in the middle of the highway.

"Let's stop and check out the next one," Connor suggested.

"I want to get a picture of a dead armadillo up close. Every one that I have seen so far was headless," I added.

"Cool." Connor straightened up and began scanning the roadside for death.

It didn't take long. I pulled over just past a mangled coyote. We jumped out and ran back to take a look. It was flattened; all four legs and the head were bent back into the body, as if something powerful had picked it up and folded the animal in on itself.

"It looks like a serial killer's bathmat," I remarked.

Connor laid down beside it for a picture.

"We should make a list of things we want to take photos of and check them off as we go," Connor suggested back inside the car.

"Connor lying down with roadkill, check!" I laughed.

"Matthew's white ass hanging out above a 'Welcome to Oklahoma' sign, check," Connor added.

"Here, write them down in this," I said, handing him my pocket notebook and collapsible pen.

Connor opened the notebook to a blank page and began to scribble.

"Ok, what else?" he asked a moment later, his eyes scanning the side of the road for dead armadillos.

56

"I want a photo of me with a working oil well. I remember seeing them on road trips when we were young. They fascinated me. I used to imagine they were giant, wild, metal bulls that had been captured and forced to buck pump the oil out of the ground. I wanted to get up close, to watch them snort and puff, but I was too afraid to ask Dad to stop the van so I could."

Connor nodded as if memories were swirling around inside his own head as he added my suggestion to the list.

"There's an armadillo," I said, pulling over to a sudden stop. I grabbed the camera, and waited as a truck blew past the car before jumping out.

The armadillo was headless, but the rest of its body was intact, the legs and tail sticking out from under the shell. It was a gruesome sight, and I wondered if its head had popped off upon impact, or if it had been devoured by something wild and dangerous.

Connor lay down on the rumble strip, putting his hand above the armadillo torso to mimic petting it without actually touching it. I took a couple of photos of him spending time with the new family pet.

Back on the road, I looked in the mirror and threw Jared a smile. After a shaky start, the trip was shaping up to be everything I had hoped it would be.

Chapter 24: Summer 1996

To call it an intervention would be a slap in the face to anyone who had ever taken part in a real one. A true intervention is a gathering of loved ones fueled by concern, understanding, hope, and support. Our sit-down with Jared at my parent's house was more a display of fear, ignorance, judgment, and threats than it was anything else, regardless of the love we felt for him.

"Do you believe in God?" I asked Jared.

"Yes," he answered.

"Do you believe that he is perfect?" I continued.

"Yes, Matthew, God is perfect. Listen, it's not that I don't believe in God, or heaven, or any of that stuff," Jared tried to explain.

I ignored the second half of his reply, intent on getting Jared to make my point for me. "Do you believe that we are created by him, in his image?" I asked.

"Of course, but-"

"Okay," I interrupted. "Then how can you say that you are gay?"

"What? I just am, I have always-"

"No you're not! You can't be gay, not if you believe that you were created by God, and in his image," I explained, the point clear in my eyes.

Jared looked at me in confusion. "What?" he asked.

"God is not gay, and he wouldn't make you gay either," I explained, settling the matter in my mind.

"But I am!" Jared said, his frustration visible and mounting.

"No, you're not, you're just confused," I assured him.

We had ambushed Jared, taken him hostage, and force-fed him a heavy dose of religious rhetoric, ignorant bigotry, and conditional

58

love. We professed our deep love for him and expressed great concern for his well being in both this life and the next, but made it clear that his role within the family would change dramatically should he continue down the dark path that he had chosen.

"Why? Why would God do that to you, or anyone?" we demanded to know.

"I don't know why, and I can't explain it to you because I don't understand it myself. But I know that I am gay, and that I have always been this way!" Jared cried, his voice desperate and his cheeks wet with tears.

Jared's response to our barrage was an unwavering, passionate plea for understanding and acceptance, coupled with his own admission of confusion and doubt. His tears, though heartbreaking for me, served only to fuel my resolve; how could he live a happy life as a homosexual if it was already causing him so much pain to be one? All I had to do was convince him to take a closer look at his miserable existence in order to revert him back into the happy young man that he had once been. I was determined to save my little brother from himself, and in doing so bring peace to our forever family.

My intentions were ignorant in their nobility. I was panicked; we were quickly becoming nothing like the family that I had wished for since childhood, and my brothers were not fulfilling their roles in my vision of the future. I had long held fast to future memories of our own children growing up together. I dreamed of summer vacations spent together splashing in the ocean, gathered around Mom's kitchen table eating pancakes, and traveling westward in happy convoys along the highways of our childhood.

In time I discovered that it would not be Harrison or Jared that destroyed any chance of even the least of these dreams coming true.

It would be our sister Becky.

Chapter 25: October 2009

We made good time through the Texas Panhandle with the cruise control set at seventy-five. The landscape was for the most part flat fields peppered by windmill farms and the occasional small town. Before long we came upon Groom, home to both a leaning water tower and the largest cross in the western hemisphere. The water tower was worthy of a slow-down as we passed, but the cross was something we had to see up close. Several stories high and visible for miles in every direction, it looked very much out of place standing above the flat plains of Texas.

"It's so white, I wonder how it stays so clean?" I wondered aloud as I turned off the highway and took the access road that led to the cross.

"Isn't this tornado country?" Connor had his head out the open window and was clicking away with the camera as he marveled at the structure that towered overhead.

I pulled the car up to the parking lot, happy to see just a couple of cars parked nearby. I didn't feel like meeting up with a crowd of people, especially should they be of a religious, zealous, testifying sort. We jumped out into the wind, and as Connor closed his door I looked into the back seat. I was reluctant to leave Jared behind again, but knew that he was content to stay where he was for the moment. I pushed the door shut with a quiet click and then ran to catch up with Connor, who was already standing at the base of the cross.

"This is massive!" I shouted as I approached.

Connor grunted in agreement, his head cocked back in an attempt to take in the whole of what stood before us. The structure provided shelter from the winds that whipped past its base on both sides. Connor took advantage of the calm, lighting another cigarette.

The cross was fashioned as a square column measuring at least fifteen feet across on each side. I guessed it to be more than twenty stories tall, with the cross arms reaching out at least five stories in either direction. The outside was a layer of white sheet metal siding, and although we couldn't see inside, I assumed that the interior had to be made of something very strong, perhaps steel beams, or rebar welded together in a zillion places.

I stood in the shadow of the giant symbol of sacrifice and wondered why I didn't feel anything more than fascination at the size of it. I approached the cross and leaned against the cold white surface, tipping my head back to look up. The sky was a beautiful blue, with just a few wisps of cloud drifting in the wind. I closed my eyes and waited, but nothing more came over me than the foolish feeling that I was trying to force a spiritual moment.

I opened my eyes and laughed at myself. I had promised Ella that I would take whatever the road west of Independence held in store for me as it came, and that I would not try to force emotions or moments. Here I was, not twenty-four hours into it, trying to do just that.

"Man, it's a bit nipply out, isn't it?" I said loudly as I left the shelter of the cross and stepped back into the wind. I zipped up my sweatshirt without a thought to my irreverence, and just then an older gentleman hobbled around the corner of the cross with the aid of a walker. I drew my hood up over my head in a useless attempt to hide my embarrassment.

"Nice, Matthew." Connor, who hadn't stepped inside a church for years and was smoking a cigarette in the shadow of a two hundred foot cross, chastised me for my crude joke.

"Yeah, that was smooth, wasn't it? I wonder if they have a bathroom inside, I've gotta piss like a racehorse," I said, making for the visitor's center.

There was a bathroom, and after using it I browsed the gift shop with Connor. There were shirts, hats, posters, necklaces, books, and anything else that Jesus could be painted, etched, or printed on. After a few minutes I signaled Connor that it was time to go, and began heading for the exit.

I was almost out of the shop when a little figurine standing on a glass shelf near the door caught my attention. I was drawn to it immediately, and picked it up for further inspection. It was a little boy carved out of wood and painted in soft brown earth tones. His right arm was extended in apparent wonderment, while his head was tipped back at a slight angle. He had no facial features, but I imagined a happy smile and wide eyes fixating on the object held aloft in his left hand. It was a balloon on a string, fashioned of fine wire. The artist had finished off the balloon by twisting the wire to incorporate a single word at the center.

Hope.

Chapter 26: Summer 1996

Becky was my older sister, my parent's second child. She had married a man from Canada and lived out west in Alberta. She had an annoying habit of coming to visit us each summer, and she always stayed longer than anyone really wanted her to. A typical summer visit from Becky would last for two weeks, sometimes even longer, in spite of the fact that our parents had always warned us to never wear out our welcome.

The nervous anticipation and build up to one of Becky's visits was dramatic and stressful. Mom would clean her kitchen like a madwoman, worrying about which of her maternal shortcomings would be put up for public scrutiny, and Dad would begin an entire new list of outdoor projects to keep himself busy and out of Becky's way.

Becky would blaze into town like a newly hired sheriff, eager to make an example of the first local to defy her authority and expertise as homemaker, mother, and power shopper. She would shower us with gifts in spite of the fact that we never bought her or her kids much of anything. Her husband's father owned a very successful business, and she would bring the latest batch of hats, pens, and shirts that had been decorated with the company name and logo. I always felt as though she were branding us like family cattle, lest we dare to forget her when she left us after two long weeks.

She needn't have bothered to brand us that year. Her actions that summer made her impossible to forget. After the disastrous intervention, Becky sent Jared a letter that outlined the direct results of his "decision" to live as a homosexual. In it she explained that she and her husband had long ago decided that should any member of the family choose to be gay, that person would no longer exist for their children. This meant that Becky and her husband would never so much as mention Jared in their home, and that their children would never see him, talk to him, or know about him. She was in essence wiping him from her family.

As if passing such hateful judgment on Jared was not black-hearted enough, she reminded him that the punishment was his own fault, the consequence for electing to live a homosexual life contrary to God's laws.

If nothing else, Becky was evenhanded in her bigotry. Harrison had been sentenced (in absentia) by her moral court, and had been mailed a poison pen letter of his own.

While the majority of the family was at odds with Jared's lifestyle, we had no intentions of cutting him out of our lives completely. In time, Jared became the other gay brother and son, the one that lived nearby. We continued to spend time together, most of it at Mom and Dad's. My children knew and loved him as an uncle.

But Becky's visits became a different story altogether, marked as they were by segregation, contention, and heartbreak. Harrison lived far away in Connecticut and had very little contact with any of us, so his punishment was easily administered. Jared lived nearby and was a regular visitor to Mom and Dad's, so Becky's efforts to keep her kids away from him became an underlying theme of her time in New Hampshire.

I did my part to maintain an unsettled peace within the family by letting Becky know when Jared would be coming around. She would pack her kids into the car and drive away until it was safe to return. I felt like a traitor to my little brother, but at the time I thought it best for all involved to avoid a confrontation.

Regardless of how conflicted I felt about homosexuality, family, God, and eternity, Becky's actions shocked me. Her behavior shined a light on my own potential for bigotry, and kept me from treading the same deplorable path. I loved Jared and Harrison, and so I would not deny them my love, or the love of my children. Ella and I welcomed everyone into our home, especially Jared. Our children worshipped him in the way that any good uncle should be.

I expected that at some point Mom and Dad would stand up to Becky and put a stop to her imposition of such hateful rules on their home each summer, but they said not a word. I stood by, hoping, waiting, and praying as Becky drove her hateful wedge through the family.

But I could only hope, wait, and pray for so long.

Chapter 27: October 2009

We stopped in Amarillo for some pizza. We had been on the road for a solid twelve hours, and I had been awake for close to thirty. Fatigued, reeking of cigarette smoke, and in need of a shower, I was right where I wanted to be.

After a hot meal, several caffeinated sodas, a whore's bath in the restroom for me and a cigarette for Connor, we were once again riding down the highway, the border of New Mexico our next waypoint. Connor had offered to spell me at the wheel, and I was happy to accept. I leaned the seat back a bit, careful to avoid crushing Jared into the back seat, then folded my arms over my chest but kept my eyes open, knowing there was little chance of even so much as a catnap in the car.

"Tucumcari?" Connor, wondered aloud, pointing at a billboard a few minutes down the highway.

"Yeah, I've heard of it, the town is named after a famous prostitute from the old west. Cari always came twice," I lied without conviction.

"Shut up," Connor snorted his appreciation at my dirty joke.

"I'm just telling you what I heard," I protested.

"Whatever."

"Maybe it was that she always let her clients come twice for the same price," I suggested, an obvious effort to keep the joke alive.

Connor didn't take the bait, but I didn't mind. I gazed out the window as the last few miles of Texas whipped past. It was a strange but comfortable feeling, to be driving halfway across the country in a tiny little rental car with Connor. It had been years since we had been close, and the fault was mine.

I had spent most of my adult life believing that my brothers needed become more like the brothers that I wanted them to be rather than the brothers that they were. I had dispensed endless amounts of counsel, offering up hypocritical advice on how to better live their lives. My brothers had slowly distanced themselves from me over time, rather than subject themselves to my self-righteous attitude. It was only in recent years, with the prodding of maturity and the patient example of an insightful wife that I had made a conscious effort to accept my brothers for who they were and how they lived their lives.

Jared had been the first to witness my eventual renaissance, but with limited access to Connor and none at all to Harrison, it had been difficult to effectively demonstrate my change of heart to them.

I was keeping the door to the jury room shut until the trip was over, but as we approached New Mexico and saw the massive sign welcoming us to "The Land of Enchantment," I was feeling rather optimistic about my new self and my chances at redemption.

"Prepare to be enchanted!" Connor warned as we sped past.

For a moment I allowed myself to believe that I already had been.

Chapter 28: 1997-2002

Several summers passed under the shadow of Becky's rules before I finally tired of the stress, guilt, and hostility that stemmed from holding the family apart at arm's length. I began to make a point of defying Becky's hateful rules. Photos of Harrison and Jared were left on display in our home, and my brothers were an open topic of conversation in the presence of her kids. I stopped making any effort to warn Becky of Jared's arrivals, and encouraged him to come over to Mom and Dad's whenever he pleased.

The resulting drama became something of a summer ritual; Jared would pull into the driveway, and Becky would scoop her kids up to either lock them in an upstairs bedroom or rush them into her rental car and speed away to the safety of wandering among strangers at the mall. I marveled at the desperate urgency with which she protected her children from her own brother. The tension between Becky and I grew thicker with each passing summer, but I felt that in the end something would give, and she would see the error of her ignorant ways.

In an obvious effort to mask her bigotry, Becky came up with the ridiculous idea that we should meet together as siblings for dinner one night each summer. She called it "The Sibling Dinner," making it easy to exclude her children. From its very inception, the whole thing felt to me like a photo-op dinner with a slimy politician eager to win over a disgruntled slice of the popular vote.

Connor refused to attend the charade, but Jared went willingly each year. The dinners were lame and uncomfortable affairs, with moments of awkward laughter at the rehashing of childhood memories peppered throughout the course of the meal. Becky would preside over these dinners, acting as if nothing were amiss. The conversation was strained at best, and every year I vowed to never again break bread with Becky.

After one such meal I asked Jared why he attended each summer, when Connor refused to go as a show of solidarity to Jared's cause.

"She's my sister," he offered in reply.

It was then that I decided I had prayed, waited, and hoped long enough. It was time to make some sparks and start a cleansing fire, one that would either purify or destroy the family for good. As luck would have it, Becky supplied me with the perfect opportunity to do just that a few months later.

Becky had announced a return visit to New Hampshire with her infant daughter in the Fall. I pointed out to my parents that it had been ten years since we had been together as a family, the last time being when Ella and I were married. I volunteered to contact Harrison in Connecticut and coordinate a family reunion of sorts during Becky's visit. Mom and Dad offered up no resistance to the idea, and even suggested that we could spend some of that time sorting out all of our childhood belongings, and in so doing clear up a large amount of space in their barn loft.

As the weeks passed and the date grew near, I allowed myself a little faith in my plan. I believed that if I played it easy and didn't force the issue, Becky would take a single step forward and allow both Jared and Harrison near her little girl, who was making the trip with her mother due to her young age. At barely a year old, Becky's daughter would have no idea that two of her four uncles were gay, so what harm could their presence pose?

I envisioned a dinner table surrounded by Mom, Dad, and all of their children, with a good portion of in-laws and grandchildren as well. While it would not be the complete family gathering that I had always hoped for, it would be a huge step in the right direction. It seemed impossible to me that Becky, when faced with the choice of being part of a happy reunion or the evil destroyer of it, would choose the less honorable of the two.

I had, however, underestimated my sister's ability to bring about the impossible. On the evening of the reunion kick-off dinner, Becky called me from Mom and Dad's house.

"Matthew, are Harrison and Jared already on their way over here?" Becky's voice sounded cheerful and innocent on the other end of the line. I ignored the hazard lights blinking in my mind's eye, and plowed right into the answer with hope wrapped around each word.

"They should be, I told everyone to be there around five so we can hang out in the kitchen and make dinner together. We'll head over in a few minutes. Are Sarah and Joshua there yet?" I held my breath upon finishing my response, a silent prayer in my head.

"Yes, they are here. I am going to their house before Harrison and Jared show up. I will leave the baby with a sitter at Sarah's and come back tomorrow for the barn cleanup." The cheerful tone remained, but the innocence was lost.

"Wait, why are you going to Sarah's house?" I asked, already knowing the answer but wanting to force her to say it out loud.

"You know why, Matthew," Becky said, avoiding an actual answer.

"Becky, you knew they were coming and you didn't object. Please don't do this, don't ruin the first chance in ten years that we have at being together." I tried to keep my tone even and calm, but knew that I sounded desperate and on the verge of tears.

"Matthew, I made a promise to Richard, and I am going to keep it. Harrison and Jared have not changed the way they live, and so they are not going to be around my children." She was on the defense, her tone sharp and biting.

"Bigot!" I shouted into the phone before hanging up.

Chapter 29: October 2009

"What the hell is that?" Connor leaned over the steering wheel and focused his stare far ahead, above the horizon. I looked and saw something dark and indiscriminate speeding faster than I thought was possible across the blue backdrop of New Mexico's sky.

"UFO? Are we looking at a UFO?" The hope in Connor's voice was infectious.

I grabbed the camera and asked, "How far do you think we are from Area 51?"

"I don't know, but that thing does not look like any airplane or helicopter I have ever seen!" Connor insisted.

My little brother was getting excited; it appeared that all his conspiracy theories were about to be confirmed by light of day, in the middle of highway 40, just west of a New Mexico town named after a very accomplished hooker from the late 1800's.

"It doesn't look like it's moving in a straight line, either." I could taste the stale breath of open-mouthed wonder as it passed over my tongue.

Our little car could not match the speed of the UFO, so all we could do was snap a few photos and watch as it crossed the highway several miles ahead of us. It soon blinked out of view, leaving us with nothing more than a few blurry photos and a sense of wonderment.

"Damn, I wish this car would go faster," Connor complained.

"I'm surprised it will go as fast as it does, eighty-five is not too bad for such a little engine," I remarked.

I was just as frustrated, perhaps even more so than Connor. I had imagined Jared being happily drawn up into the bright light of a tractor beam and taken away from a world that he didn't understand. I could not picture a more fitting compliment to our odyssey.

We drove on for several miles, listening to more screeching guitars of the Eighties. The music took my mind on a road trip of its own, back to four lousy years in high school, a string of girlfriends better forgotten, and countless hours spent listening to records in the attic bedroom I shared with my three brothers.

"There it is again!" Connor's voice once again served to tear me from a waking dream.

I grabbed the camera and switched it to video, then stuck it out the window and held it up against the rushing wind, aimed in the general direction of the mystery craft.

"It looks like it's turning around for another pass! I'm going to try to get us underneath it when it crosses the highway!" Connor shouted.

I watched as the strange dark object began to turn in a wide arc.

"Whoa! What the hell? Tell me those aren't wings, and that they aren't moving up and down!" My mouth hung open again as I watched the UFO bank slightly, giving us our first view of something fluttering on either side of the fuselage.

"It's a dragon! Matthew, *that* is a dragon!" The childlike excitement in Connor's voice suspended my own disbelief, and my fantasy moved from an alien encounter to the discovery of a real dragon with beating wings, sharp teeth, and fiery breath.

I held the camera up like a talisman, willing the beast to come closer and fly alongside our little black rental car. My juju wasn't that strong, however, and we were still a few miles short of driving directly underneath it as it approached the highway. Acknowledging that we wouldn't get a closer shot, Connor pulled the car over and jumped out. I followed suit, and as I steadied the camera I noticed the distinct and disappointing sound of a helicopter.

A moment later, I could easily discern the twin prop rotors of an Osprey aircraft. The props were tilted forward on an angle, creating the bizarre shape that from far away had appeared to be flapping wings.

"Damn, it's just an Osprey aircraft! What the hell is an Osprey doing out here in the desert?" I shouted the question, angry at the inevitable outcome of our fantastical chase.

"Well, it was still pretty cool, chasing a UFO down the highway. Look at it this way, it was an adventure, and now we have the story to tell." A blend of disappointment and adrenaline fueled Connor's words.

"Yeah, I know, but think about how much more of an adventure we'd have to tell had it really been a UFO *or* a dragon," I countered, sucker-punched by reality.

I switched off the camera and turned back to the car. As I did I noticed something large and white lying in the tall grass. It looked like a discarded roof top luggage carrier missing its bottom half. Upon further inspection I noticed that not only was it made of a plastic too weak to hold luggage, but that the several rows of vents down two sides would have made it less than waterproof.

"What is it?" Connor asked.

I stood it up on one end for a better look. "I think it fell off an RV, maybe it's a housing for a refrigeration unit or some other piece of equipment on the roof," I suggested.

"Yeah, you're right," Connor said.

"Get a shot of this," I said, handing him the camera. He took a few steps back as I squatted down and squeezed myself inside the plastic housing. "Matthew on a half shell!" I laughed, holding my hands together as if in prayer.

Connor laughed and snapped a few shots of my efforts to look pious inside my makeshift roadside shrine.

"Well, it wasn't on the road-trip bucket-list, but it is now," I said, shedding my shrine.

Connor handed me the camera, then bent over and grabbed the housing. He looked down the highway before running out into it, dragging the housing behind him. I watched as he set it down on the tarmac and sat inside it, facing oncoming traffic. A semi truck was maybe a mile away and coming fast.

"Matthew, get some pictures!" Connor put his hands up in front of his chest as if he were holding a steering wheel.

I ran out into the road behind my little brother and took a few shots of him sitting in the westbound lane of highway forty with a semi truck barreling down on him like mechanized death in the background.

Chapter 30: Fall 2002

Sarah had never been one to miss out on a chance to throw herself into the middle of a family fray. She called me from Mom and Dad's to inform me that I had ruined everything. Mom and Dad, ever exemplary in their behavior, had jumped in their car and driven off in a huff after the heated phone conversation between Becky and me. Becky had done the same. The reunion was over before it had even started.

"I am not the one that ruined everything, it was Becky and her bigot of a husband, with their homophobic promises to each other," I replied evenly when confronted by Sarah's high-pitched anger over the phone.

"Matthew, how can you call her that?" She asked.

"Look up the word in any dictionary, and you will see why. She is intolerant and prejudiced against gay people, and that makes her a bigot. If she doesn't like being called a bigot, she should stop being one."

"So, that's it?" Sarah asked.

"I'll be over for dinner in a few minutes," I replied, and hung up.

The decision to go alone needed no explanation; Ella had heard enough of both phone conversations to know that she was not going to drag our children into the middle of the emotional mess that the reunion had become. Over the ten years we had been married she had witnessed her share of the contention, sarcasm, and selfishness that made up so much of my family. There was plenty of happiness and love, but they came at a high price, and Ella was beginning to tire of paying it.

I said goodbye and kissed her. She grabbed my face with both of her soft hands and looked me in the eyes. "Matty, be careful over there. Remember that you have a family of your own now. We have to stop the drama and anger from spilling over into our home." Her eyes brimmed with tears. I felt the shame of what my family had become billow around me like hot steam.

"I know. But I have to go, I planned this nightmare and I can't leave Jared and Harrison to face it alone." I kissed her again before leaving the warm comfort of our home.

The quick drive to Mom and Dad's took a little longer than usual. I made a few extra turns in order to calm down and allow me time to think. Ella's cautionary words and the fear in her eyes played on a loop in my mind. Our relationship had come a long way. We had been making a more conscious effort to talk, to love, to forgive, and to forget. While we were not quite out of the proverbial woods, we were well on our way to the bright, clear, meadow of happiness that we truly believed lay somewhere down the path that we were on together.

The distraction of an extended family in turmoil had been a constant source of derailment, and it seemed that no matter how far we managed to distance ourselves from it, the swirling vortex of discontent that was my family had the power to pull us back in, putting all that we had accomplished at risk.

The extra drive time failed to calm me down. I was tired of being blown about; this time I would be the wind. As I neared Mom and Dad's house I couldn't help but imagine myself as a tornado ready to tear across the driveway and into the kitchen.

Chapter 31: October 2009

We passed the next hour or so of highway by listening to more music from our past. I had taken the wheel back, leaving Connor free to play deejay. I took another bittersweet voyage through time, but with Connor at my side it was more sweet than bitter. I pulled the car off the highway and into Santa Rosa, New Mexico, a tiny little town that boasted a classic car museum.

"Holy crap! Check out all these cars!" I couldn't contain my excitement at the sight of all the shiny paint and polished chrome as we stepped inside the museum.

I had never been much of a car enthusiast, but I did appreciate the look, shine, and muscle of a classic. The museum had it all. There must have been at least fifty cars, most of them restored and gleaming with the pride of American craftsmanship.

We spent an hour weaving our way through the maze of machines, admiring the leather, the wood, the chrome, and the bright, rich colors. We passed the camera back and forth, taking photos of our favorites, posing with them as if they were our own. Connor bent down inside the open hood of an old white Dodge and pretended to work on the engine. His sleeves were rolled up, exposing the tattoos on his forearms, which added a genuine touch.

My favorite car was an old Buick painted in a pearl-finished military green. Its grill was a heavy, toothy monstrosity. I knelt down, stuck my hands into it, and made a tortured face, as if being devoured by the metal beast.

Cars were not the only items on display. There were bikes, signs, gas pumps, and a stuffed iguana, which Connor had to lay down next to and pretend to kiss for the camera. We wandered our way to the back of the museum, and both stopped upon spotting an old silver telephone booth standing amid the auto memorabilia.

"Are you thinking what I'm thinking?" I asked Connor.

He was already on his way into the booth. I snapped a sequence of photos while Connor played Clark Kent tugging at his collar and pushing the door shut as if making a quick change into Superman.

We left the museum after using the bathroom and drinking some Orange Crush from classic glass bottles. Back at the wheel, I stifled a yawn and fought the urge to set the cruise control.

"Let's get a room in Albuquerque, I'm not going to be able to stay awake for much longer," I said.

Connor searched for his lighter. I rolled down the windows, and we put some more mileage on the meter to the sound of angry lyrics that cried out against hypocrites and the self-righteous. The guilt of decades spent preaching righteous behavior to my brothers while ignoring so many of my own imperfections grew more intense with every song on the play list. I was soon overcome by my emotions and on the verge of breaking down into a sobbing mess on the side of the highway. I silenced the music with a jab of my finger, and searched the landscape for a distraction.

"What do we have left on the road trip bucket list?" I asked.

Connor opened up the notebook and read aloud, "Abandoned building, oil well, windmill, car parked across the highway…"

I yanked the wheel to the right and hit the brakes. "Let's check off abandoned building," I said, grabbing the camera and throwing my door open.

Chapter 32: Fall 2002

I pulled into Mom and Dad's driveway to find Joshua and Sarah waiting for me outside. We spent a good twenty minutes arguing about Becky and her immovable position. They refused to accept that in enabling Becky to impose her rules over the reunion they were condoning her bigotry.

"We aren't agreeing with her, but they are her children, and she can raise them any way she wants. She made a promise to Richard and she doesn't want to break it. You should respect her choice," Sarah said, planting herself right where she loved to be, dead center of the drama.

"I cannot respect her choice because it infringes upon the rest of the family and their wish to be together. She has no right to force her ignorance on the rest of us, and I refuse to grant her the power to control this family!" I was almost shouting, and I was just getting started.

"Matthew, if you made a promise to Ella to protect your children from something, wouldn't you do anything you had to in order to keep it?" Sarah persisted in her misguided need to defend our older sister.

"What are you saying, that she is protecting her children from Jared and Harrison? What are Jared and Harrison going to do, molest them? Make them gay? Hurt them? You'd better be careful with what you say, because you know damn well that Jared and Harrison would walk in front of a truck to save her kids, and they don't even know them. I can't believe you are defending her homophobia like this!" I countered.

Sarah's attempt at reasoning made my stomach churn with disgust. She and Joshua had always allowed Jared to interact with her own little boy, and though I had always hoped their attitude would serve as an example to Becky and Richard, my constant fear was that Sarah would eventually follow in Becky's footsteps.

"We are not defending her," Joshua said.

"Do you think she is a homophobe?" I asked point-blank.

79

"That doesn't matter, what matters is that we need to try and get along this weekend. What good will come from all your yelling and name-calling?" Joshua was studying to be an attorney, and was very adept at avoiding direct answers. Normally I admired that quality in my brother-in-law, but there was nothing in this particular response that endeared him to me.

"No, it does matter! If you turn a blind eye to the reasons behind her choice and allow her to dictate when and who and where the family spends time together, you are ignoring the feelings of others and condoning her behavior. As for the yelling and accusations, I have been quiet for too long, and these are not accusations, these are facts!" I was in full swing, countering with conviction.

"We are not turning a blind eye to her reasons, we are just trying to support her. If we don't stand with her then she stands alone." Sarah's voice was passionate, and it made me sad to hear her pleas for Becky's sake.

"Evil people should stand alone! How can you choose her over Jared and Harrison if you truly don't agree with her?" Shivering in the cold night air as I was, I must have appeared to be trembling with anger.

"Come on Matthew, you don't really believe that she is evil, do you? She believes that she is doing the right thing, and just because you disagree with her doesn't mean you can attack her and call her a bigot," Joshua said, making a play at reasoning with me.

It didn't work. "Actually, I do think that she is evil. She is prejudiced, intolerant, and hateful, which makes her a bigot." I rubbed my arms to keep them busy as much as to keep me warm.

"If you want to hate someone, hate Richard. She is afraid to betray him," Sarah explained.

"No, no, no, she can't blame this on Richard! She knew that Jared and Harrison would be here, and that she was bringing the baby. She could have talked to her bigot of a husband and told him that she wasn't going to hide their kids from her brothers anymore, but she didn't, and now she wants to hide behind him, selling him out as the reason behind all these years of hate. She's sold you a bullshit sandwich and you've swallowed it whole!" I was pacing, the cold no longer the reason for my fidgeting. The regret of standing by for so long and allowing, even enabling Becky's behavior was boiling over from within me.

"Ok, we are getting nowhere, and I think we all need to calm down before we say anything more that we might regret later on. Let's just go inside and try to have a peaceful dinner. This will not get fixed standing outside in the cold all night." Joshua seemed to understand that I had not yet begun to fight, and was doing his best to keep some sort of reasonable peace for the time being.

I stood still and quiet for a long moment, staring up into the starry autumn night before calmly stating my final argument. "Fine, but let me say something first. Becky is wrong and you both know it. Mom and Dad know it too, but they are cowards and won't stand up to her. Maybe they agree with her, but who can tell, since they don't say anything about it. I am just sick of her ruining any chance of peace in this family. She claims that Jared and Harrison have a choice about being gay, but she has a choice too. Becky could be the bigger person, but she is too stubborn and mean-spirited to do so. She is an evil, black-hearted, bigot, and this is not over."

With that said, I walked between them and headed into my parent's house for the reunion that never was.

Chapter 33: October 2009

I was climbing through the fence before Connor had even opened his car door. As I slipped through, my pants caught on one of the barbs. It took me a moment to extricate myself without injury. By the time I was free, Connor had caught up to me.

"Ranchers mean business in these here parts. Their fence barbs are sharper than an Arkansas toothpick, and they pull their wire tight, just the way they like their jeans." My western drawl was in my opinion, passable.

Once through the fence, we ran towards the abandoned town like sixth graders let off the bus on the last day of school. We slowed to a walk and surveyed the area as we approached the front steps of the nearest building, a little house with front porch and boarded windows. To one side of the house we could see an ancient truck. The yellow paint of the cab was mottled with rust, and it had long ago settled comfortably onto flat tires that dug into the red earth beneath them.

I followed Connor up the steps and onto the sagging porch. He entered the house, but I stayed outside, fascinated by the yellow truck. I imagined the family that had lived there long ago. I pictured a husband, his wife, and their two little girls. The young couple had spotted each other across a dance hall in Albuquerque. He had been too scared to ask such a pretty girl to dance, but both his friends and hers had pushed them out onto the floor. They were married three weeks later. Soon a baby was on the way, and he had moved them out to their own little house, far away from the pressing matters of the "big" city.

They had been happy. A second baby girl had added to their joy, and his modest trucking business had provided well enough. His weeks were long, but coming home after a haul was the greatest feeling in the world. He would honk his horn as he drew up, and his girls would come running out, waving and laughing as he parked his bright yellow truck next to the little house. He would leap from the cab, scoop his daughters up in his arms and spin them around, kissing them and loving on them, their laughter and adoration renewing his will to live. As he put them down and they spun away in dizzy circles, his wife would step out onto the porch, an apron tied tightly around her tiny waist, a smile on her face. He would approach the porch, stopping before the top step so as to look straight into her happy eyes before kissing her deeply.

It was their heaven on earth, their own private eternity. Everything they could ever want was growing old within the walls of that house.

"Matthew, check this out!" Connor's voice cut my dream right down the middle, but it was just as well, because I was sure to imagine something bad happening to that happy family.

"Take a picture of me on the floor, like an addict passed out in a crack house," Connor laughed, breaking open my somber mood.

I followed the sound of my brother's voice into what might have been a family room at one time. The floor was littered with trash, broken furniture, and dust. I kicked at an old toaster full of straw. "It does look like a crack house," I marveled, turning on the camera and taking a few photos of Connor lying on the floor with an old jar in his hand.

We spent the next several minutes exploring the inside of the house before heading out to the back yard. There was a time-weathered water tank set atop an old concrete shed, and Connor scrambled up the side of it to peer inside and snap a photo.

We worked our way around the outside of the house to the truck, and I climbed into the cab. There was a large hole in the windshield, and Connor took a picture when I stuck my head through it and made a nasty face, as if I were flying out onto the road.

"We should get going," I said with great reluctance. I could have explored the little town for the rest of the afternoon, waiting for dark when all the ghosts would appear. I was sure that Connor would have been up for it too, but we had to make tracks.

"Wait," Connor said. I watched him run into the road and pick up a long, narrow piece of shredded tire. He leaned back, spread his feet in a powerful stance, and held the piece of tire up into the air like a longbow made from black wood. His other hand rested against his chest, as if pulling back on the bow's string, an arrow nocked and ready to fire.

"Hold it, don't move, you look so cool right now. Let me get a picture!" I hurried to turn the camera back on and get a good shot. The sun cast a shadow of Connor and his bow, reminding me of the Native American petroglyphs that I had seen on my last trip to Arizona.

"Got it," I said, allowing Connor to drop his tire-bow and run for the car.

Once back inside the car, I checked on Jared before merging onto the highway. He was right where we had left him; quiet, content, and cozy in the back seat.

"Keep your eyes peeled for a windmill and an oil well, we need to check them off the list," I reminded Connor as he checked "abandoned building" off the list.

"Will do," he replied, replacing the notebook and pulling out a cigarette.

I rolled the windows down and wondered about the owner of the yellow truck, and what could have brought such an abrupt end to his living dream.

Chapter 34: Fall 2002

Becky returned to the house during the final preparations for dinner, but she circumvented the kitchen and made her way upstairs. After hiding her daughter in an upstairs bedroom, she entered the kitchen looking defiant, seemingly determined to preserve her proper place as the most important member of the family. A large part of me wanted to lash out. I imagined slapping her across the face with the back of my hand, but I never would have, no matter how badly I wanted her to suffer. I knew that the most effective weapon for taking Becky down was her own prejudice. To use Becky's own words against her and allow others to see for themselves what kind of a person she truly was would eventually be her undoing.

After a short and awkward dinner, we dispersed, with plans of returning in the morning for the toy cleanup out in the barn. Back at home I filled Ella in on all that had transpired, and her reaction was just what I had expected.

"How can she do that? Matthew, your sister is crazy! It's like she doesn't even have a soul." Ella sat on our bed while I pulled off my clothes for a shower.

"I know. She's a borderline sociopath. She and Dad are a lot alike; they are both so full of pride that they can't admit when they're wrong. I remember the first time I saw it in her. We were walking home from the bus stop one day, and I bragged about getting a perfect score on my spelling test. She said she was better than me at spelling, so I challenged her to spell all the words on my test. She did fine until she got to the word *dirt*, which she spelled with a *u*. I corrected her, and she went mental!" I said, dropping my clothes in a pile on the floor of the closet and grinning at the memory.

"I bet she did, you were such a little snot," Ella laughed.

"Yes, I do admit to taking great pleasure in making my older sister angry," I said without guilt before continuing my story. "Becky screamed at me, and I laughed at her, so she came after me. I turned and ran away, right into Dad's wheelbarrow. As usual, Dad got mad at me, and not at her. He has always defended her, no matter how crazy wrong she is. To this day, if I so much as say the word *dirt*, she explodes and Dad gets angry. It's like they made a promise to forever defend each other, no matter how deranged they both become!" I exclaimed. My bare-assed tirade at an end, I headed for the shower.

We spent the next day in the barn, digging through the past by way of the many boxes packed full of toys, clothes, and books from our childhood. I ignored Becky and stuck close to Harrison, Jared, and Connor. Each new item that we found in the dusty boxes sparked memories of growing up together, which in turn brought about laughter and happy teasing between brothers. I hoped that our overt happiness would demonstrate to Becky just how isolated she would become should she continue down her ignorant path. The tension between us crackled and snapped like electricity arcing across empty space.

I was comfortable with my decision to speak out against her, and felt that I had made my position clear enough. She would soon leave for the frigid North, and her destructive influence would fade with the contrails of her plane as it passed over the Midwest. Fade but not disappear, of course, because she was bound to return.

But the climate of her visits would never be the same again. No longer would I allow Becky to have absolute control. For years I had hoped for a peaceful end to several years of silent discord, but with this latest display Becky had moved us from a cold war into a red-hot conflict.

As for Mom and Dad, it was all I could do to refrain from hurling obscenities in their direction. I was beyond frustrated with them for abdicating their responsibilities as parents. Dad had issued no patriarchal decree, no gentle command to lay down our arms and love each other, and Mom had done little more than grit her teeth. There was no mistaking their own frustration with the situation, but rather than address it, they had resorted to their usual reaction to friction between their adult children, which was to run away and hide from it.

Over the following few summers I continued to ignore Becky's rules, bringing Jared over to swim at Mom and Dad's whenever it pleased us. We would invade the kitchen as we had since childhood, our swimsuits dripping wet trails across the linoleum. We chewed sandwiches, crunched chips, and guzzled soda while laughing and chattering away like brothers should. Becky would scoot her children up the stairs, hiding them away like Anne Frank's parents hiding their daughter from the Nazis. I would sometimes listen at the base of the stairs, half expecting to hear the sound of a dresser being dragged in front of the door.

The yearly sibling dinners continued without Harrison, who remained in Connecticut, and Connor, who still refused to go along with such madness. The tension was thick and undeniable, growing more so each summer. We forced smiles and laughter, recounting the safe and neutral memories of childhood.

In spite of all my efforts to weaken Becky's stranglehold on the family, she seemed to be tightening her grip.

Chapter 35: October 2009

Within a few miles Connor and I standing at another barbed wire fence.

"Hey, was 'plastic eating cow' on our list of photo ops?" I asked, pointing at a large brown bovine chewing on a long piece of lightweight black plastic.

"Nice, get a picture of the plastic eater." As he spoke, Connor was stretching his arms high into the air and tilting his head back, face to the sky. His words were accompanied by a loud groan of satisfaction; he looked and sounded like a dog standing on his hind legs to stretch and yawn after a long nap.

I climbed the fence carefully and dropped down on the other side between two fresh piles of cow manure. "Watch your step," I warned Connor as he followed me over into the minefield.

I had noticed the state of Connor's shoes when we stopped for lunch in Amarillo, and they were not fit for running carelessly through a field of moist cow crap. They were old and worn, the leather soft and pliable, like that of a well-used but beloved baseball mitt. Not only were they creased with wear and shiny from age, but the heels were mashed flat. Connor no longer pulled them up over the heels of his feet, choosing instead to slide them on like leather slippers.

"I wouldn't want you to get cow shit on your SHOEPERS!" I shouted over my shoulder as I ran toward the comical cow.

"Ha!" Connor caught the meaning of my word combination joke immediately, laughing as he caught up with me.

"How can you run in those things?" I asked, not really looking for an answer.

Connor didn't offer one anyway, he was too focused on his stealthy approach towards the plastic-eating cow. He needn't have bothered with sneaking, because the cow was committed to munching her synthetic snack, and she ignored the both of us completely.

"I think I'm gonna grab that out of her mouth," Connor said, looking at me with a grin.

"She's gonna kick you," I warned.

"You ready?"

"Yeah, I'm filming," I answered, stepping in closer to capture the action.

Connor took a few quick steps alongside the cow, then reached out a hand and grabbed the plastic as he ran past. Instead of pulling free from the cow's mouth, the plastic parted with a snap. Connor kept on running, turning in circles while I laughed myself breathless. The cow chewed on, impervious to my little brother's attempt at stealing her treat.

Once the laughter faded, I turned my attention to the real reason for jumping the fence and risking a shoe full of cow manure. I stood at the base of the windmill and listened to it creak as a warm breeze turned it slowly. The metal blades sifted the afternoon sunlight, creating a dizzying pattern of shadows and light on the ground. I took a deep breath and held it in as a wave of unexpected emotion washed over me. I couldn't suppress my sadness at the thought of passing countless windmills over so many years worth of family road trips. Regret and anger merged inside of me, just as it had so many times over the past several months.

But I was becoming more proficient at converting the familiar cocktail of emotions into fuel for change within myself. I chose to enjoy the moment, rather than regret the ones that I'd missed. In an instant I felt the bitterness pass, as if blown away by the same warm wind that turned the windmill.

It was silly and I knew it, but standing in the shadow of that giant metal flower, I felt as though I had chased down and conquered a windmill of my own. It felt good, and I shouted for joy as Connor and I ran back to the car, jumping over crap mines along the way.

Chapter 36: April 2004

While Becky's blockade had pushed me closer to accepting Jared and Harrison's homosexuality, my mind and heart remained at odds over how to define the terms of that acceptance. I wanted to love my brothers and treat them just as I did any straight and righteous person, but that was an ideal more easily imagined than fulfilled.

Just as it had to other states, the fight over the definition of marriage soon came to New Hampshire. Before long, the hallways and classrooms at church echoed with fearful comments and excited arguments against gay marriage. I was confused and frustrated; I loved my brothers, and I knew that Jared wanted nothing more in life than to be joined in happiness with someone that would love him without qualifications. That seemed reasonable to me, since it was exactly what Ella and I had been fighting for in our own marriage. The issue for most church members seemed to be the threat posed to the institution of marriage by legally joining two men or women. It was to me a silly notion, the thought that anyone could threaten a marriage other than the two people in it, but I listened earnestly to many of my fellow Mormons as they argued their case. I spent several weeks waiting for a clarity that never came.

I felt like a homeowner standing on his lawn with a dribbling garden hose, watching as a menacing brushfire crept ever closer to everything he owned. I could stand and try to fight back the inevitable, or I could admit defeat and run away. The trouble was that I wasn't sure which side was the menacing fire.

In an effort to figure it all out and put a permanent end to my wondering, I accepted an invitation by church leaders to carpool up to a public debate on gay marriage at the statehouse in Concord.

We sat in the large auditorium-like chambers of the state legislature and waited for the debate. The government was as slow in action as it had ever been, and we spent a fair amount of time just growing ever more impatient.

I watched as a constant flow of citizens entered the room. The line of demarcation was clear; a long aisle between the many rows of seats separated the opposing points of view. Upon walking through the double doors, people would step almost immediately to the left or the right, heading for the security of their fellows. I found it disheartening that the very room in which people were meant to come together for the good of all had been built as if division were in fact its intended purpose.

Not everyone had clued in on the obvious segregation, however. At one point two men holding hands crossed in front of our group, the limited space between seats causing their legs to brush against the knees of everyone in the row. I was horrified as my father made a show of pulling his legs up into his chest to prevent the gay men's legs from touching him. As he did so, I heard him half-mutter, "I wouldn't want it to rub off on me."

My head was floundering in a pool of disbelief. I knew Dad to be intolerant in private, but had never seen such an outward display of hatred from him in public. I felt a large measure of the respect I had for my father disappear before the two men had reached the end of our row.

At last, the debate began. A microphone was set up in the center of the room, and after a reading of the proposed amendment the floor was open to the public. A few of the state legislators sat behind a table at the head of the room, listening and scribbling notes as the people of New Hampshire stood to voice their opinions, beliefs, and arguments on the topic of gay marriage.

The arguments made against gay marriage seemed poorly prepared, most of them based upon religious beliefs and having nothing to do with the legal rights of human beings. One man quoted a few verses from the Old Testament, and then warned that the state of New Hampshire would suffer the wrath of God should marriage be legalized. Another stood and said in a loud voice, "God created Adam and Eve, not Adam and Steve!" Both men were cheered amid thunderous applause.

In stark contrast, the gay and lesbian supporters came off as smart and respectful, their arguments based on the freedoms upon which our country was founded. One man read a portion of the Declaration of Independence, emphasizing the equality of man and their

91

unalienable rights, stating that he believed in a God that inspired the precious document that set our nation apart from any other.

After several arguments and opinions from both sides, a man stood at the microphone to share his personal experience as a gay man unable to marry his long-time partner and thereby enjoy the benefits allowed any other legally married couple in New Hampshire. He was a prominent member of the local clergy, and having seen him in the papers and on the local news in recent weeks, I knew enough about him to understand that he had taken great personal risk in making his private life public. His argument in favor of gay marriage was eloquent, respectful, and impassioned.

As he spoke, I felt compassion for the man, and with it a swelling of regret for the way I had treated Harrison and Jared. Years of confusion slipped away as I felt the need to erase the asterisk that I had applied to their names when speaking, thinking, or feeling about them. My brothers were deserving of the same rights to happiness that I enjoyed, rights that had been given to them at birth, by the only Being worthy of judging them.

"Boooooo!" The hate-filled cry thundered across the room and against my ears, disrupting my emotional moment of realization. I looked down the row towards the sound and saw a man from my church, a man that I had known and respected for years, standing, shouting, and waving his fist in the air like a member of the angry mob storming Dr. Frankenstein's castle. My immediate reaction to this abhorrent behavior was embarrassment, but that was quickly replaced by the thought that he was in fact booing my brothers in absentia.

The din of murmuring filled the room, a direct result of the booing and fist waving. The man who had so respectfully conveyed his personal experience and feelings stood at the microphone, his head bowed as if in silent prayer. He seemed accustomed to such treatment. I felt shame wrap around me like a blanket, one that would not hide me from the men and women on the other side of the room. I sunk into my seat and began to wonder how much a cab ride home would cost. The thought of the return trip with these men disgusted me. I broke into a sweat and began to fidget. After several minutes of panic I stole away and placed a frantic call to Ella.

92

"I have to get out of here! This is horrible! Bill Rivers just stood up and booed at the gay Episcopalian Bishop while he was speaking. I feel like I'm in a Kafka story." I couldn't breathe, pacing the empty corridor in desperation.

"He did? Oh, that is just wrong! What are you going to do?"

"I don't know, a cab ride home would cost a fortune. You should have seen it Ella, two gay men walked past us in the aisle and Dad freaked out. He pulled his legs up into his seat so that they wouldn't touch him, and he muttered something about *it* rubbing off on him. Two of his own sons are gay, what does he think of them?" I was close to tears, but too angry to cry.

"I have wondered that for so long, and I don't think we'll ever know. I don't think it matters anyway. Look at today in this way, you went up there wondering what this gay marriage thing was all about, and it sounds like you figured it out..." Ella paused. I could hear her breathing.

A few tears burst through the dam of anger.

"There is no love here," I whispered.

"You'll be home soon. Listen, I know this sounds corny, and that you hate cliché, but ask yourself what Jesus would do, and then do it. I will love you either way, you know that." Ella's words calmed me down before the tears got out of hand. I felt my spine straighten, a direct result of her confidence in me.

I said goodbye and pocketed my phone. Having felt the calm of clarity, the debate was for me, at an end. I spent the rest of the afternoon wandering the state house hallways while nearby, angry and fearful men imagined themselves to be acting in the name of their God.

I walked back to the car with my father and the other members of the carpool in silence. The door of the minivan slid shut, trapping me inside with men in whose company I didn't want to spend another moment. I leaned my head against the window and watched the landscape whip past while wishing for time to fold in on itself and shorten the trip home. The car was filled with men that believed in a

93

God who fathered and loved all mankind, and who had extended to all of his children the free agency to live as they will, but their actions that afternoon had demonstrated hate and fear, and the words they had uttered betrayed their ignorance and self-righteousness.

I was grateful for the clarity that had come to me in their presence, but saddened by the cost.

Chapter 37: October 2009

The victory at the windmill was still fresh in my veins when I spotted the oil well. I pulled the car over, jumped out, and approached the sagging fence at the edge of the highway. After a look around and a moment's thought, I made to climb the fence. The crotch of my shorts got hung up on a stray wire, putting my most personal property in danger.

I heard Connor laugh as he watched me carefully extricate myself.

"You wouldn't be laughing if this were a barbed-wire fence," I said, feigning a hurtful tone.

"Yes I would."

"Yeah, you probably would." I pulled myself free and ran over to the oil well.

As I approached it, I slowed to a reverent walk and stuck both hands into my pockets. The beast bucked up and down with a rhythmic groaning accompanied by the constant squeak of a tiny belt driven by an electric motor no bigger than a five-gallon bucket. With the help of two massive counterweights and the laws of perpetual motion, the motor kept the monster nodding its head up and down at a steady pace

I walked around to the front in order to get a better look at the pump head. It bobbed up and down, driving a shiny metal rod into the ground and pulling it back out into daylight over and over again. The slight groaning of its movement was therapeutic. I closed my eyes and listened for a spell. I heard Connor walk behind me, the camera clicking as he captured my moment, thirty-plus years in the making.

"I have waited since we were kids to stand this close to one of these. I don't know what it is about them that fascinates me so much, but I love it," I said.

"Maybe they remind you of the happy times on all those road trips, and your subconscious believes that getting up close to one will bring those times back for you." In spite of all of his shortcomings (perceived or otherwise), Connor's waters were proving to run deeper than I had ever thought possible.

"Maybe, but right now it's reminding me of something else." I looked over at my brother and grinned like an idiot, putting an intentional end to the emotions of the moment.

"What, sex?" Again, I had not been giving Connor enough credit, he knew me better than I had thought.

"I prefer to call it making love..." I said with a smile.

I turned the camera on and filmed the pumping action for several seconds before heading back to the car. I had enjoyed seeing the oil rig up close, and could have spent the day watching from the comfort of a camp chair while sipping cold lemonade, but I couldn't risk another bout with anger and resentment.

Back at the car Connor said, "Wait, park sideways on the highway. I'll take a picture and we can cross it off the list."

I started the car and drove it across the road, stopping so that it straddled the center lines. Connor took a picture of me smiling in my illegally parked rental car. The moment was frightening, but exhilarating.

"Hurry up!" I called out.

I could see that the highway was empty for miles in either direction, but I shivered at the thought of an oncoming tractor-trailer.

"I'll drive," Connor offered.

I climbed out, slid across the hood of the car like an action hero, and jumped in on the passenger side.

"Two more items checked off the list," I said, marking them down in my notebook.

I picked up the Ipod and resumed our musical run through the best of the Eighties. We drove with the windows open, and Connor smoked another cigarette. The warm air of the southwest swept not only the smoke from the car, but the emotional clutter from inside my head as well. The trip had already been so much more therapeutic than I had expected. It had started out heavy, but the weighty hour spent at the lonely motel seemed so far away, and the odometer wasn't the only indicator of how far we had come.

I reached into the back seat and rested a hand on Jared for a few miles. I wanted him to know that although he wasn't jumping out of the car and running around with us, he was still very much a part of everything Connor and I did on the trip.

He couldn't respond in any way that would let me know for sure, but I was pretty confident that he had received my unspoken message.

Chapter 38: Summer 2004

When he wasn't sharing an apartment with Connor, Jared lived with Francis, a boyfriend at least twenty years his senior. Francis taught at one of the local high schools and sang in his church's choir. The relationship was an on again, off again affair. The differences in their ages and interests often caused conflict that led to temporary break ups. Jared was young, handsome, energetic, and fun. Francis was of a different generation, and while he may have been handsome, he was less than energetic and definitely boring.

Jared was looking for a secure future with someone who loved him unconditionally, but Francis was just looking around. After devoting several years of his life to him, Jared discovered that Francis had been unfaithful from the very start of their relationship. This betrayal was for Jared one more source of crippling pain in a life awash with rejection. Still, his need to be loved never wavered, and he was determined to make their relationship work. He returned to Francis more than once, a pattern that reminded me of the way he returned each summer to the sibling dinners with Becky.

As the years stacked up behind him, Jared would remind me of his simple need to be adored by someone special.

"Matthew, I just want someone to sit on the couch with and watch stupid movies with, or sit and do nothing with. You know how you and Ella can sit and say nothing, watch nothing, do nothing, but you are still happy? That is what I want, someone who is so comfortable with me that we don't have to talk. Of course, when we do talk it will be fun and interesting, but even when it isn't fun and interesting it will still be fun and interesting to us. Does that make sense?" He would laugh at himself, unsure that his message was getting through to me.

I would reply with my well-rehearsed speech on true love. "I know what you mean. It feels good to be that close to Ella, and to share everything with her because she loves me no matter what. I know what she is thinking without her saying it, and we can spend time doing nothing together and still enjoy every minute of it. True love, that's what you want," I would say, believing it more and more each time. Ella and I had worked towards such happiness for years, and were at last starting to see the fruits of our labors.

But Jared had tried to find true love with Francis, and had nothing to show for his efforts but the inevitable end of their relationship. The failure had jaded him. The loving peacemaker whose joy for living had done much to preserve my marriage was slowly overcome by loneliness, betrayal, and sorrow. Jared became an angry shadow of his former self. His mood could turn a corner quickly, and without warning he would rant and seethe about growing up in a home void of affection and attention, blaming our parents for his unhappiness.

Of course, his anger towards Mom and Dad was not entirely lacking in justification; Mom and Dad had rarely shown affection for each other. From early on we siblings had noticed the lack of warmth between them, and often worried over the consequences in secret.

I could not deny that Mom and Dad's lack of physical interaction had made an impact on my own life. I had long doubted their love for each other, and often wondered just how close to divorce they actually were. Eggshells covered our floors for much of my childhood, and I had both stressed over and prayed for my parents and their marriage as far back as I could recall.

In addition to the anger he expressed over Mom and Dad's lack of affection for each other, Jared often voiced his rage over their failure to encourage and believe in their children. Self-esteem had long been my biggest challenge, and I was unable to defend Mom and Dad as inspiring and supportive parents. I had never felt that my parents believed in me, and their lack of encouragement had made its mark. My marriage had fallen victim to my insecurities from the start. I didn't value myself as worthy of success and love, and so I found it hard to succeed and be loved. Lucky for the both of us, however, Ella had seen the potential within me and had refused to surrender to my insecurities.

But Jared had not been blessed to find such a devoted believer in his own worth, and so he continued to flounder in the deep waters of self-doubt.

I would try to defend Mom and Dad, telling Jared that as an adult he could no longer blame our parents for his miserable life. The trouble was that I didn't believe my own argument. I had long blamed Mom and Dad for much of what was wrong with my life, and felt I had substantial evidence to convict them in the court of public opinion should I ever have the platform or the courage to present my case.

It soon became clear that time spent with Jared had become more detrimental to my life than it was beneficial. I would return home, the chip on my shoulder swollen by our time together. If my life were to remain steady on its course towards happiness, I would have to either become impervious to Jared's attitude, or distance myself from him altogether. I didn't want to abandon my little brother in his time of need, but I could not reconcile the damage done to my wife and children.

In the end, Jared made the decision for me, inexplicably disappearing from my radar for several months. I worried about him, but that concern faded with the passage of time. It helped that my own life, though not quite as happy as I had expected, was getting better every day.

I no longer bothered with Jared's life, and so I didn't know that it was circling the drain.

Chapter 39: October 2009

A few miles outside of Albuquerque the traffic slowed to an eventual standstill. It was early evening, so the sun shone hot on the windshield as we sat motionless on the highway. We were exhausted, having been awake and traveling for thirty-six hours.

"I have really got to pee!" My bladder was repaying me for the deluge of caffeinated soda I had poured down my throat over the miles in order to stay awake.

Connor smoked his umpteenth cigarette of the afternoon and ignored my whining. I watched him blow a lungful of smoke out the window, and imagined the tension billowing out of him in the bitter cloud that drifted away.

"What the hell! We haven't moved for ten minutes! I bet that if I got out and walked, I would be in downtown Albuquerque, checked into a hotel and showering before you even reached the city limits!" I shifted in my seat, the confines of the car becoming smaller and more uncomfortable with each minute that passed.

"What's that?" Connor asked, pointing out his window at what looked to be a large, flat, yellow circle on the side of the road.

"I dunno, maybe it's a wormhole," I snapped, looking across the road at whatever it was that Connor had spotted. "If it is, I hope it leads to a bathroom." I released my seat belt, opened the door, and jumped out of the car. I stood and stretched with a loud groan before crossing two lanes of stagnant traffic to get a better look at the wormhole.

"What is it?" Connor shouted.

I lifted my hands and shrugged my shoulders without turning around. I was standing right next to it and I still wasn't sure what it was. I gave the wormhole a kick with my toe. The yellow fluttered, and my tired eyes almost tricked me into believing that it was a wormhole, and that I had just stuck my toe into some inter-dimensional fluid.

101

"It's not a wormhole, it's a giant fabric Frisbee," I turned and shouted to Connor.

"Grab it," Connor ordered.

I bent down and picked up the defunct wormhole, only to find that it was also defunct as a fabric Frisbee. The edging, made of plastic tubing, was broken in two places, causing the whole thing to sag and fold over on itself.

I must have looked rather stupid, crossing lanes of dead-stop traffic to inspect a large, broken, yellow-fabric flying disc, all the while shouting like a crazy old man at the little rental car from which I had emerged. This thought occurred to me, but didn't bother me. Everything we did on this trip was to be part of the adventure, and we had already seen a dragon-UFO, so why not shout across the highway that we had not found a wormhole after all, but rather just a large, broken, yellow-fabric flying disc?

I stood on the side of the road with my discovery in hand and looked at the line of vehicles behind us. It stretched as far back as the nearest curve almost a mile away, and probably extended well beyond that point. Looking ahead towards Albuquerque I saw the same thing, and knew that it was going to be some time before I stood in front of a toilet to relieve the pressure building inside my bladder.

Back inside the car, I stuffed the Frisbee behind the passenger seat and grabbed an empty bottle that I had tossed there several hours before.

"Desperate times, little brother. I need to piss." I held up the wide mouth one-liter bottle and gave it a shake.

Connor returned to ignoring me. I leaned my seat back a bit, turned onto my right side and faced the door. We were in the right hand lane, so I didn't have to worry myself with any neighboring cars full of gawking passengers. I twisted the lid off the bottle and looked for a suitable place to temporarily stow it until my task was accomplished. I had no desire to hold an open container of warm pee while searching about under my seat for the lid. Unable to find one, I hesitated for a moment before clenching the cap between my front teeth.

I unzipped my pants and fumbled around for a moment while extricating my equipment and positioning myself so that all of the pee would go directly into the bottle. I didn't want to wet my pants, or worse, soak down the passenger side door of the little black rental car. Once adjusted, I looked out the open window and waited for the rush of relief.

But nothing happened.

I adjusted my configuration, hoping a little movement would clear any kinks, whether mental or physical.

"Come on bladder, let go!" I shouted.

Connor continued to ignore me. I was hot, tired, sad, and full of piss. We were not moving any closer to that hotel room with its toilet, shower, and soft bed. I felt yet another slip in my grip on sanity.

"Why can't I pee?" I wondered aloud, before breaking into manic laughter. The mental threads that had months ago begun to unravel were in danger of giving way altogether. I felt the sting of tears at the edges of my tired eyes.

"Finally!" Connor shouted.

Startled, I almost dropped the bottle as a hot stream of urine burst from within me. I felt the pressure drain away as the traffic broke, allowing Connor to roll the car forward towards Albuquerque.

Chapter 40: Summer 2005

"Ooh, I like it, it really shows off your sexy calves!" Ella cast a seductive gaze over her shoulder and disappeared into our walk-in closet.

I spun around, making the kilt billow. A breeze rushed over my nethers.

"Well that's one mystery solved!" I exclaimed.

"What?"

"The answer to the question, 'What do Scotsmen wear underneath their kilts?' is simple; nothing at all. If I wore one of these every day, I wouldn't wear anything underneath. Talk about cool and breezy!" I twirled several times, making myself dizzy.

I flopped onto the bed in a daze. Ella emerged from the closet wearing her bridesmaid's dress. It was a long, simple, flowing affair that reminded me of the spank-crazy maidens of Castle Anthrax in the movie "Monty Python and the Holy Grail." My mind wandered for a moment and in an instant I understood one of the more carnal reasons for wearing nothing underneath a kilt.

"Fair maiden, be warned! I shall storm your ramparts this very night and give you a spanking!" I boomed with a wicked smile.

"That had better be a promise, because I'm serious, you look good in that kilt." Ella crossed the room and kissed me, both hands reaching for my pleats.

"Of course, my lady, ramparts and soft parts, I shall storm them all!" I insisted.

I had long wondered how it would feel to wear a kilt, but it was my youngest sister Meghan that had at last provided me with a legitimate excuse for doing so. She was getting married, and she had asked Ella and me to be members of the wedding party. The ceremony was to be held in my parent's garden in the style of a renaissance fair. I took it as an opportunity to buy a kilt for keeps. I was very pleased with my purchase, and had already made a short list of public places to wear it.

The day was sunny, happy, and warm as we set off to my parent's house. Ella was wearing her maiden's dress, ready to serve as a lady-in-waiting, and the kids were decked out in medieval apparel of their own. They also carried weapons. Our two boys each brandished a wooden sword/shield combo, while our daughter carried a wooden dagger. The kid's clothes, as well as their weapons, had been sewn and crafted by my mother over the past several weeks.

We pulled up to Mom and Dad's and the kids scampered out of the car, across the driveway, and onto the lawn. I watched them go, Noah dressed like a knight in training, Isabel as a beautiful young maiden with a crown of flowers in her hair, and Samuel in a little kilt that my mother had fashioned from some tartan fabric. I soaked in the happiness of the moment in preparation for the tension that was sure to be lying in wait no more than a few dozen steps from where I stood.

"You ready?" Ella asked, squeezing my hand in hers and kissing me softly.

"Let's do this," I sighed, leading her by the hand towards the house.

Meghan was marrying an idiot, but he was her idiot. I had expressed my opposition to their relationship early on, and had at one point threatened to beat the stupid right out of him. I had never heard him utter a single sentence worth repeating. He was uncommonly immature, an accomplished liar, and worst of all he harbored no respect for Meghan that I could see. But he talked a good game, and she was devoted to him.

I was not alone in my reservations, but if anything, the family's dislike for him seemed to have pushed Meghan deeper into her misconceptions of the love she felt for him. My intentions were pure. I had Meghan's happiness in mind, but my methods were too dividing and my arguments too fatherly to be those of a big brother. As had been my practice over the years with all of my siblings, I had for a while tried to direct and lead Meghan's life instead of allowing

105

her to live it as she saw fit. This had resulted in an inevitable distance forming between us, but in recent months I had made great progress in allowing her to make her own choices, no matter how foolish I might believe them to be. For whatever value it might have been to her, Meghan had my blessing.

We entered the house and found Harrison standing in the kitchen, freshly arrived from Connecticut. We greeted him with hugs and smiles. I had not seen him since the stressful reunion years earlier. Happy and chatty as ever, he was carrying around a few extra pounds in the shape of a protruding belly. I chose to ignore the urge to ask him when his baby was due and instead picked up the conversation right where we had left it several years ago. With Harrison, the topics always revolved around television, books, movies, and video games.

Meghan came into the kitchen with her moron in tow. I looked up and saw that he held in his hand a very large sword sheathed in a leather scabbard.

"Matthew, this is our gift to you. As a member of the wedding party and kinsman to the bride, we thought you might need a claymore to fend off attackers," Meghan said.

Her husband-to-be held the sword out with both hands.

"Wow, thanks! I've always wanted a real sword," I said rather lamely. I accepted the gift, pulling it free from its sheath and admiring the blade as if I knew something about the craftsmanship of swords. I slid the weapon back into its sheath and slung it over my back using the thin leather strap provided. I gave Meghan a hug and shook hands with the moron, thanking them once again for the gift and wishing them a great day.

Meghan led her groom back upstairs, leaving me alone with Harrison and Ella.

"I'm not sure it's such a good idea for you to be carrying a Scottish claymore around with Becky here. Maybe you should give that to your wife for safe keeping," Harrison joked.

106

"Hey, you just gave me an idea! I could solve all the family problems with one swift stroke." I reached back and fingered the grip of the massive weapon, a devious smile on my lips.

"Sorry officer, it was an accident! Becky just ran in front of me while I was practicing my thrust and parry!" Harrison's belly bounced as he laughed at his own joke.

"Seriously though, is she here?" I asked. The tone of my voice couldn't have sounded more conspiratorial.

"Yes, she's back. She drove her kids down to Sarah's yesterday before I got here. Apparently she left them with Sarah's babysitter," Harrison answered.

I shook my head in disbelief. The lengths that Becky had gone to in the past had surprised me, but to leave her children over an hour away with a stranger, just so they wouldn't come in contact with their two gay uncles was proof to me that she was stark raving mad.

"Where's the chocolate fountain, bitches?" Connor's voice burst into the room ahead of him.

I turned to see my youngest brother enter the kitchen like a conquering hero returning from battle to the lusty sighs of chesty maidens. He was all smirk and fashion, wearing a pale blue button-down shirt, dark tie, and black pants. On one wrist hung a massive watch and his fingers flashed with silver rings. Above the smirk he wore a pair of kick-ass-and-take-names sunglasses.

Jared walked in behind Connor without any fanfare, as if he were Connor's painfully shy plus-one. His thin face was barely beefed up by a goatee, and his hair was, as ever, a model example of coiffing perfection. He was wearing a brown shirt tucked into faded blue jeans. His black belt, with two rows of silver grommets running around its length, was cinched tightly across his skeletal waist.

I wondered later that night if Jared had noticed my immediate, knee-jerk reaction to his appearance. To say that he was gaunt was beyond an understatement. He was wasting away, and couldn't have weighed much more than a buck-twenty-five. My mind had raced back to a thick book on World War II that still sat on a shelf in my parent's library. Jared wouldn't have been out of place if pasted into any of the black and white photos taken of the malnourished Jewish prisoners stacked like living cordwood on bunkhouse beds inside concentration camps. The book had commanded so many hours of my attention as a child, the inhumanity of it all troubling me late into the night every time I looked at its pages. Jared's frail condition at Meghan's wedding had the same effect on me. I hadn't seen him for some time, and although I had heard the rumor that he was drinking heavily, I had figured that it was limited to the occasional angry bender.

But after seeing him that morning at Meghan's wedding I couldn't deny it; my little brother was an alcoholic.

Chapter 41: October 2009

We checked into the first hotel in Albuquerque that didn't advertise hourly rates. I was ready to shower, eat, and hit the pillow, but didn't want to wake up scratching at bug bites and mysterious rashes, or to spend the night listening to the sounds of casual hookups through paper-thin walls. As we pulled around the building and into a parking space in front of our room I noticed a Volkswagen camper van parked two spaces away, in front of the room next to ours.

"Oh great, hippies," I remarked with a heavy dose of sarcasm.

"Maybe they'll have a party and invite us over," Connor quipped, pushing open his door and climbing out of the little car.

The thought that a vanload of hippies would be throwing a party near the pillow where I was about to lay my head was not a happy one. We had been driving for at least eighteen hours, and awake for thirty-six. I was beyond exhausted and needed several hours of restful sleep. I pulled my suitcase from the trunk and led the way into our lodgings for the night.

I jumped into the shower to clean the road from my skin and the smell of cigarettes from my hair. Fifteen minutes and an empty water heater later, I felt renewed enough to stay awake through a late dinner in front of the tiny television.

After dinner Connor disappeared into the bathroom for a long soak in the tub. I drifted off to sleep beside Jared with the television on, the shrieking of acid-for-blood aliens sounding in my ears.

I was out of bed early the next morning, which came as a surprise not because I had been so fatigued from our travels, but because it had been months since I'd had the energy and willpower to get out of bed before nine. After a warm shower and some clean clothes I was out the door and on my way to the dining room to take advantage of the hotel's free breakfast. The sun was warm but the temperature mild, with a blue sky and few clouds above. It seemed a perfect day to drive across the desert.

Inside the dining room I dropped two slices of bread into the toaster, poured some cereal into a tiny joke of a bowl, and picked a couple of bananas from a basket of fruit on the counter. The toaster jumped, and I pulled out the two pieces of under-browned bread. There were several empty tables, and I sat at one that would allow me a view of the silent television hanging on the wall. Captions scrolled across the bottom of the screen in letters too small to read.

Seated nearby was an older, slender couple with salt and pepper hair. I watched as they finished their own breakfast, smiling at each other and speaking in soft tones that suggested a long love affair and a lifetime spent together. They appeared to exist so comfortably together; each movement, each gesture, each sentence offered up a working example of how familiar they were with each other, yet they seemed not at all tired, frustrated, or bored by such intimacy. I marveled as he cleaned up her dishes, wiped down the table, and took her hand in his as they left the dining room, nods and smiles in my direction as they did.

As they disappeared around a corner, I felt a sudden sadness, as if I had been a part of their happy life for more than those past few moments and had reason to miss them.

Connor wandered into the dining room, and his frustration with what was on offer for breakfast quickly distracted me from my thoughts on aging happily with Ella at my side.

Ten minutes later we were packing our gear into the tiny black car, ready to move westward. I saw the breakfast couple exit the room next door to ours. The man carried their only piece of luggage, a slender suitcase that didn't look big enough for a single set of clothes. They made their way to their vehicle, which just happened to be the Volkswagen van that I had imagined to be full of party-happy hippies. He slid open the side door of the camper van and placed the case behind the passenger seat.

Looking past him at the inside of the van, I could see a little countertop with a tiny sink, a miniature stove, and cupboards that would barely fit a couple of dishes and cups. To the rear of the vehicle was a very narrow bed that looked to be a tight squeeze for one, and a very tight squeeze for two, no matter how familiar they might be with each other.

"Someone's in love," I said aloud without thinking.

"Well, we have our moments, but yes, we are quite comfortable with each other by now," the woman said as she turned around to face me. Bright eyes accompanied her warm smile.

"You guys traveling far?" Connor asked the couple.

I was amazed at the sound of his voice, because he never spoke to strangers unless it was heavily warranted.

"Well, that depends on how you look at it. We *have* far to travel, but not as far as we already *have* traveled. We left our home up in Vancouver last September and have been on the road ever since." The man offered up his answer as a friendly matter of fact, with a proud-without-pride like tone to his voice.

"Are you serious? Thirteen months on the road?" Connor's mouth dropped open in unison with mine.

"Is that how long it's been? We kind of lose track of time and space every now and again." The woman's smile had yet to slacken, and for a half a second I thought of my mother-in-law's never ending smile.

"You guys must have seen it all, have you been back east as well?" I asked, my amazement lingering.

"Oh yes, we've been all over the lower forty-eight. Let me show you our map." With that, the man pulled out a much-used road map and unfolded it onto the hood of our car. It was peppered with the notes and marks of their many months on the road.

We listened for several minutes as they both shared some of their favorite sights, routes, and memories. I couldn't help but notice that they seemed incapable of interrupting each other. The gentle ebb and flow of their conversation was so comfortable and familiar, the result of what appeared to be many years spent in mutual adoration. I thought of Ella, and hoped that we would someday reach such a happy level of comfort together.

"You wouldn't believe how hard it is to find qualified mechanics and parts for this silly machine," the man said, jerking a thumb back at the van.

"A Volkswagen? I thought they were pretty straight forward and common, I didn't know they broke down a lot," I replied.

"Oh, no, the van has been great. Don't get me wrong, we love it," he said, waving his hands in retraction. "It's just that when things do break down on it, we typically end up stranded in some podunk town in the middle of nowhere, waiting for parts to be shipped in. We spent three days in a real sleepy place last month, but it didn't matter, we weren't in a real rush to get anywhere."

Our conversation continued for some time, and we were happy to listen as they shared some of what they had learned living on the road. They knew how to travel light and fast, taking only what they truly needed, a short list of items that included a photo book of their family and a single cell phone for emergencies or occasional updates on their location for their children. They carried a GPS device with them, but expressed their love for their folding map with its markings and notes.

We had our own road trip story to tell. We shared with them our quest to get Jared to the Grand Canyon and the heartache we had faced over the past several months. They listened with genuine concern and empathy, and then expressed their sincere admiration for our crusade. They eluded to a history of mental illness in their family, and shared some of the trials they had faced throughout their life together.

"We learned long ago that we had to love our kids without conditions," the man said. "They are our children and they need our love, in spite of what they may say or do sometimes to push us away."

I nodded my head and blinked away the threat of tears. Their commitment to both feel and demonstrate the love they felt for their children and each other touched and shamed me at the same time. Their marriage had not been a perfectly framed photo of constant smiles, but they had made the active choice to appreciate and nurture it through adversity.

After a lengthy exchange which none of us seemed eager to wrap up, it was all we could do to thank them for sharing their time and experience with us. We wished each other well in our separate journeys and drove off in different directions, each of us better off for having met.

As we pulled away, I wondered what their names were, and why I hadn't felt the need to ask.

"Your brother was arrested for drunk driving last night." Dad sounded tired on the other end of the line.

"Seriously?" It was sad, the fact that I hadn't had to ask to which of my brothers he was referring.

"Seriously enough that I had to go down and bail him out early this morning."

"So, where is he now, and what happens now?" I asked.

"Well, he'll get a court date, and since he has no money he'll get a public defender. His car was impounded, but he won't need it for a while since his license was automatically suspended. He'll probably lose it for two years, and he is looking at the very real possibility of some jail time. New Hampshire is tougher on drunk driving than other states." It seemed that my father had been asking some questions of his own.

"Where is he now?" I asked again.

"He's here, sleeping upstairs." Dad's answer was not what I had expected, but was the one that I had hoped to hear.

"How was he when you bailed him out?"

"Oh, he was pretty scared. The officer that brought him out said that he was very quiet, even polite, as if he had been waiting for this to happen. Who knows, this might have done the trick." Dad sounded tired but encouraged.

"Let's hope so. What about his job at the inn? How's he going to work without a car?" I asked, allowing the practical matters to take their rightful place at the head of the line.

"Well, his boss is not going to like this, and he'll lose his job if he doesn't shape up right away."

"If he hasn't already lost it! They have probably been waiting for something like this to give them a legal excuse to let him go," I warned.

"I don't think so," Dad said. "They may not know he drinks; he works alone, and not too many of the guests are downstairs after eleven o'clock at night. We'll see. Anyway, we will have to find him an apartment within walking distance so he can continue to work. I just hope we can find him something that he can afford."

Dad's answer was for me a mixed bag of signals. His use of "we" indicated that he and Mom were going to be an active part of Jared's recovery and rehabilitation, and that encouraged me, but the fact that they were looking to stuff him into an apartment rather than taking him into their home at a time when he seemed to need them most was disappointing. They wanted to help their son, but it would be on their terms and under their conditions.

A few more minutes on the phone with Dad confirmed my suspicions. He made it clear to me that if Jared disagreed with any of their assistance or the form in which it was proffered, he would face the consequences of his "bad decisions" alone.

The conversation over, I sat in my car and tried to decide how I felt and what I should do. As much as I wanted to help Jared, I didn't think that taking him into our home was an option. It had only been a couple of years since we had let Connor live in the attic bedroom during a rough patch in his life, and that had not ended well. He had spent his nights watching movies, eating chocolate, and playing video games, while wasting his days away by sleeping. After several weeks of patience that I could ill afford, I had chased him out in disgust at his inability to better his life. Since then I had only seen him at Mom and Dad's on major holidays.

I was not going to stick my neck out or risk the safety and happiness of my wife and children again. Regardless of the fact that I loved him dearly, Jared was a drunk, and his presence was a burden too heavy to bear. I decided to help him if I could, but to keep him at arm's length while doing it.

Besides, I thought, it was about time Mom and Dad did something other than look on with contempt as their children self-destructed.

Chapter 43: October 2009

I didn't want to spend all of our time in the car, so before leaving New Hampshire I had searched online for a few things to check out while on our way to the Grand Canyon. The Rattlesnake Museum seemed worthy of a visit, so we had driven there straight from the hotel. I parked the car next to a plaza in the heart of old Albuquerque.

"Check out the denim jeans gang," Connor said, pointing across the grass at a group of old people making noise. Most of them were playing some form of string instrument while singing in Spanish, and all of them were wearing blue jeans.

"Let's get this on camera," I suggested, leading the way over to the group. We merged into the small crowd of people that had gathered to listen. I began to shoot video, and upon closer inspection counted among the instruments a massive harp, a fiddle, three guitars (one of which was very fat), and a mandolin.

"Looks like someone forgot the lyrics," Connor mocked, nodding in the direction of a woman at the center of the group. She was shaking her hips and waving her fists to the beat as if they held maracas, but her mouth wasn't moving in synch with the words that everyone else was singing.

"She looks happy though, maybe it's her first time. Maybe the only way into the gang is via dead man's boots, and she's been number one on the waiting list for years, just hoping for someone to die so that she can don her denim and spend her mornings in the plaza with the gang," I mused.

Every one of the denim-clad revelers had a smile on their face and a sway in their hips as they sang about a girl named Maria. I had retained enough Spanish from my missionary days in Paraguay to understand that Maria had gone to the beach to swim, that she had been flirting with someone, and that they went dancing.

We watched the denim jeans gang for several minutes before dropping a few dollar bills into the open guitar case lying on the ground.

"Do you think they use their tips to buy new jeans?" I wondered out loud as we crossed the street on our way to the museum.

The sign on the door warned us that the museum wasn't for everyone, most particularly the close minded, the ignorant, and the know-it-alls.

"I guess that rules out Becky," I muttered, pulling open the door.

Once inside, I paid the nominal entrance fee and we passed through a doorway into the first room of displays. The first few glass cases housing reptile skulls, insects, and dead or otherwise harmless species were interesting, but we spent little time browsing their contents, having come to see the live rattlers, spiders, and anything else that could kill us while visiting the Southwest.

"Whoa, look at that ugly sucker!" I moved in close to the glass for a good look at a tarantula that looked to be as big as my head. The beast had propped its hairy yellow and black legs up against the glass, as if considering a climb up the side and over the top in order to sink its fangs into my face.

"Nice," Connor said softly. He was on the other side of the tank, hunched over with his hands resting on his knees. I snapped a photo of the tarantula with Connor's face in the background, his eyes wide with true surprise.

"Hey look, it's Whitesnake," I joked, pointing at a snow-white Texas Rat Snake.

"Ha! That's a good one, Matthew, I bet no one has ever said that before." A jovial sarcasm dripped from each of Connor's words.

"Someone had to be the first, might as well be me," I came back, a stupid grin on my face.

We moved on, growing more reverent as we progressed deeper into the museum, surrounding ourselves with venom.

"Look at that," Connor whispered, his face nearly touching the thin wall of glass that separated him from a diamondback's fangs.

As the viper coiled back, its head held high, I heard my brother gasp, and then whisper, "Strike!" but the deadly animal lost interest and turned to explore the rear corner of its pen.

We spent over an hour in the tiny but well-stocked museum. We took dozens of photos and shot video of our favorite snakes as we whispered our way through the many displays. By the end of the tour we agreed that it had been well worth the time spent. Before leaving I sought out the restroom. The short hall leading to it was covered in reptile-themed license plates. Words like slither, rattle, serpent, and venom were all there, but there was one that caught my eye, a Nevada plate with the word "COBRA" standing out in bold red letters.

"Connor, we have to get a photo of this," I called out. Connor turned the corner and scanned the plates. It took him but a moment to focus in on the COBRA plate.

"Nice!" he said, rolling up the shirt sleeve of his left arm.

A G.I. Joe fan since childhood, Connor still read the comics, watched the cartoon, and collected the action figures. He held his arm up beside the license plate, exposing his tattoo of a red cobra head with hood open and fangs poised for a strike. It was the symbol used by Cobra, the terrorist enemy of the Joes. I snapped a photo of Connor's tattoo beside the COBRA plate.

After I used the restroom we left the museum. The morning remained sunny but mild, and a light breeze kept my spirits up as we walked around the plaza, checking out the shops on our way back to the car.

"Ella would love all the jewelry shops here. I am going to have to bring her someday."

Outside one of the tourist shops stood a cigar store wooden Indian, some chains around its feet and waist holding it fast to a pillar. I examined the painted wooden carving, complete with a full black and white headdress lined in turquoise trailing down its back.

"Just how far have we come?" I protested, handing Connor the camera. I grabbed the chain in one hand and cast a solemn look of shame across my face as Connor laughed and took a photo.

"Grandma would have loved that one," I joked, thinking for the first time in years about my maternal grandmother, a Native American born on a Blackfoot reservation in the Northwest.

The memory of a photo taken of my grandmother and me standing outside her home in Paradise, California popped into my head. In it I was eleven or twelve years old, dressed in red shorts, a red tee shirt, and Grandma's full-length eagle-feathered headdress. The photo fully conveyed my awkwardness, not only of the moment, but of my age. On the other side of the camera, Dad had demanded without a hint of humor or warmth that I do a better job of smiling, just as he always did when taking photos of his kids.

I wondered if my own children would look at photos that I had taken of them and remember more about my bad attitude in the moment than they would about whatever family event it was that had spawned the photo. Scanning my memory, I could not recall ever barking at them to show the straightened teeth that I had paid for, frowning at them from behind the tripod, or facing them into the sun and demanding that they stop squinting. I figured I was okay, and returned to the moment, standing outside a tourist shop in the historic section of downtown Albuquerque, New Mexico.

"Let's go, we've got a long way to go, and a lot to see along the way," I declared.

After a quick stop to gas up the tank and stock up on road treats, we hit the highway with the windows open wide. Warm air, acrid cigarette smoke, and the fresh memories of snakes, wooden Indians, and cowboy hats swirled about us as we headed west.

Dad sold Jared's car, and also managed to find a tiny and relatively cheap studio apartment within walking distance on the inn. After moving everything out of Jared's old apartment and over to the new place, Dad called me.

"Your brother is all moved out of his old place, but he still has some boxes in storage over at the jerk's house. I think it best if he breaks all ties to the past, and that means getting his stuff out of there as soon as possible. Could you go over with him and get it? I don't want to risk jail time by going over there and seeing that predator."

Dad sounded stupid repeating the same idle threat to Francis' well being that he had been muttering for years. Francis had been Jared's partner for some time, but I doubted that Dad or Mom could pick him out of a line up if he had been offered the chance.

To the best of my knowledge, the only encounter that either one of them had shared with Francis had taken place at the wedding reception of a family friend. Jared had led Francis right up to Mom and introduced him without warning. Francis had held out his hand, offering up a warm smile as a greeting. Mom had held out a cold glare, offering up the grinding of teeth behind her squared jaw in return. She had looked like a fool in front of several people, and upon hearing of it Dad had ranted and railed without action.

Over the years Ella and I had reminded Mom and Dad that Jared was his own person and was therefore responsible for choosing the man he slept with, lived with, and had his heart broken by. I was no fan of the man, but it wasn't as if Francis had held Jared down and raped him late one night in a poorly lit parking lot outside a porn shop.

"You may have to load and carry everything by yourself, because Jared is pretty weak. He tried to help me by lifting a few smaller things, but he didn't even make it to the top of the stairs. I finally told him to sit down and let me do it all myself. He's a good example of what alcohol and cigarettes can do to a body," Dad said.

I was no longer surprised at Dad's knack for turning a loving moment into a hollow lesson. I would have been touched by his willingness to carry all of Jared's belongings up the stairs and into his new apartment by himself, but he had wiped away any chance at endearment by pointing out his son's sad physical state and the choices that had brought him to it. He said nothing of the depression, loneliness, and anguish that had driven Jared to the bottle. In the eyes of my father, alcohol and cigarettes were habits for the weak, stumbling blocks for those unwilling to overcome the natural, physical appetites of man.

But I knew for a fact that Dad had his own share of bad habits and carnal appetites to overcome. I had witnessed his hypocritical self-righteousness first hand. When I had once called him out on one of his own stumbling blocks, he had shared with me the ever popular "the spirit is willing but the flesh is weak" excuse that gave him and so many others the right to sin and run away from the consequences.

There was nothing to be said at the moment, however, so I promised to help Jared out, then hung up as soon as I could.

"Did I hear him say something about Francis?" Ella asked as I put down the phone and stretched, letting out a groan to make known my frustration with the situation.

"Yep. Jared has some boxes over at his house, and Dad refuses to go over there because he might hurt Francis for making Jared more gay and taking advantage of his innocence," I explained, my voice heavy with sarcasm.

It was the same story on a different day, and I was growing tired of telling it.

"So you are going to go?"

"Sure, I have no problem helping Jared get his stuff out of there," I said, crossing the bedroom and entering the closet, as if to hide from any further discussion on the matter.

I pulled my belt free from my jeans and hung it on a hook in the closet.

"But?"

"But nothing! The kid needs to wise up and quit drinking or I am done with him. I have come a long way; I am about as okay as I am ever going to be with him being gay, but he has to stop drinking if he wants to be a part of my life." I stood in the closet, one leg free of my jeans, the other kicking its way out.

"What does that mean?" My sweet wife sat on the bed, a clean tee shirt in her hand and several piles of laundry surrounding her. They looked like colorful cotton ramparts meant to protect her from my response.

"It means that I am done with him, and I am going to tell him that. I'm tired of reaching out to my brothers and getting nothing in return until they need something from me. I won't do it anymore. If Jared wants my help, he needs to wise up and make an effort first, because I refuse to be burned again." My brief tirade complete and both my legs free of my jeans, I began to fumble with the buttons of my shirt.

"Matty," Ella began. My ears burned red.

Whether she knew it or not, my wife only called me "Matty" in moments that mattered.

"What do you think your responsibility to Jared actually is?" Ella continued.

I stood half-naked in the closet, watching as she folded a pair of my jeans. The soft manner of her question and her use of my pet name had set me at comfortable odds with myself. I knew the answer she hoped to hear. It was the answer I wanted to give. It just wasn't the answer I felt I could put into practice. Not without some sort of divine intervention.

I held my breath and waited for a miracle.

Chapter 45: October 2009

Fifteen minutes down the highway, Connor and I were walking into the Route 66 casino to play some slots. Road signs along the highway had made heavy on the implication that were we to stop and gamble, we were sure to get laid, but we went inside because Connor had never chanced his money away in a slot machine. I had, so it was my turn to play corrupter.

We walked the floor before choosing a machine. Hundreds of white-haired, chain-smoking, fanny-pack-wearing retirees sat trapped inside the labyrinth of gambling machines. I fought the urge to grip my wallet tightly and run back to the car.

"It's like a kitty cat sweatshirt convention in here," I muttered. If he heard it, Connor didn't acknowledge my keen sense of observation.

He probably hadn't heard me. Bright lights flashed. Levers clunked. Bells rang. The lever and bell sounds combined with the constant click of weathered palms on bet buttons to drown out all casual conversation.

"Check it out, the perfect one for you to lose your virginity on!" I led Connor over to a Star Wars themed slot machine. He sat on the stool as I fed in a five-dollar bill.

"I don't know what I'm doing, but at least I can smoke while I'm doing it," Connor said happily. He slapped at the bet buttons like a chimp learning to sign in exchange for bananas. The five dollars was gone in less than a minute.

"Let's try the nickel slots, we might last longer over there," I suggested.

We did last longer, but not by much. It took Connor ten minutes and the rest of his cigarette to lose fifteen dollars. He had been winning until Lady Luck seduced him into slapping the maximum bet button a few too many times.

"Okay, we're done here. You can now add playing the slots to your list of vices." I headed for the door, and Connor followed.

124

We took one last look around the casino floor before pushing through the doors and into the sunlight.

"Man, there are so many people in there, and it's not even noon yet. How many people do you think fart away their life savings inside this building each year? That's crazy!"

Connor ignored my commentary on the financial perils of gambling addiction. Instead, he took off running. I watched him approach and then lie down beneath a large, three story arrow that stood in the center of the parking lot. It served as a towering compass needle for the weak-willed, guiding them to the true North of chance, bankruptcy, and free drinks.

I took a few photos from an angle that made it look like the arrow was sticking out of Connor's back. Gamblers gawked at him as they hurried past, but not one of them stopped. Curious though they were about the man lying face down in the parking lot of a casino with the tip of a titan's arrow protruding from his back, they were far more curious about the elusive fortunes hidden deep inside the temple of risk.

Moments later we were speeding west. Connor resumed his role as deejay. The songs he chose were an angry blend of instrument and voice; indignant demands for answers to spiritual questions and passionate cries of grief over the mess that mankind had made of living were accompanied by screaming guitars and thundering bass. The frame of the little black rental car threatened to shudder into pieces around us as we raced towards the elusive horizon.

Chapter 46: Spring 2006

"To accept him for who he is, instead of hating him for the person he'll never be..." The divine had stepped in, the miracle occurred, and the right answer escaped my mouth in a frustrated rush of air.

I looked across the room and into my wife's eyes. "I have spent so many years trying to fix Jared. I have been so focused on what was wrong with him that I have forgotten all that is right with him," I continued.

Ella sat on the bed, my jeans half-folded in her lap. I loved her for not speaking, a mother hen watching as her baby chick began to peck his way out of the shell.

"No wonder he disappears from my life for months at a time. He must hate me for my self-righteousness and conditional love. I have to let go of what I think Jared should be," I said.

Ella finished folding my jeans and placed them on one of the many piles surrounding her.

"I am not his father. For whatever they are worth, he already has parents," I admitted. The shell weakened against my pushing. Cracks had formed. Bright veins of light bled through.

"I need to love him," I concluded.

The shell gave way and a rush of cool, fresh, life-giving air followed. I pulled the rest of my clothes off and dropped them to the floor. Standing naked in our closet, I looked over at Ella sitting on our bed with a clean pair of my underwear in her hands. She smiled at me, a perfect curve of love, free of condescension or conditions on her lips.

"I feel good," I said after a long moment.

"Good, I'm glad," Ella replied, true happiness in her voice.

I enjoyed the weightlessness of being both physically naked and spiritually unburdened. I had spent years fretting over Jared's spiritual well being, and in doing so I had lost sight of my little brother, the very catalyst of my concerns. I had always proclaimed a great love for him, but had in fact held him at arm's length, propping up conditions between us that served to dig into his side and keep him away should he try to approach me on his own terms.

"What?" Ella's voice cut softly through my realizations.

"I just realized that I have been so busy trying to save Jared because I love him, that I have in fact forgotten to love him." I choked on the last few words, their impact heavy on my conscience.

"Now that you know that, what are you going to do about it? You can't change what has happened, only what happens moving forward." She looked at me, patiently willing me to look ahead with hope rather than dwell on the regret of the past.

"I know, I know, but it's so hard not to look back and regret. I've been a real ass, and it makes me mad. Just help me look ahead, will you? If you see me being a dick to Jared again, hit me, hard!"

"Sure, no problem, I'll hit you anytime you want me to!"

I walked over to the bed and pushed my butt out in her direction. She gave it a hard slap.

"Hey!" I shouted, leaping out of her reach. "That hurt!" I rubbed my butt cheek and pouted.

"You stuck your butt out right after telling me to hit you! What did you expect me to do?"

My beautiful wife, to whom I had just confessed a great regret, laughed at me.

I twisted my head around to get a better look at the damage from her slap, and the sight of me naked and chasing my tail while rubbing my ass tenderly with one hand added to her joy. I was not exhibiting any of the more traditional sexy behaviors, and yet something in her laughter assured me that I was, in that moment, just what she wanted in a husband.

My cup of self-esteem overflowing, I headed off to the bathroom for a smiling shower. As the water heated up, I stole a glance at my backside in the mirror. A red handprint began to show across my ass. I considered it a light punishment for my behavior over the past several years.

Chapter 47: October 2009

One hundred and some-odd miles later, I pulled off the highway so that we could check out the Continental Divide marker. It was nothing much to look at, just a state park sign made from wood sitting off to the side of a dirt road. Across the way sat a tourist trap, covered with signs painted in loud yellows and reds that trumpeted the items sold inside.

"Do you think they sell fireworks, t-shirts, or blankets in there?" I asked, pointing over at the obnoxious signs.

Connor snorted in polite reply to my lazy attempt at humor. I grabbed the camera as he slipped into his shoepers, and together we exited the car and walked over to the marker. The words "CONTINENTAL DIVIDE" were painted just above a tiny little white arrow pointing down at the ground.

"Stand next to it," I instructed Connor.

He walked over to the sign and with one swift motion flipped himself over into a handstand in front of it. His body was blocking the little white arrow and most of the words.

"Spread your legs," I commanded, and then chuckled at the sound of my voice demanding that my brother spread his legs for me.

Connor obeyed. The words became visible, but the little white arrow remained covered.

"Your crotch is covering the arrow, get lower." I watched as Connor struggled to comply. It didn't look easy. He was upside-down with legs akimbo. His arms began to shake at the strain of keeping his hair out of the dirt.

"Screw it!" he muttered, and dropped his head to the ground.

I snapped a couple of quick photos, and then gave him the okay to stand. Connor folded over and got to his feet. He steadied his dizzy self on the sign as I scrolled through the photos on the camera's tiny screen. I heard him clapping his hands free of dust as he approached to get a peek.

"How do they look?" He asked, leaning over and shaking the Continental Divide from his precious hair.

"Sweet, the arrow is pointing right at your crotch!"

I handed him the camera so he could take in the results of his effort. When he bent over to create some shade before peering at the camera, I could see the top of his head. His hair was a mess by my standards, longer than mine would ever be and deceivingly unkempt. It called out to me for scissors and a comb. But I knew that each strand was familiar to Connor. Over the years he had trained each hair on his head to merge with its fellows into a tousled, classic, James Dean sort of look.

Connor's carefully planned dishevelment had always been a flint struck against the steel of jealousy I had carried around since childhood. I had forever marveled at how casually stylish Connor and Jared carried themselves, seemingly without effort.

"I'm glad the photos look good, because my head is pounding now." Connor handed me the camera and took his head in his hands, as if to hold it together against an unseen pressure from within.

I looked over at the large sign advertising authentic Native American merchandise and wondered about a more natural solution to his headache. A sweat lodge, complete with peyote and a vision quest held a certain and strong appeal to me in that moment. The chance to sweat out toxins, chase away demons, and get lost while finding my life's purpose all in the same afternoon would have been a difficult temptation to resist.

After a moment of pipe dreams I did what was expected of me, and offered my brother chemicals that had been approved by the federal govt. "I have some ibuprofen in my bag. Take as many as you need," I said as we reached the car.

Though I had always known Connor to claim immunity to modern medicine, he accepted my offer and dumped several of the small reddish-brown tablets into the palm of his hand. Against his white skin, they looked like little pellets of the red earth that had surrounded us for so much of the day's drive. The comparison conjured up more illusions of what it would be like to spend a starry night in a state of self-induced sensory deprivation. The illusions appealed to me. All of my senses had been on high alert for far too long. I could do with a temporary shutdown.

Chapter 48: Spring 2006

After just a few minutes spent in Jared's company, I realized that loving him without conditions was easy to want, difficult to visualize, and almost impossible to do. While my heart had always been free to love, my mind had long ago been hobbled by the strong influence of a conservative, religious upbringing and my own version of the extreme expectations that came with it.

The challenge to love him without conditions began in earnest the moment Jared pulled a large frame from the pile of his belongings we found at the house he had shared with Francis.

"Be careful with this, it is very important to me," Jared said with a smile.

My brother held the frame up, and I took it with both hands. Jared had always been an exceptional artist, and I assumed that the frame held a precious drawing that he had spent hours perfecting, so I was surprised to see that it was in fact a typewritten letter. I noticed at once the familiar letterhead of the church in which we were raised, the church that I still attended but both loved and feared. My eyes blurred as I realized that what I held in my hands was Jared's letter of excommunication.

The church looked on homosexuality as a sin against God and an intolerable lifestyle choice. Choice was the operative word, because the sin existed in the decision itself. As young men, Jared and I had not been taught that homosexuals were born with same sex attraction. We were made in God's image, and to admit to any sort of inborn proclivity towards homosexuality was to suggest that God himself could be guilty of the same, and that was just not possible.

Since then the church had expanded its views on homosexuality. Same sex attraction was indeed a reality, but it was something to be controlled and overcome, just like any other challenge or obstacle that stood in the way of personal exaltation. It wasn't a perfect explanation or complete acceptance, but it was progress, and I felt an increased measure of hope for my brothers in the eternities.

But Jared hadn't been to church in years, and so the same increase of hope that I had experienced had eluded him.

To hold in my hands the actual declaration of Jared's willful separation from God and his truths horrified me, and I fought to maintain my composure.

"I heard that you asked to have your name removed from the records of the church." I almost whispered the words. The frame felt heavy in my hands. My fingers numbed and my knuckles whitened from gripping the edges.

"I told them that if they don't want me the way I am, I don't want them the way they are." Jared took the frame from me and looked at the letter, bitterness in his eyes. I watched, and wondered if I were included in his use of the word "they."

"So you went to your disciplinary council? That must have been, I don't know, weird?" I had wanted to say "difficult" but wasn't sure that it had been.

"Yeah, it was weird. I got drunk before I went. When I walked in I felt bad for Dad, but only for a moment." Jared put down the framed letter down gently and sat on a box of books. He lit up a cigarette and took a long drag.

"Did you say anything?" I asked, assuming that he would have been given a chance to speak.

"Hell, yeah I said something! I told them I would be better off without their hateful church, and that I was happy with who I was. I don't remember everything I said because I was drunk, but I know that I told them I was born gay, and that they were wrong about it being a choice. They sat there pretending to listen and care, but they were judging me the whole time..." Jared paused for a moment.

"I don't think-" I started to say, before Jared interrupted.

"Whatever, it's over and I am glad. If God doesn't want me to be gay he shouldn't have made me this way, and if he doesn't want me in his heaven, I don't want to be let in," he concluded, his tone heavy with anger.

133

I watched exhaled smoke billow around my brother's head. Listening to Jared talk about God in such a way made me uncomfortable, but I couldn't disagree with his argument. I too had always struggled to dovetail God's love for me with his command that I work towards perfection. I had been sent to earth to live a life of choice so that I could learn right from wrong. Had I not been given freewill, a forced obedience would have profited me nothing. My imperfection meant that I would not always choose the right, which would result in sin. Sin made me unclean, and being unclean prevented me from entering God's presence. It was only through repentance made possible by Christ that I could become worthy of heaven.

It seemed to me that salvation depended an awful lot upon sin, the very same thing that prevented it. I had heard it said that God would never place in your path a mountain you could not climb, but I had also heard it said that homosexuality was a test given to some in this life. Did that mean that Jared had been born gay and was supposed to overcome his inborn feelings? If homosexuality was a test, and Jared was indeed born gay, that fact cast shadows of doubt over God's love for Jared. What kind of loving father would give such an impossible task to a child that he loved?

The questions outnumbered the answers, dooming my renaissance before it had even truly begun.

Chapter 49: October 2009

We exited the interstate and drove into the Petrified Forest National Park, located within the Painted Desert. After parking the car we headed over to use the bathroom. Without warning, Connor took off running into the small courtyard outside the visitor's center like a bloodhound on the scent. I followed close behind, pulling the camera from my pocket. I had no idea what my brother was about to do, but I knew that it was sure to be photo worthy.

It was. Connor dropped down to the ground in front of a mountain lion. The big cat had been sculptured from a single piece of long, flat iron. I watched as my brother rolled onto his back beneath it and made like he was fending off the animal's attack.

Connor picked himself up after I took a picture, and we started back across the courtyard towards the restrooms. On our way I noticed a large, empty, rectangular fountain. It was about a foot deep and bordered by river-rounded stones on all sides. The inside was painted light blue, and a metal sprinkler head stood silent and dry in the center.

"I'm going in," I said, handing Connor the camera before wading into the empty fountain.

I lay down on my stomach and began to swim over the blue, pushing my hands and kicking my feet through imaginary water. I stretched my arms out long and straight, turning my head to take a breath after each stroke.

I heard the camera clicking away in Connor's hand. I swam out to nowhere and back before relaxing my body and letting my head drop. The sun was comfortable and warm on my back, while the hard sea of blue beneath me felt cool and comforting against my cheek. I could have fallen headlong into a nap, but the temptation disappeared with the sound of Connor's voice.

"Look over there at those windows, people in the restaurant are watching us," he said.

I twisted around to take a look at a long string of windows in the visitor's center building no more than forty feet away from my

135

swimming hole. I squinted through the sunlight and focused my eyes on one window after another.

"Yep, they sure are." I rolled over onto my back and swam a few more yards before leaping to my feet. I took a bow for anyone watching.

"Dinner and a show, folks! Try the veal, we're here all week!" I said with a smile.

As we began our drive through the park, it was clear to me that Jared had at least one thing in common with God. They shared the ability to take hold of an empty canvas and work a beautiful blend of colors and imagination into something capable of making me cry. I couldn't help but think that we were making our way through God's personal art studio.

I pulled over at a marked overlook. Connor was out of the car and running into the red yonder before I could even unbuckle my seatbelt. I opened my car door and stepped out. I watched as Connor disappeared through a gap in the short rock wall marking the edge of the tiny parking lot.

A crow was perched on the corner of the wall. The big black bird didn't so much as flinch when Connor sped past, despite the fact that he could have reached out and swiped the bird across the beak as he did. I stared in wonder at the confident creature.

He seemed to be looking right at me, his head cocked to one side as if he were scrutinizing me.

"What do you want?" I asked the bird. He jumped down from his rock wall perch and waddled a couple of steps in front of the car.

"This is incredible!" I heard Connor shout. The joy in his words pulled my attention away from the fearless black bird. I had not expected to ever again hear such happiness in my brother's voice. I skirted around the crow and followed the path that Connor had taken.

I held my breath at the sight of a red landscape that could not have been anything other than God's rough draft of Mars, done with pastels.

"Matthew, it's like running around on Mars!" Connor's unwitting agreement with my own thoughts made me feel good inside. I smiled as I watched him run down into a little valley below me. His shoepers left odd-looking tracks in the red dust.

I snapped a few pictures as Connor bent down, grabbed handfuls of red earth, and flung them into the air above him. Even from my position far above, I could see the smile of absolute joy on my brother's face.

Like a puppy off his leash in a park full of fire hydrants and littered with bones, Connor ran around inspecting the terrain for several minutes, hooting and hollering as he made new discoveries. I watched from my vantage point. Tears wandered their way down my cheeks at the sight of my littlest brother acting so happy and free.

Connor ran up a trail on the other side of a little valley, stopping at the top of a hill that matched my vantage point in height. He turned to face me, both arms hanging at his sides. Warm winds tousled his hair and lifted an un-tucked corner of his pearl-buttoned western style shirt. His dark blue jeans and black bracelet-wristwatch stood out against the indigo sky behind him. In my mind's eye we were acting out a living metaphor of our own past, standing atop two distinct hills, a deep chasm separating us.

I took a few pictures of him and wondered if I looked half as cool, dressed as I was in brown shorts and a light blue tee shirt with a red dinosaur printed on the front.

"You're right, it feels like you're on Mars," I whispered, feeling self-conscious as the words left my lips and blew away into the Painted Desert.

Chapter 50: Spring 2006

"Jared showed me his excommunication letter," I said, standing in the doorway of Dad's home office, my shoulder settled comfortably against the doorframe, both my hands deep inside the back pockets of my jeans.

My father turned to face me. He leaned back in his chair and clasped his hands together behind his head. "Do you have any idea what that was like for me? When they ask you to sit in on a disciplinary council they don't tell you who it is, or why they're being brought before the council. I had no clue that own my son would be walking through that door..." Dad paused, and I couldn't help myself from wondering how much of the pause was for dramatic effect, and how much of it due to emotion.

"I was sitting there in that room with my friends, men that I have known and respected for years. Some of them I have known almost as long as I have known you," he said at last.

I wondered if my father considered me his friend, and worthy of his respect.

Dad continued. "The door opens, and in walks your brother. He was drunk, and he reeked of cigarettes. He was belligerent the whole time he was in the room..." Another pause. I wanted to believe it was less for effect and more for emotion, but couldn't.

"When it became his turn to speak, he was angry, and he said so. He told us we were spiteful men who had judged and hated him, while living hypocritical lives ourselves. He wanted nothing to do with 'God or his church.' Do you have any idea how I felt? I mean, my children have done some really stupid things over the years, but I have never been so embarrassed in all my life." My father looked less defeated than he did offended, angry, and humiliated.

I stood silent in the doorway, staring at an oil painting of a naked woman on the wall above Dad's desk. Over the years I had escaped many of my father's long and angry lectures by focusing on the one thing he seemed to truly enjoy. While he boiled and raged, I would stare long and hard at the artwork he had hung around our house. I would daydream my way into landscapes, fight monsters, and seduce beautiful, scantily clad women.

Dad leaned forward in his chair, his sudden movement pulling me away from my daydream escape. I looked at my father as he spit one final, bitter string of selfish words in my direction. Even as he uttered them, I knew that they would be forever etched across the windowpane through which I would look when remembering my father.

"And do you think Jared even cared how I felt?"

The words were so cold, and so void of compassion for his own son, that I wanted to knock my father to the floor, grab him by the throat, and bury my knees into his chest. I imagined pinning him there until Jared could come and shout the heartless question right back into the gasping mouth from which it had hissed.

For the first time in my life, I didn't love my father, but I didn't hate him either. I pitied him.

Somehow that felt much worse.

Chapter 51: October 2009

Connor returned from Mars. We spent a few minutes standing side by side, looking out across the desert.

"Damn!" I exclaimed.

"What?"

"It's pretty as a picture here!" My drawl had returned.

Connor said nothing.

"A man could just walk out into that landscape and disappear," I mused aloud.

"Uh-huh." Connor stood beside me, both hands crammed into his back pockets. Our elbows were almost touching.

"I can see forever," I said, my voice stuffed with as much wonder as I could muster without laughing.

"Yep."

"It's so...I don't know, it's just so...ethereal..." I wrapped this final platitude inside a throaty whisper.

"Shut! Up!" Connor shouted, reacting at last to my onslaught of cliché. "I hate that word! People use it because they think it will make them sound deep and poetic!"

I laughed, happy to know I hadn't lost my touch when it came to scraping my fingernails down Connor's mental chalkboard. When something got him ranting, my little brother was fun to watch. His eyes would go wild and his face would darken. If the situation allowed he would pace the floor, his arms jittering like a junkie only two days sober. Long and loud groans accompanied his powerful blusters as he ranted against someone he deemed to be an affront to common sense, their actions in conflict with his concept of basic intelligence. Earlier in the day I had belly laughed for ten miles of Texas highway listening to his tirade about a group of fat people gorging themselves at the buffet of the Pizza Hut in Amarillo.

"Just because you start lunch with a salad does not mean you can then eat four plates of pizza and wash it all down with a gallon of Mountain Dew!" This shout had served as his opening statement, and from there his case against the overweight citizens of Amarillo rapidly escalated into a frothing attack against the entire state of Texas. Connor had artfully braided his arguments, colorful expletives, and derogatory terms together into an elaborate condemnation of the obese.

Much to my surprise, I had laughed to the point of tears and a side ache. It was for me a new reaction to Connor's attacks on other people.

My youngest brother's opinions of others had always been in conflict with the life he lived. By my standards his life was on a slow boat to nowhere. His diet consisted of chocolate and cigarettes, his love life was a mess, and his job history was sporadic at best. As capable as Jared when it came to drawing and painting, Connor had done nothing to develop and make a living from his God-given talent. He was hardly in a position to comment on other people's bad habits, idiotic behaviors, and general lack of common sense. I had always figured that until he had a mortgage, a wife, three kids, and a career, his judgments of others were to be looked upon as nothing more than the jealous rants of an absolute failure. My lack of respect, combined with my self-righteous and fatherly way of treating him, had pushed my little brother so far away over the years that I could no longer say that I knew anything about his life.

But none of that mattered anymore, and so I laughed because I loved him. No matter how twisted, what he had said about the fat people at Pizza Hut was funny, and more than a little true.

Minus the disparaging remarks and expletives, of course.

Chapter 52: Summer 2006

Jared became a welcome and regular visitor in our home that year. I would pick him up in the afternoon and take him to a late lunch as often as I could. He seemed to have quit drinking without much effort, the threat of losing his job fortifying his will to stay sober. His appetite had quickly returned, and he often ate more than I did. He gained back most of the weight that he had lost to alcohol and the vomiting that came along with it. In time, Jared began to look like the handsome little brother that had lived with us out in Seattle.

Jared's demeanor improved as well. My brother was once again fun to be with. Every time I picked him up, he would make me come into his tiny apartment and watch the short movies he had created using his video camera and the editing software installed on the refurbished computer I had given him. He would take self-portrait photos dressed up in odd costumes, and then run them together with music. He made use of special effect features, filling the movies with bizarre sequences in which he ripped the skin off of his face or morphed from one costumed Jared to another.

I would watch the clips in mouth-opened awe. In spite of several years of drinking and self-abuse, Jared had clearly retained his creative talents. His silly but amazing movies gave me hope that he would someday turn his skills into a modest income. My dream for him was that he would quit the inn, put his creative talents to work, and live the simple and happy life he yearned for, one with a man that loved him.

After catching up on his latest creations, Jared and I would head out to my car. Jared would wave to the crazy man who sat on a chair inside his front window all day, then shout a bright hello to the old lady who was always sitting outside, rain or shine. She would wave and smile, one hand rocking the antique baby carriage beside her. Inside it napped her baby, a cat that was most likely her only earthly companion.

"Your apartment building would make great material for a television series or an independent movie," I said one day as we pulled out of the parking lot.

"Yes! A bunch of crazy people living in tiny apartments next to the train tracks," Jared agreed.

"It would be a dark comedy about a young alcoholic artist that is trying to stay sober and all the weird but loveable people that live in his building. What would we call it?" I wondered.

"Making Tracks?" Jared suggested.

"Yes, that's perfect! The artist is eager at first to move out, thinking he is better than all the crazies. Then one day they pull him from the train tracks when he passes out on them after a drinking binge. He realizes that he is no better than they are, and that he actually needs them in his life. The train tracks could be a metaphor for both his desire to jump a train and escape their crazy antics, and the fact that he is a recovering addict." I was on a roll.

"You should write it," Jared encouraged.

"Maybe someday," I snorted, no confidence in my writing abilities.

I loved bringing Jared home. Ella would light up when Jared walked in behind me, and would dote on him with cookies and conversation. Had he not been gay, I might have even been a bit jealous of the connection they shared. I was his brother, but she was his friend. The kids loved to see him too, and although Jared had never been comfortable with the sort of frantic attention that children pay to uncles and aunts, he endured it out of love. They had long stories to tell him, drawings to show him, and toys or games they wanted him to play with. He adored them, and so he suffered through their barrage of attention with smiling patience.

Since he worked nights, Jared had to sleep at some point during the day. He would often crash on our couch, covering himself from head to toe in a blanket so that he could sleep in relative darkness. Ella would chase the kids outside or upstairs so he would not be disturbed.

While I loved having Jared there to laugh and joke with, it was while he lay sleeping on our couch that I felt the happiest. My little brother was asleep on my couch during daylight hours, and I was okay with it. I felt that I had become the loving brother that Jared had always needed, rather than the self-appointed surrogate father that I had always been.

Chapter 53: October 2009

We drove through beautiful desolation. A man could indeed lose himself in the Painted Desert, but for me the wide and colorful expanse felt like a homecoming. Unable to see, think, or feel with any sort of clarity for months, I had longed to escape the canopied forests and emotional tunnel vision of New Hampshire. The open skies, colorful stretches of earth, and sweet-tempered winds of the Southwest afforded my body, heart, and mind the healing space that they had been missing.

We drove along like visitors from another planet, marveling at the terrain, pointing out each new rock formation or color like it was something never before seen by members of our species. Each curve in the road brought us to a new vantage point, each vista more striking and inspiring than the last.

"Oh, we have to pull over and get some shots of us sitting in that," I said, pointing into the distance.

"Cool," Connor agreed, grabbing the camera.

A short minute later, I pulled over and parked the little black rental car on a small patch of pavement. We climbed out and approached the rusting corpse of an old Ford Model T that must have been eighty years old. It was obvious from the cement footings beneath it that the car had been placed there intentionally, but I decided that it had been abandoned years ago by a couple of bank robbers on the run. It had been stripped of its interior, windows, tires, and engine not long after, as if the robbers had left it in a bad neighborhood knowing there would soon be little evidence of their getaway car for the police to examine.

The paint had long ago been stripped away by the harsh elements in which the car sat. Over the course of decades, it had broiled under the summer sun, and iced over in the bitter cold of the desert's winter winds. The metal had rusted into a dark rich color that blended in naturally with the surrounding landscape, so much so that it seemed intentional on the part of the car, as if it were trying to hide itself away from its wretched past.

Over the years the Ford must have become such a popular attraction for tourists that the park authorities had put in a small parking lot and a bench made of car parts, transforming it from an old wreck into an official piece of the landscape. Thousands of people from all over the world must have stopped to snap a memorable photo of the antique car sitting alone and quiet in the middle of a beautiful desert.

Connor and I climbed into the car through the open roof.

"I'll set the camera up on the hood and hit the timer," I said, leaning over the windscreen.

Connor climbed behind the wheel, squatting above the rusting floor where the seats had once been.

I placed the camera on the hood, pointed it in our general direction, and poked the timer button before squatting beside Connor. I unfolded the paper map given to me by the park ranger when paying the entrance fee to the park, and stared at it, feigning confusion.

"So, where the hell are we? Don't you know how to read a map? What are you, stupid?" Connor shouted in my ear, the angry husband berating his wife for not being able to read the map under the pressure of his watchful and impatient eyes. The camera beeped rapidly and took a photo.

We repeated the process a few more times, acting out a spiteful couple lost somewhere in the southwest while trapped inside a marriage that neither of them felt they could escape without risking embarrassment or eternal damnation.

Finished with our fun at the Model T, we jumped back into the rental car and set off through the desert once again. The next stop was a bridge spanning a dry riverbed. The mud below was parched, and had cracked into odd scaly shapes of varying sizes. It reminded me of the first time I had looked at my own skin under a microscope.

We stood on the bridge for several minutes, watching a train that looked to be at least a mile long pass in the distance. I lost track of the car count somewhere in the seventies.

Once the train had disappeared, Connor dropped to his knees. I watched as he crawled under the bridge's railing and lay down so that his torso hung out beyond the cement edge of the bridge, over the dried riverbed below. I took several photos of him stretched out into the air with one arm tucked to his chest, the other extended ahead of him, and both hands balled into fists. The angle of the photos hid the bridge from view, so it appeared as though my little brother was flying high above the cracked mud shingles of the riverbed.

From the bridge we drove to a parking lot complete with restrooms and a drinking fountain. Once again I noticed a single crow waiting for us. After a pit stop we raced each other past a sign indicating a pathway that led to some petroglyphs. We spent the next thirty minutes contemplating the characters and symbols that had been etched into the rock hundreds of years before our visit.

A grave-sized hole in the ground captured Connor's attention as we made our way back to the car. I followed as he left the marked path to get a better look.

"Maybe it's a baby meteor crater," I suggested.

"Or the grave of a Native American zombie," Connor said, jumping into the hole.

"Dude! Spiders, scorpions, snakes; do you want me to keep listing everything that might be waiting in there to bite you?"

"Just hurry up and take my picture!" Connor insisted.

I watched as he leaned forward, pressed his chest up against the rim of the hole, and began to claw at the ground in front of him. His face took on the mindless drive of a zombie pulling itself up from the earth.

"Oh, that's awesome!" I laughed, snapping away with the camera as he clawed at the earth. He raised one hand above his head, as if reaching for the leg of a passing meal.

"Ok, got it. Now get out of there before I have to suck venom from your leg," I begged.

147

Back at the car, I saw that the crow seemed to have waited patiently for our return.

"What do you want?" Connor shouted at the bird.

"So you've noticed it too?" I asked.

"You mean the fact that every time we park the car, a single crow is waiting for us?"

"Weird, isn't it?" Connor and I exchanged conspiratorial looks across the roof of the car, but we both stopped short of voicing any suspicions of supernatural activity.

I climbed into the car and rolled down my window. Connor yelled at the crow, then started over towards it. I pulled out my video camera and started filming as Connor began to run and shout.

"What do you want?"

Just as Connor got close, the crow hopped into the air and then landed several feet away. Connor slowed to a sneak, doing his best to creep up on the bird several times. Whenever Connor got within a few steps, the crow would leap into the air again, and then drop back down out of range.

I laughed, watching from the car with the camera rolling, as Connor and the crow played cat and mouse. At last the bird tired of the game, and flew high above the ground, landing on the side of a small hill a hundred feet away. Connor turned and started running back to the car. He stuck his hand on top of his head, as if holding onto a hat.

"Start the plane!" He shouted, his voice an excellent imitation of Indiana Jones running from the tribe of warriors sent to kill him by his rival, the cunning and cutthroat Belloq.

Connor skidded across the hood of the car as I reached out to push open his door. He leapt in and I pulled away as fast as the little black rental car could muster.

148

Chapter 54: Christmas 2006

Dear Jared,

You do not have to read this out loud if you do not want to. I know sometimes people start reading very personal cards out loud and end up reading something they don't want other people to read, but this is not one of those letters; I just thought you might not want to read it out loud.

This gift was not wrapped because I wanted to remind you and everyone else that sometimes the best gifts aren't tied up neatly with a bow (who am I kidding, none of the gifts I give ever have a bow, and the wrap job I do usually sucks!). Anyway, some gifts are not tangible, cannot be purchased with money, and are not very easy to give or receive. Those types of gifts are often the best ones.

Jared, this year you are a gift, and I am happy to have received that gift, and I am sure the rest of the people in this room today are as well. To be friends with you again, to see you healthy again, to be proud of you for overcoming something I can't imagine possible; these are the gifts you have given me this year. I admit that I was quite skeptical at first, and imagined you would disappear from my life again in a flash, leaving me wishing for a brother to spend time with, and wondering when I would see you again, if ever. So far you have proven me wrong, and I hope it never ends.

We decided to get you this box of sustenance, because you have come to appreciate the finer foods in life. The kids helped to pick it out. We hope you enjoy.

Love,

Matthew

I folded the letter and placed it, full as it was of commas, run-on sentences, and emotions, inside an unwrapped cardboard box. I had filled the box with macaroni and cheese, cans of soup, cake mix, and other foods that I had seen Jared devour in earnest at our house that year. The kids had helped me raid the pantry, with a few suggestions from Ella shouted down the stairs.

After spending Christmas morning exchanging gifts as a family, we drove the five miles over to Mom and Dad's for the rest of the day. Sarah and Joshua had come up from Boston with their two boys, and even Meghan showed up with her husband in tow. Most importantly, Jared was there. It was the first Christmas I had spent with him in some time.

The tradition in our family had always been that we would open our gifts one at a time in age order, starting with the youngest child. Since my parents had done their part to "be fruitful and multiply" the Christmas day unwrapping had always started after breakfast and gone on until dinner.

This way of spending Christmas Day had its ups and downs. It certainly made the suspense last longer, and the fact that we sitting amidst piles of gifts sent a happy tingle through our bodies every time we surveyed the scene. But Dad would insist that we all pay attention as each gift was unwrapped, often with a loud, reprimanding voice. This could be distressing and tedious, especially if you had just unwrapped something spectacular that you had been waiting for all year. This suffering would be compounded as the younger kids slowly unwrapped another stuffed animal or Mom unwrapped her umpteenth box of cherry chocolates.

Ella had encountered quite a bit of resistance from me when she had first suggested, then pleaded, and finally demanded that we try unwrapping blitzkriegs in our own home on Christmas mornings. In the end I had come to enjoy the chaos of our yearly holiday free-for-all.

But the tradition remained in place at Mom and Dad's, and so the older grandkids pulled gifts from under the tree one at a time and read the tags out loud. Each gift was then passed to a younger cousin, who in turn passed it to the recipient. Even in my thirties the process seemed to take forever.

As the unwrapping began, time seemed to slow itself into a belly crawl through quick-dry cement. I was growing nervous about the gift I had chosen for Jared. Second-guessing myself, I thought that it would have been more fitting had I just filled the box with cream style corn. My letter was so loaded with sweet, mushy sentiment that it would soon be dripping from the corners of the cardboard box.

I began to worry that the letter would make me vulnerable to Jared. I had a tendency to prematurely confess my feelings, expose my self-doubts, and over-commit myself to anyone that showed me any measure of love and attention. This behavior had left me vulnerable many times in the past, and put an extra strain on relationships that were already unbalanced. These situations rarely ended well. My marriage to Ella was one of the few relationships that had survived this behavior, and only after years of hard labor.

I also feared that the embarrassing weight of my sentiments, coupled with my unwavering faith in his strength to overcome would pressure Jared into a drinking relapse. I knew enough about alcoholism to understand that my little brother would be in recovery mode for the rest of his natural life, ever tempted to take the one drink that would bring months, years, and even decades of sobriety to an abrupt and devastating end. The fear of failing to live up to the expectations of loved ones could send an alcoholic back into the bottle. I did not want to be a trigger for Jared.

Still, the letter conveyed how I felt about Jared and all that he meant to me, and I wanted him to know it. I didn't think he fully understood all that he had done for me. Jared had unwittingly given me the gift of opportunity and a view of life from a different angle. His struggle to overcome had in fact extended itself to my own life. In his fight I had found the strength for my own crusade against the person I had been for so long. The only other individual that had made such a lasting and positive impact on my life was Ella.

At last Jared lifted the plain brown box from his dwindling pile of gifts. He set it down in front of him on the floor between his feet and pulled it open. I was relieved when he picked up the letter and chose to read it to himself, his lips mouthing each word. As he worked his way down the page through my poorly expressed gratitude for our renewed relationship, I felt the weight of the man that I had been shift, the scales of my personality dipping in favor of the man that I was trying to become.

Jared sat contemplating the letter. He looked at me, a subtle smile on his lips. He nodded his head, and I no longer cared about being vulnerable or embarrassed. Jared knew that I loved him, and if he walked out of my life that afternoon, he would do it knowing how I felt. If he failed to draw a line of understanding from the sustaining food inside the box to my new life and his part in making it a reality, it didn't matter.

What mattered was that for the moment he was a part of my life again. He was healthier, happier, and most of all, overcoming.

Or so I believed.

Chapter 55: October 2009

We continued down the road, which led us through a landscape known as the Blue Mesa. The area could have served as a backdrop for any number of cheesy science fiction movies and television shows. A layer of odd grays and blues coated the wandering maze of hardened earth domes. It was hard to imagine the amount of time, and the patient force of the elements that it had taken to create it all. I felt guilty rushing through it the way we were, but felt that no amount of time spent gazing out over all the beauty before us would do it justice. Still, it felt irreverent to spend so little time admiring it all, as if taking a motorcycle tour through the Louvre.

We parked the car and followed a walkway that led us to the Agate Bridge, a large petrified tree lying across a ravine. As we approached the site, I noticed a couple standing together, their attention focused on the view. I stopped, and held out my arm as a signal for Connor to do the same.

"Shadow grab," I whispered.

The sun was behind us, casting our shadows down the path and towards the couple. I moved my right hand around in the air until its shadow was resting on the woman's butt. I cupped my shadow hand below her left butt cheek for a moment, and then patted the air as if spanking her. Connor and I fought to hold back the immature laughter that rolled upwards from our bellies. The woman turned around, perhaps sensing our mischief. I dropped my arm, started walking up the path, and threw a camouflage of serious interest in the Agate Bridge over my face.

After staring at the petrified bridge, we jumped back into the car and headed for the next stop, a landscape strewn with chunks of petrified wood. As we entered an area in which you could approach and touch the ancient stone logs, the concepts of time and patience took on a whole new meaning. Millions of years meant nothing inside the Petrified Forest, and that fact made it a good place for me to spend the afternoon.

Connor squatted as if taking a dump, his rear-end hanging over a large solitary chunk of petrified wood.

153

"Hold it," I laughed, taking out the camera for the obligatory shot.

We wandered over the terrain for some time, inspecting each block and marveling at the colors and patterns made by minerals that had replaced the wood long before man and his opposable thumbs came along to slap price tags on nature's artwork.

The museum at the southern end of the park was small and just what one would expect. There were plaques and informational displays loaded with so much scientific knowledge that had we stopped to read half of them we would have been there late into the evening. We browsed through it briefly before making our way to the trail outside the museum.

Behind the museum, a concrete walkway looped around through a garden of petrified wood. Some of the chunks were bigger than cars, coming from trees that must have stood upwards of two hundred feet. As we rounded the first turn, I spotted a young Japanese couple standing to one side of the pathway up ahead of us. I turned to point them out to Connor. He smiled and nodded, having already noticed them.

I was not sure when his fascination for all things Asian had started, but I knew that Connor had been obsessed with Asian culture for some time. A collector of Asian movies, he had recently introduced me to a good number of Korean and Japanese movies that had been mind blowing in their ability to jump-start my imagination and induce skin-prickling fear. His knowledge of Asian anime, music, movies, and culture was equaled only by his love for all things Star Wars and GI Joe.

Connor took the lead as we neared the young couple. They were standing to one side of the path, chattering away in Japanese and gesturing at a massive chunk of petrified wood. I stole a long look at the girl. Her face was beautiful and clear, her eyes as dark as her smile was light. She was thin but not too skinny, and quite tall for an Asian girl. The tails of a long white button-down shirt hung over her short skirt, and her legs were covered by black tights tucked into brown suede boots complete with fringe. Her long black hair was pulled into a ponytail that hung off center from the back of her head.

154

As we passed them by and continued our way through the fallen stone trees, I felt sad for Connor. He knew what he wanted out of life, but for some time he had harbored less than little hope of getting it.

Had he asked me, I would have told Connor that he would know a relationship was worth having if the changes he was willing to initiate within himself to make it last were the most ambitious and difficult of his life. They would not be the juvenile changes that stem from an initial attraction. They would eclipse the willingness to shop for shoes, watch chick flicks, or enjoy the company of her overbearing best friend. The changes would be almost impossible to initiate, painful to follow through on, and would at times test his resolve beyond belief and reason.

Had he asked, I would have also told him that they would be worth it in the end.

Chapter 56: February 2007

We took Jared and the kids to a sledding party at a local golf course that winter. I was happy to see him walking up the hill without pausing for breath. He hadn't quit smoking, but he was sober, and still gaining strength.

Dad had come along to watch the action from the top of the hill, taking a rare break from the endless list of home and garden projects he always had going. After a string of downhill slides, Jared called it quits and sat down next to Dad. In between runs with the kids, I watched Dad and Jared from the corner of my vision. It was good to see them spending time together on neutral ground, out in public with the grandkids around to keep things light.

All of Dad's children seemed to suffer emotional shrinkage in his presence. Conversation with him seemed to be made through a curtain that filtered anything you said into baby talk. I doubted that my father had ever listened to me share an opinion or express a feeling without looking down upon me as a small child. Jared had for some time seemed determined to tear his section of the curtain down, soak it in gas, and throw it on a fire.

But since he had quit drinking, Jared seemed calm and unbothered by the filtering curtain. Dad had made strides of his own in Jared's direction, and they seemed to have settled into some form of silent understanding. Jared had overcome something that his father did not understand, and Dad seemed to respect the effort and willpower it had taken.

I snapped a photo of them sitting together in the cold. Dad was wearing the same red and white scarf with matching winter hat (complete with yarn pom-pom on top) that he had worn every winter for at least twenty years. He wasn't smiling, but he did look as happy as he could be without a painting, a tool, or an antique in his hand. Jared looked to me like a younger and cooler version of Dad, wearing a bright green winter ski jacket and a dark knit cap. His own lips stopped just short of curling into a smile below his dark sunglasses.

I dared to imagine that attitudes were changing within the family. If Jared stayed sober and involved, and if Dad could find it within himself to take the lead, accepting Jared as he was and loving him without expecting too much of him, then perhaps Becky's upcoming summer visit would prove to be a groundbreaker.

A few minutes after leaving the Petrified Forest we ran into a small herd of dinosaurs. There were seven of them standing at the side of the road in downtown Holbrook, Arizona.

"I had no idea dinosaurs were so colorful," I remarked, pulling the car over for the obligatory photo-op with the painted statues.

Connor grunted a reply that I had finally figured out to be his non-verbal way of telling me that a joke was at the edge of being funny, but not quite worthy of laughter. I sensed my face flushing red, and felt like an embarrassing father trying to fit in with his son's friends.

The dinosaurs stood behind a locked fence that surrounded a large lot piled high in petrified wood and other mineral samples for sale.

"Look at all this petrified wood. How can they sell all of this if it is illegal to remove from the park?" Connor shook his head in apparent disgust and confusion.

"Maybe there is some loophole in the law, or maybe this was all picked before it was made illegal."

We looked through the fence at thousands of hand-sized samples of ancient history piled high for easy browsing and purchase. I was no tree-hugging weirdo, but it seemed irreverent to me, as if the earth's patience had been gathered and put up for sale.

"Remember that commercial with the huge piles of trash and the crying Native American?" Camera in hand and at the ready, Connor's words acted more as a cue than a question.

"Yep, here goes." I laced my fingers through the fence and tried to look mournful to the point of tears.

Connor took a picture, and I laughed at the absurdity of the moment. Standing in the shadows of colorful cement dinosaurs, we were re-enacting a public service announcement from our childhood that seemed almost racist by modern standards of political correctness.

We posed for several photos with the dinosaurs before pulling the car into the gas station next door.

"Check it out, an A&W sign! I have not eaten at A&W for years. Root beer float here I come!" I grabbed my wallet and stepped out of the car. As I shut my door I glanced in the back window and checked on Jared. He was in the middle of the back seat, tucked comfortably inside my sweatshirt.

I twisted off the gas cap, and then turned to the pump, credit card in hand. The pump was so old that it didn't have a scanner, only a hand-written sign that told me to pump my gas before paying inside.

"Connor! Come here and check this out. This gas station is old school!" I lifted the nozzle and flipped the lever that activated the pump. The numbers clinked as they rotated back to zeroes. I turned and began filling the car's tank.

"It even has a trigger lock so you can clean your windshield while you pump!" I had not been this happy to buy gas since the first fill up of my first car in 1986.

As Connor approached, I pointed at the metal numbers spinning upwards with a rhythmic series of clinks.

Connor seemed to be more amazed at my joy than at the old style pump itself. He pulled out the camera and I hammed it up for yet another photo, pointing at the numbers with my mouth open in awe, my eyes wide with excitement.

"They don't make 'em like that anymore, do they?" The words came from a throat roughened by a lifetime of sucking on cigarettes.

I turned to face a scruffy man wearing a maroon tee shirt stretched over a potbelly and tucked into grey sweat pants that were held up by black suspenders. Topping off his ensemble was a dark ball cap with "MARINES" stitched in bold red letters across the front, with the anchor and globe insignia beneath.

"Hi guys, you look like you've been on the road a piece. My name is Simon, and that's my van over there at pump number two." He extended a pudgy hand. His grip was strong, his skin rough.

159

"We have been driving for some time, but it's not the hours, it's the mileage," I joked.

My Indiana Jones reference went unnoticed.

We chatted about a lot of nothing, accompanied by the synchronized clinking of the gas pump. Simon was from Denver, heading for California with his wife and mother. We told him we were headed for the Grand Canyon but left it at that, other than to say that we were from New Hampshire. Our tank topped off with a click, and we said a polite goodbye and Godspeed before heading inside to pay.

After paying for the gas, we headed to the back of the station to order an A&W lunch.

"This is just like I remember, so delicious and the perfect size to boot. Not a fat chunk of greasy beef, but not a thin sliver of meat substitute either." I took another bite, savoring the taste of childhood. A long pull on some root beer made the moment complete.

"They know how to make a burger, don't they?" The gruff but friendly voice from the pumps had returned, its owner close behind.

Simon took a seat at a table across from our booth. After moving a chair so that her mother-in-law could pull her wheelchair (complete with oxygen tank attached) up to the table, Simon's wife sat down and began eating her own late lunch.

A conversation that lasted for the better part of an hour ensued. It was put on pause long enough for me to order a root beer float, but other than that the three of us swapped stories without interruption. Simon's wife and mother seemed used to his conversational nature, and since they had probably not only heard, but also lived his stories over and over again, they kept to their own quiet conversation.

Simon was a llama and emu rancher from Denver. He considered his ranch hands to be part of the family, and boasted of the freezer he kept stocked with their favorite foods.

160

"Emus are mean when they need to be," Simon warned us, sitting with his hands clasped around his pot belly.

"They can kick, can't they?" I asked.

"Hell yes, they can kick! They kill coyotes out on the ranch all the time. They kick them dead, and then they stomp on the carcass, pounding it into the ground. I don't bother to clean up the mess. Nothing will discourage a coyote from attacking my herd more than a dead, flattened Wile E. rotting on the ground."

I laughed at the thought of so many early morning cartoons in which the unfortunate coyote had been pounded into the ground time and time again. Maybe truth had been the basis for all those silly and impossible scenarios after all.

During the lesson on emus and their capable kicks, I watched as Simon's wife finished her meal and then turned her attentions to her mother-in-law. She cleaned her face and wiped up her dinner mess, and then wheeled her carefully into the restroom. I was moved by her humble patience and selfless service, not sure that I would ever find myself accused of the same for anyone other than Ella one day, heaven forbid she should ever need it.

His mother and wife in the bathroom, Simon shifted topics to the reason for their road trip. His mother was old, and she had wanted to visit family and friends she had not seen in a long time before it was too late. He had bought the van and fitted it for her wheelchair so that they could spend a week making the trip.

"I don't think she's gonna make it to the end of next week, but we're gonna try to get her to California to see her sister before she goes." His words were sad, but his face smiled. He was happy to give his mother such a special, perhaps final gift.

I looked across at Connor, and in a rare moment of complete connection, felt his desire to share our story with Simon. He seemed to read the imperceptible nod of agreement in my eyes; it was okay to share our innermost with this man.

I listened as Connor told Simon about Jared's suicide attempt at the motel in Independence and our quest to take him to the Grand

161

Canyon. I had never heard my little brother talk to anyone else other than Ella about all that had transpired that year. It was heartbreaking to hear it retold, but more than that, it was unbelievable, to know that I had lived through it all myself.

As it turned out, Simon had once made a serious attempt on his own life but had (obviously) failed. His own failure at suicide had been followed shortly by his brother's success.

"That's heavy," I said in reaction to his sad tale.

"Sure is. After my brother died, I was stuck in a wheelchair of my own for several years, not because I couldn't walk, but because I wouldn't. I had myself a nice, long pity party..." Simon's voice trailed off as he re-lived his past.

"How'd you get out of it?" Connor asked quietly, as if asking for advice, rather than a asking polite question.

"I learned to love myself. It took some time, and it wasn't easy, but once I learned to love myself, I could love my wife. I started to be the husband I should have been all along, and the son that I should have been to my mother. I had caused them both a lot of pain, and had to spend a lot of time making amends for it all." His hand reached up to stroke his salt and pepper beard, which I took to be his acknowledgement that age and experience had brought him wisdom, humility, and the ability to forgive himself and others.

"Nothin' matters more than family. You can't take nothin' more than family when you go," Simon concluded, as his wife wheeled his mother out of the restroom.

As she rolled past me, I reached out to take his mother's hand in mine and say goodbye.

"You have a good boy there," I said, nodding in Simon's direction.

"He'd better be good! I raised him, and I'm a good mother!" She laughed, the sound graveled by years of smoking.

162

I smiled at Simon's wife and she offered a shy goodbye. I watched as she pushed her mother-in-law outside and helped her light a cigarette.

"I could sit and talk for the rest of the afternoon, but we've got to get moving," I said at last, with a bit of reluctance.

"Come on out to Denver sometime and stay at the ranch." Simon offered this invitation while squeezing my hand inside his friendly vice-like grip.

"We just might do that on our next road trip," I smiled.

After Simon had finished shaking the dust from Connor's skinny frame with his powerful handshake, we made for the highway.

Though he had looked nothing like a therapist or a counselor, the time spent with Simon over a root beer float seemed to do more for me than the time I had spent with trained professionals over the past few months.

"Who knew emus could kill coyotes?" I shouted over the wind as Connor sucked on a cigarette.

Chapter 58: Summer 2007

That summer was to be my best chance at change within the family. I figured that Jared's arrest and his subsequent year of sobriety and recovery must have had some sort of opening effect on the door to Becky's heart. No matter how small the crack, I was determined to assist her in prying that door open enough to let Jared slip inside.

I thought long and hard about the best way to handle her visit, and asked Ella for advice. She suggested that perhaps when in her own home far away, Becky was nothing like the person we saw each summer.

"You know how it is with families. When I go out to see my family I settle back into my role as the youngest of eight. It's not always easy for me to feel like I fit in, especially since so many of my family members live close to each other and see each other so often. Becky is facing the same thing each year, only it's worse for her, because you are all so passionate," Ella explained.

I laughed at her use of the word passionate. "Don't you mean crazy?"

"You know what I mean," Ella said.

"I get what you're saying, but that doesn't justify her hateful behaviors," I countered, resisting the urge to feel empathy for my sister.

"I'm not saying that she's right, I just think that it's hard for her to admit she's wrong," Ella explained.

"Remind you of anyone?" I asked.

"Yeah, you," Ella said.

"I was thinking of Dad," I joked.

"Him too," Ella agreed.

I thought a lot about the Becky situation in the weeks leading up to her summer visit, and came to some conclusions. Pride, partnered with insecurity, had road blocked my own road to change throughout several years of marriage. Change had only come to me after learning that I could trust Ella to champion rather than ridicule my efforts. She treated any desire to improve myself as natural and expected, without any hint of self-righteous pageantry.

I decided that I would handle Becky as if she wanted to change but needed a gentle, non-threatening push in its direction. During her visit, I would act as if nothing were or ever had been wrong, making it easier for her to take a step forward. Forgetting the past with all of its turmoil and bitterness would be difficult. To do so without appearing sanctimonious and judgmental would be close to impossible. Still, I felt that I had to try. To abandon the hope that we could all spend time together as a complete and happy family someday was not an option.

Summer came, and so did Becky and her three kids. The first few days went very well, with lots of swimming, eating, and laughing. My hopes for a breakthrough were cautious, but higher than they had ever been. My own attitude adjustment seemed to be working. I began to think that perhaps my forceful nature had played a greater role in keeping Becky from ending her embargo than I had realized.

After spending the week in her company, I was convinced that Becky was ready to ease Jared into her children's lives. We had discussed him at length during the week, and she seemed genuinely concerned for his happiness. My plan was to suggest that the family come over to our house for a barbeque and some air conditioning. All I needed was a moment of opportunity in which to extend the invitation.

The moment arrived in Mom's kitchen early one afternoon. I was looking for something sweet to snack on, and was digging through the pantry in search of cookies. Dad was in the kitchen with me, having come in from the barn with his empty lunch plate.

Becky walked in and asked, "So are we doing the sibling dinner tonight? Mom said she'd watch your kids if Ella wanted to come too."

I paused my search for cookies and took a moment to clear my head before turning to answer. "I talked to Jared already. He said he'd be home this afternoon, so I can go get him anytime. Instead of going out, why doesn't everyone just come over to our house for steaks and burgers? The kids can ride bikes and play in the tree house while we hang out inside with the air conditioning on full blast. I can pick up Jared and grab whatever we need at the store on the way back." I lobbed the suggestion into the air, hoping that my tone sounded as innocent and non-threatening as I intended it to be.

Becky stood in the center of the kitchen with one hand on her hip, the other holding aloft an index finger as if to halt the ticking of time itself because everything in the world depended upon the words she was about to speak. "I have just one question," she said.

"What is that?" I asked, hoping that the next words out of her mouth would not be horrible.

"Is Jared still gay?"

Chapter 59: October 2009

"Do you get the feeling that people and things have been put in our path on this trip?"

Connor's question didn't catch me by surprise, in spite of the fact that he had long expressed a serious doubt in the existence of any form of higher power other than aliens.

"Of course, how could I not? Ziggy's doppelganger at the airport, the traveling couple at the hotel, the crow, Simon? I'd be stupid not to imagine something bigger than my own understanding is at work on this trip," I admitted.

"I won't say that it was God putting it all together, but it feels like something more than just chance," Connor said, offering what I thought to be a fair and honest assessment of the situation.

"Don't get me wrong, I don't believe that everything happens for a reason. I mean, I believe in God, but I don't believe that he cares about every little detail of our lives. People that say he does are stupid. If everything happens for a reason, then why make a single decision in life? Why not just let things happen for a reason and blame God when it all goes bad?" I was almost shouting at the thought of how many mindless drones had vomited cliché into my lap over the past several months.

"Most people are stupid. They can't or won't think for themselves. They'd rather believe anything that sounds deep and mystical," Connor agreed.

"Or anything they hear at church," I added.

"True," Connor nodded. He turned and grabbed his backpack from the back seat. He dug around inside it for a moment before his hand emerged gripping a toothbrush.

"Oh, I could use one of those right now. My breath tastes like the inside of your shoepers," I joked.

Connor ignored me and reached into his mouth.

"Something stuck in your teeth? I hate when that happens. One time on my mission, I had a little sliver of meat stuck between my teeth for almost a week. I didn't have any floss, so I tried using thread. That made it worse. By the time it came out I had an infection that hurt like hell and bled for hours." I glanced at Connor, who was pulling something much larger than a sliver of meat from his mouth.

"Hahaha!" Connor burst into a fit of nervous laughter as he held aloft a set of dentures.

"Wha-?" I watched as he began to brush his removable teeth.

"You didn't know I had these did you?" Connor grinned.

"Uh…" I stammered. The speech center of my brain had not yet recovered power, since the rest of it was working overtime to comprehend the signals sent to it by my eyes.

"I've had them for a while. Dad paid for them." Connor finished brushing his false teeth and slid them back into place with a soft click.

"Wow, Dad paid for them? How did you get him to do that?" I wondered aloud. Dad had paid for a lot of cars, apartments, and airline tickets, but I had never imagined him buying a set of teeth for one of his kids.

"I just called him and told him that I couldn't work unless I got my teeth fixed. They hurt so bad that I could only sleep standing up, and only for an hour or so at a time. I had migraines for days, I couldn't eat, and my mouth bled all the time." He put his toothbrush away and flipped his phone open.

"How long ago was all this? I shook my head in wonderment.

"It's been a few years. Look at this." He held up his phone. There was a photo on the little screen.

"Gross! What is that?" I gagged and looked back at the road.

"That is my sink, covered in blood and pus from my teeth. One night it was so bad I just stood over the sink and watched it drip until I almost passed out. That was when I called Dad." He closed his phone and stuffed his backpack into the back seat next to Jared.

"Nasty! I remember taking you to get some of your teeth pulled when you lived at our house, but I didn't know that there were more after that," I said with a shudder. Memories of Connor's time in our home filled my head as I stared down the long, straight highway ahead.

Connor had been married, and then divorced at a young age. His ex-wife was not Asian, but rather an American brunette from New Hampshire that he had met at a church youth activity. The relationship had been the first serious romance for both of them, and had endured on and off status for several years. At one point when she had gone to school out in Utah he had followed, living in his car through an entire mountain winter just to be near her. I had thought it an act more stupid than romantic.

They got married not long after, and from a distance they seemed to be happy. Connor attended church regularly, which led me to believe that he had decided to give maturity a try.

Maturity hadn't stuck. After a few years that included at least one separation, they announced that they had come to the mutual and amicable agreement to end their marriage.

In the judgmental and narrow-minded tradition handed down to me by my father, I held Connor to blame for their divorce. He had not held a steady job, smoked too much pot, and seemed to have no interest in growing up. His unwillingness to go to church and to change had in my opinion been the cause of the break up.

It had only been in the past few months, several years after their divorce, that I had taken the time to hear Connor's version of events. He was not the only driving force behind the end of their marriage. His ex-wife was just as much to blame, having played everyone for fools as she led the same double life that so many Christian girls live. It was heartbreaking to listen as Connor cracked open the shell of pain and regret that he had long kept closed and hidden from me, knowing that I had long been incapable of empathy.

In the past I had ruined every chance to have a meaningful relationship with my youngest brother. There were many moments for me to be ashamed of when it came to my history with Connor, but the guilt stemming from one specific incident had never faded, the memory of my behavior having plagued me ever since.

It had happened while Connor was still married, but separated. His wife had once again moved west, but this time he had not followed her. One night we had just finished our family dinner, and were about to eat chocolate pudding when Connor knocked on the front door. I had not seen him for some time.

"Oh, I see how it is. You only show up when we are about to eat something chocolate." My comment was meant as a joke, but the words carried the attitude I had long harbored towards my brothers. They only ever needed something I had, and never actually needed me.

Connor stood silent and still on our front steps. The moment became awkward, the limits of conversation having long been at an end between us.

Connor burst into tears, and then ran past me into the house. I stood in the doorway, listening as he made his way up two flights of stairs and into our finished attic.

"What the-?" I wondered aloud, as Ella and the kids came running from the table, curious about the commotion.

We all climbed the stairs to the attic to find Connor sobbing, his body shaking with the force of his sadness. He looked lost and confused.

"I miss her!" Connor's explanation burst through his blubbering. It was the saddest sound I ever heard him make. Ella herded the kids downstairs to set them up in front of a movie. I sat down on the couch but said nothing. I thought it best to wait out the silence; Connor would talk if and when he was ready.

170

He opened up once Ella returned, and then didn't stop for a couple of hours. It was a rare occurrence for me. Not only was my brother exposing to me a part of his life that I knew nothing about, but I was keeping my mouth shut and listening rather than correcting and directing his life.

By the end of the conversation Connor was feeling lighter for having vented his sadness. Ella and I invited him to live with us, up in the attic bedroom, for as long as he needed. He moved in the next day.

We asked that Connor remember that our children came first, and that he be respectful of our roles as parents. There was also to be no smoking of any kind in the house.

Part of Connor's sad story was the state of his mouth. His back teeth were rotting out of his head. He denied the suggestion that it was his diet and lack of dental hygiene, and blamed it instead on the ear infection medication prescribed by doctors during his younger years. He was convinced that the medicine had had lasting effects on his teeth.

It never occurred to me to that there might be some validity to his argument. I just assumed it was another one of his many excuses for things in his life being the way they were through no fault of his own. I should have remembered that Mom and Dad had bottle-fed me on grape flavored Kool-Aid well into my toddler years. I had always offered this excuse for the many fillings in my teeth, so why then couldn't I accept Connor's excuse? It was just another example of the contempt I had for my brother's care-free lifestyles and attitudes, things that I denied myself in order to be more obedient.

I took Connor to see an oral surgeon, who removed a good number of his teeth. Connor put the substantial bill on his credit card. It was understood that with the money he saved from living in our home, he would be able to pay off the debt faster.

The trouble was that I wasn't sure Connor was even working all that much. He stayed up all night watching movies and playing video games, slept during the day, and left dirty dishes and clothes scattered about the attic. He would come and go at odd hours without notice, disappearing for a day or two at a time. I asked him one afternoon about his odd hours, and where it was that he was off to in the middle of the night. He replied that the painkillers given him by the oral surgeon had no effect on the pain, and the only place he felt comfortable was driving his car.

I was concerned. My little brother was out driving the roads at night with incredible pain in his head. That sounded both dangerous and foolish to me. I also did not believe that he was just driving around to escape the pain. I was sure that he was taking off in order to smoke weed, spending his nights tripping in his car like a homeless junkie.

After a few weeks of sleepless nights spent worrying, I reached the end of my patience and sympathy. I decided to confront Connor, demanding that he use the time in our home to better himself.

I waited for an afternoon when only Connor and I were home, then made my way up to the attic, my mind in lecture mode. Connor was asleep, and the sight of him laying there with dirty clothes, moldy dishes, and video games spread about the floor triggered a reaction much more heated than the one I had planned.

"I want you out! You don't respect me, you don't respect my rules, and you don't respect my family. Get out!" My voice was just shy of a shout, and portrayed all of the distain and contempt that I harbored for my little brother.

Connor stirred, sat up, and said nothing. He made no argument. He stood, grabbed a few things, and left the house. I had expected something more, a fight, a protest, a plea for forgiveness or a promise to change. He gave me nothing to work with, and so I was left alone with my anger.

Over the course of the next several days I felt heavy with regret. I had lashed out, attacking my brother as if he were a thief invading my home. I realized that I missed him, and was genuinely worried about him.

Not long after this onset of regret and concern, I was home alone one afternoon, eating lunch in the kitchen. Connor walked in suddenly from the basement, having come in through the garage and up the stairs without me hearing. He stood looking at me without saying a word, another awkward silence building between us.

I shoved my pride aside and spoke first. "Connor, I am sorry about the other day. I was out of line and said some stupid things that I should not have. I love you, and you are welcome to stay and live here. I promise that I will not say another word about you coming and going, or about anything else you do or don't do while here. Please stay as long as you like." Sincerity strengthened my words, and for the first time in our adult relationship I felt as though I was saying the right thing to Connor.

"Thanks, for the apology and for the offer to stay," Connor replied, surprise in his tone.

"I meant both," I said.

"I know. Can I leave some stuff in your basement for a while?"

"Yeah, sure, no problem. Leave whatever you want for as long as you need," I replied, eager to demonstrate my sincerity. In that moment my little brother could have asked me to sign over the title to my car and I would have gladly searched the kitchen for a pen.

I didn't see Connor again for several months.

Chapter 60: Summer 2007

I felt a collapse within as hope spilled out of me like blood through a belly wound. It pooled on the floor around my sister's feet. Becky's question had made quick work of gutting my spirit. I could not believe it; after all that Jared had been through, after all the concern she had expressed for him, she remained steady on her course of ignorance and bigotry.

I looked at Dad. His mouth was closed and quiet, his face loud with abdication. I knew in an instant that he would not be stepping up to guide the family through yet another storm.

I put a hand up as if to fend off a wild, swinging blow from an assailant. "I cannot talk to you right now," I said, rushing out of the kitchen and onto the back porch.

The sun was hot on my back, but the layer of sweat I felt pushing its way through my pores had nothing to do with the summer heat. I made my way past the happy kids splashing in the pool, through my father's garden, and out to the swinging bench where Ella was seated reading a book. As I approached, her face took on a look of concern, her senses elevated the moment she saw me.

"I need to get out of here. I cannot spend another minute in this house of hate," I said, my voice cracking.

"What happened?" She asked. Before I could answer, Becky came thundering around the corner and over to the swing.

"Matthew, how dare you!" She began.

I cut her off. "Please do not talk to me right now. Just walk away. I do not want to fight." I did my best to keep my voice from turning into a shout.

"No, I will not walk away!" she continued.

I dropped to my knees in front of my sister. "Please stop! I cannot take this anymore! I do not want to fight about this, please leave me alone. I cannot control myself, and I do not want to say something that I will regret," I begged, my hands clasped together in supplication.

Becky continued to rant, despite the fact that I was clearly in distress. I could see the kids in the pool behind her. They had stopped playing, their attention focused on the chaos. My heart ached at the sight of the puzzled looks they cast in our direction, and I could no longer understand the words flying around me, wrapped in a high-pitched shriek that clawed at my ears.

I watched as Dad walked across the yard and disappeared into his barn. I had never before thought of my father as a coward, but in that moment I was sure of it.

At last Becky finished her tirade, her face a snarling mask of anger. I stayed on my knees, silent in my misery. After a moment she turned on her heels and stormed off, throwing her hands up in the air, both her middle fingers held aloft in a final gesture that only served to demonstrate her ignorance.

I turned back to Ella. Her eyes were wide in wonder at all that had transpired in a matter of seconds. Taking a seat beside her on the swing, I reached out and took her hand. My breath was fast and shallow, my heart beating a dance club baseline.

"Did you see her flip the double bird?" Ella stole the question from my lips.

"Yeah. What a bitch. I think I am done with her for good." I settled back into the swing. I needed a moment to gather myself.

"So, I guess you suggested dinner with everyone?"

"Yep. I thought she would go for it. Dad was right there and did nothing but walk away. What a coward." I shuddered at the memory of Becky's cold-hearted question and Dad's indifference to it.

"So what are you going to do?"

"Well, Jared is expecting me to pick him up for the stupid sibling dinner from hell. Maybe I'll see if he just wants to go out to a movie with me. No way am I going to sit across a table from that evil woman tonight." I leaned over and gave my wife a kiss.

Ella reached up and grabbed my face between her hands. "Look at me," she said. "This is not about you, this is about Jared."

"I know," I mumbled.

I kissed her once more before crossing the yard and climbing into the car. Before I could drive off, Sarah jumped into the back seat.

"Just let me say something before you go away mad," she said, applying a mousy tone to her voice.

"Make it quick. I am out of here," I demanded.

"I just want everyone to get along. Why can't you just leave it alone?" As she always seemed to do, Sarah had come to plead Becky's case.

"If you really want everyone to get along, why don't stand up for Harrison and Jared, and tell Becky that she is wrong?" I countered.

"I am not choosing sides, don't tell me that I have to choose sides," she whimpered.

"You already have, Sarah! By not saying anything to her, and by supporting her decision to keep the family apart, you have chosen her side! And how stupid is it that we are even using the term *sides*? We are a family, there shouldn't be any *sides*," I shouted, tired of making the same argument every summer.

"I hate that you guys do this to me! You always put me right in the middle and I hate it!" Sarah said, her voice trembling as she cried harder.

I laughed at the pitiful sound. "Oh, Please! No one puts you in the middle. Besides, you aren't even in the middle! You could be in there telling Becky that enough is enough, and that you want the family to be together, but you're not. You're sitting here telling me that I need to leave it alone and respect her evil decision. Give me a break!"

176

Sarah jumped out of the car and slammed the door. I drove away, happy to be rid of her. She had tried to play the martyr, having learned the role so well from our mother. I wasn't having any of it. This was not about her.

But in truth I often felt bad for Sarah. It seemed to me that Becky was always pulling at Sarah's strings and taking advantage of her younger sister's devotion. The power she had over Sarah was often a topic of discussion within the family, so I knew that I wasn't alone in my assessment of their relationship. I did not begrudge them their bond, and Sarah and I had long enjoyed a healthy brother and sister relationship. What bothered me was Sarah's need to please Becky to the point of ignoring her abhorrent behavior towards our own brothers.

Jared's apartment wasn't far away, but I took my time getting there, making extra turns and doubling back more than once while en route. I had not yet cooled down enough to mask my emotions when picking him up. I planned to act as if nothing had happened rather than tell him that his older sister still feared that his gayness would rub off onto her kids and send them straight to hell.

"What happened?" The first words out of Jared's mouth confirmed that I had not taken enough time to cool down.

"Is it that obvious?"

"Look, can we just get together for dinner and pretend that nothing happened?" Jared looked out the window, away from me.

"If that is what you want, although I am not sure why you would want to break bread with that bitch." The instant regret I felt at saying them could do nothing to retract my words. I suddenly wondered if I was the one causing all of the tension, not Becky. Did Jared even want me to stand up against her behavior?

"Please, just call them and tell them to meet us somewhere. We'll eat, we'll hang out, and it will be over for another year." There was a tired sadness in Jared's voice. I hated myself for being part of the reason for his emotional fatigue.

"Sure, anything you want. Just tell me why first. Why do you want to go out to dinner with her? Connor won't even go, why should you?" I asked.

"She's my sister. Of course I don't want to go to dinner with her, but she's my sister. That's it, Matthew. She's my sister," he said, his voice cracking as he repeated the answer he had already given to the question I had already asked.

We drove in silence for several minutes before I pulled out my phone and called Mom and Dad's house. I spoke with Sarah, and we set up a time and a place for dinner. The conversation was brief, the pleasant tone of my voice contrived.

The atmosphere at that summer's sibling dinner was more synthetic than ever before. Manufactured conversation, hollow laughter, and the pretense of warmth engulfed us like an invisible fog. In my mind's eye I saw myself leaping across the table to wrap my hands around Becky's throat. Jared played the happy little brother, giving rise to several moments of disgust and loathing within me. I had lashed out in his defense, but had Jared seemed more disappointed than grateful. I felt confused and embarrassed.

By the end of the night, my heart and head were spent from a day of dirty family politics. All I wanted was to be close to Ella.

"I promise to you now that I will never again attend another one of those stupid sibling dinners," I announced upon walking into our bedroom.

"I can't believe you went tonight." Ella put her book down as I collapsed onto the bed fully clothed.

"I had to. I wasn't going to send Jared into the lion's den alone." I closed my eyes and felt her soft fingers running through my hair.

"Your sister came over and sat next to me on the swing after you left."

"Did you jump up and run away screaming?" I laughed.

"No, I wanted to hear her side of the story. She was willing to talk, so I listened. I'm not sure you want to hear what she said." Ella's hand moved over my forehead and down across my face. Her skin was soft, cool, and relieving.

"Whatever it is, I'm not sure it can make me despise her any more than I already do. Let's hear it," I said with a sigh.

"She told me that she and Richard haven't discussed the Jared and Harrison situation since they made the decision years ago. He doesn't even know about all the fights you two have had over the years. She's never said a word about them," Ella told me.

My eyes popped open. Light peeked between my wife's calming fingers. "Are you shitting me?"

"Nope, she said that they don't talk about it at all, ever. She even confessed to not knowing if he still feels the same about their decision. She said Richard might even be okay with the kids meeting Jared and Harrison, but since they never talk about it, she doesn't know."

I sat up and looked Ella in the eyes. "Are you serious? She said all of that with her own mouth?" I asked.

"With her own mouth, and she sounded sincere. I felt bad for her. She can't even talk to her own husband about her family and the mess she walks into every summer."

"Oh, boo-effing-who!" I almost shouted my reaction, leaping from the bed to pace the floor. "I don't feel anything but hate for that bitch! She has ruined every summer for years, she won't let the family be together, and she treats Jared and Harrison as sub-humans! Am I supposed to feel sorry for her because she can't talk to her husband?"

"I knew you wouldn't want to hear it," Ella said softly.

"No, this is not your fault. It's her fault, all of it. She comes out here for two weeks out of the year and dictates what will and won't happen while she is here, and then jets back to her mansion in Canada, leaving us to flounder in the wake of her hate. I am officially done with her. I will not waste another moment of my life on that

179

evil, nasty, hateful, empty shell of a human being. Becky can eat shit and die!"

I stripped off my clothes, stepped into the bathroom, and turned on the shower. I brushed my teeth facing the mirror. Hate stared back at me. I tried to convince myself that it felt good.

But it didn't.

Chapter 61: October 2009

"Stop, that tire looks perfect." Connor pointed at the remains of a truck tire on the side of the road.

I pulled the car over and we jumped out for yet another photo from the bucket list. Connor lay down on the rumble strip, inside the almost complete circle of black rubber. He curled up his body and closed his eyes. The tire wrapped around his back like a protective shell. I took a few photos of my brother as a human-armadillo hybrid escaped from Area 51.

A few miles later down the road we passed a train crawling westward on tracks that ran parallel to the highway.

"Pull over, I'll take a photo of you running past the engine like Superman," Connor suggested.

I needed no further encouragement and pulled the car up far enough to allow me some running room.

As I raced the locomotive, my heart sped into action, my muscles begging for blood. My lungs sucked in the fresh dry air of the dessert. For the past two days they had known only the smoke of Connor's cigarettes, which was as foreign to them as exercise was to the salad-eating Texans that Connor had ranted about. I imagined sprinting until my body quit and collapsed into a pile of flesh, allowing my spirit to slip free and continue running west.

After several yards reality set in and I panted to a halt. I watched the train roll by, then returned to my brothers. Connor was waiting for me beside the car.

"Want me to drive?"

"Sure, why not?" I was weary, and perhaps it showed.

Sometime later we left the highway and headed for the middle of nowhere, otherwise known as Winslow, Arizona.

Winslow had been the site of a meteor crash some fifty thousand years prior to our visit. The crater made by the meteor's impact was almost a mile wide and over five hundred feet deep. It had been featured in the movie "Starman" starring Jeff Bridges back in the Eighties. Ever since seeing the film as a teenager, I had hoped to one day visit the crater so that I could stand on the rim of it and imagine the moment of impact.

We paid the entrance fee, and Connor followed me into the museum that would eventually lead us out to the crater itself. We wandered through the hallways lined with photos and exhibits that explained the history and science of the crater.

"Hey, take a photo of me dropping trou' at the bottom of the crater," I joked, handing Connor the camera and running over to a diorama that was supposed to give visitors a sense of standing on the crater floor. It was a poor imitation of what must have been a breathtaking experience, but it was as close as I was going to get, since visitors were no longer allowed into the crater itself.

"Quick, before someone comes around the corner and sees my bare white ass hanging," I laughed, my pants down just below my cheeks.

Connor reluctantly took a couple of shots. I was still buckling my belt as an older couple rounded the turn with their grandkids in tow. The woman looked me over with suspicion in her eyes, and directed her young wards across the hall and away from me.

Bored by facts and tired of reading placards, we made for the door that led outside to the crater's rim.

A breathy "Wow!" left my mouth as I looked down into the massive, beautiful scar in the Earth's skin. "This is unreal. I knew it was big, but damn!" I marveled.

Connor nodded beside me. We stood together in silence, taking in the enormity of the crater below. I tried to envision the moment of impact, imagining the sight and sound as the meteor hit, sending a few hundred million tons of dirt and rock flying into the air.

"I wonder how loud the sound of the impact was. You could probably hear it hundreds of miles, maybe thousands of miles away. It must have felt like the earth was cracking in half," I said aloud,

182

sounding like my teenage son leaving the theater after a super hero movie.

Wild rabbits scampered along the steep slope below us, nibbling at small patches of vegetation growing among the dirt and rocks. I wondered if the rabbits were born, lived, and died without ever leaving the crater.

Connor had said nothing for several minutes, prompting me to look in his direction. He stood across the cement platform from me, one hand scratching the crown of his head, the other scratching at the crotch of his jeans.

"Whatever, Dad!" I laughed.

Connor had no rival when it came to imitating our father. He knew all of Dad's little tics and could mimic them to perfection. The head scratch was something Dad did when uncomfortable in a conversation or thinking of a way to signal the end of his participation in a discussion. The crotch scratch was just something he did all the time.

"Wait, move over here so I can get a shot of you doing it with the crater in the background."

We traded spots, and I snapped a photo. As if reading my thoughts, Connor moved from the crotch and head scratch combo to my all-time favorite, the not-so-secret nose pick.

The fact that as kids we had studied all of our father's habits was not lost upon me when I became a dad. I knew that I had my own tics and tells, arguably more than my father. To know that my kids watched me for shortcomings and idiosyncrasies did not bother me in the least. In my opinion, my imperfections made me more human and therefore more accessible to my children. I made no secret of my faults. My children would not be shattered to learn that I was not superhuman.

One of my few memories of feeling close to Dad was of the time he carried me into the house after I had undergone hernia surgery at the age of four. The strength of his safe and loving arms holding me against his chest, the roughness of his stubbled cheek, and the fatherly smell of his aftershave were details that I had never forgotten. He may have carried me to bed a few times in years that followed, but never again had I been wrapped up in his embrace the way I had been on that night. It was such a brief taste of his capacity for love, but the sweetness of it lingered, and I had longed for it ever since.

I loved my father, and had tried all my life to draw closer to him. As a child I had begged my mother for work boots and a jean jacket just like Dad's, in the hope that dressing the way he did would make me more like him. In church I would sit beside him, and if courage struck me, I would lay my head down in his lap and pretend to sleep. I followed him everywhere, shadowing him in the garage, the garden, and the lumberyard, spending as much time with him as I could.

To his credit, Dad had never told me to get lost when working on a project, but in sticking around I suffered severe blows to my ego on a regular basis.

"You're supposed to hit the nail, not the wood, dummy." He would make the same joke every time I dimpled wood rather than hitting the nail. Although his tone was never mean, the message was clear. I felt that I was not as good as he was, nor was I good enough for him.

As I grew older, I tried to let my father know that I needed him to believe in me, rather than criticize me. His defense was that his criticism was always intended as inspiration to succeed. In telling us that we would fail at something, he hoped that we would get angry enough to prove him wrong.

One example of Dad's methods of encouragement occurred at a Boy Scout meeting, and the moment had stayed with me. It was announced to the troop that any boy achieving the rank of Eagle Scout by the following summer would be invited to attend the high adventure trip to the Florida Keys Sea Base. I already had every intention of earning my Eagle that year; the trip would be a bonus.

After the meeting, I was talking to my scoutmaster, the man rapidly replacing Dad as my hero. Jim was a Vietnam vet, a skilled hunter, and a true modern mountain man. We were a rag tag bunch of teenagers, and Jim led us like the Dirty Dozen. He taught us respect for God, country, and self, sprinkled with a generous dose of authority bucking. Under Jim's instructional eye we shot guns, hiked tough trails, canoed white rivers, and burned things. He talked to us as if we were men, sparing us the typical condescension handed down by grownups. In return we believed that there was nothing Jim couldn't do, and we would have followed him into the breach under any conditions. Jim believed in me and had told me so.

As Jim and I were discussing my path to Eagle that night, my father approached us.

"Well, too bad that won't be you going to Florida. You won't make Eagle," he interrupted, his face conveying a subtle sneer.

Embarrassment shook my frame. My cheeks reddened and my eyes warmed with the onset of tears. My father had drained away my confidence in the presence of my living hero. I walked away, unable to face Jim and unwilling to face my father. Sometime later, when I had mustered enough courage to tell him how hurtful his words had been, he excused himself by claiming to having said what he did in order to motivate me.

At my Eagle Court of Honor later that year, I sobbed into the microphone as I dedicated my Eagle rank to my father. Even as the words blubbered their way through the drool and tears, I wondered why I was uttering them, and I felt like a dog returning to lap up a puddle of his own vomit.

In spite of his ability to make me feel inadequate, I had persisted in shadowing my father well into adulthood. It seemed that the more he hurt me, the more I needed to try and earn the praise that never came. My brothers had given up on Dad long ago, but I had refused to quit. I told myself that deep inside my father was a wellspring of emotions waiting to be tapped, and that I would one day be the one to break through the crusty layer of whatever it was that prevented him from sharing those emotions with others.

I looked past Connor, down into the meteor crater. At the center of the crater floor stood a plywood cutout of an astronaut. Placed there to give visitors a perspective on just how big the crater was, the life-size figure appeared as a featureless speck of white against a brown background. I wouldn't have seen it had I not read about it on one of the many signs posted around the observation deck.

Looking down at the tiny astronaut, I marveled that a relatively small piece of iron had left such a massive and lasting impact.

Chapter 62: Summer 2007

Crowded with chatting people, the sidewalks in Ogunquit, Maine moved along like a babbling brook. Herds of people typically bothered me, but that night's crowd was too upbeat and friendly for the usual bad vibes to sour my mood. We drifted with the smiling current of people heading for the beach. There was to be a fireworks display that night, and we didn't want to miss it.

Ella and I had picked up Jared and made the short trip north for a night out together. Before losing his license, Jared had frequented the quaint New England town known for its high concentration of gay and lesbian visitors. He had wanted to return to Ogunquit for an evening of adventure, and the promise of good food and great dance music had convinced Ella that we needed to take him.

The events surrounding Becky's visit, and the drama of the sibling dinner had faded into the darkness that overshadowed a number of unpleasant moments in family history. I had decided that time spent with Jared would be focused on happiness. Becky would not be discussed any more. She was not worth the time or the breath.

We had already enjoyed dinner at a restaurant owned by one of Jared's friends, and were following the happy throng down to see the fireworks. The night was warm but comfortable, the typical humidity of New England having taken a welcome leave of absence. I was looking forward to whatever the evening held in store.

"Curlers in your hair, shame on you!" A silly voice rang out in a sing-song tune. We turned to see a woman with large curlers rolled into her thick blonde locks and a large smile spread across her over-rouged cheeks.

"Curlers in your hair, shame on you!" She wagged a finger in our direction as she repeated the line several times. We laughed, entertained but cautious of her odd behavior and abrupt approach. Without being invited, the strange woman slid in between Jared and Ella, matching our casual gate. We sang along with her despite our lack of understanding. Anyone who passed by was handed one of the many flyers the strange but joyful woman carried with her. She explained to us that she was a comedienne performing at a local club, and that she was handing out the flyers to drum up an audience for her show that night.

As we neared the beach, she broke ranks and drifted away. Before the crowd ahead swallowed her, she made us promise that we would check out her act. She thanked us by repeating her ridiculous song one more time as she disappeared from view.

As a child Jared had always hidden in the bathroom to avoid the loud noise of fireworks, but that night he stood with Ella and me, his mouth hanging open, his head tilted back, and his eyes reflecting the bright colors of the explosions overhead. We cheered en masse at the outlandish finale.

The fireworks were over, but the night was just beginning. We made tracks for downtown, but Jared and Ella soon fell behind, my pace much too fast for their easygoing gait. I glanced back at them walking together but didn't bother to hurry them. Ever since the days when Jared had lived with us in our tiny Seattle apartment I had known that Ella and Jared would forever be close. To see them side by side, all smiles and laughter, made me happy.

I turned back towards town and forged ahead. After several steps I felt a warm, soft hand slide into mine. I squeezed it and continued walking for a few moments before turning to smile at Ella. Instead, I smiled at Jared, his arm swinging in time with mine, his hand held snug in my own.

"What the heck?" I pulled my hand away and felt my face flush warm.

"Did you really think I was Ella?" Jared asked, his hand reaching up to cover his mouth as it often did when he laughed.

"Yes, of course I did, you dork!" I gave him a playful shove. He stepped back to maintain his balance just as Ella caught up to us.

"You should have seen your reaction!" She giggled.

"Gee, I'm glad I could amuse you both." I feigned a hurtful tone, but my smile gave me away.

188

We relived the moment all the way to the ice cream parlor, where I ordered a sugar cone piled high with my standing order of chocolate and peanut butter. It was rich, it was cold, and it was perfect. We munched our way through the streets, taking in the scenery of the shop windows and jabbering on about nothing important.

Once we had finished our ice cream, Jared led us to the local dance club. It was open, but there was no dancing that early in the evening. Instead, a large crowd had gathered around a spot lit singer with a husky voice.

Seated on a tall stool in the center of a small parquet floor, the 'woman' wore a bright green evening gown that shimmered beneath the lights and matched the green streaks in her perfectly coiffed silver hair. Her legs were crossed like those of a Bond girl sitting on the hood of an Aston Martin, and every movement she made exposed more of her very long, very feminine legs. We watched as she sang, her lyrics loaded with innuendos that sparked rounds of laughter, much to her feigned surprise. She flirted without shame, and carried herself in a way that I imagined Marlene Dietrich might have long ago.

It was the first time I had seen a drag queen up close. I was fascinated, conflicted, and entertained, all within the space of a few minutes.

Since the dance floor had yet to open for dancing, we left the cross dressing singer behind and headed back up the street to the local piano bar. The large upstairs room was filled to beyond capacity with happy, singing people, most of them men. From one corner came the sound of a piano, but I could only catch glimpses of it through the ebb and flow of bodies that surrounded it.

Everyone in the room swayed to the music, singing along with arms wrapped around waists and shoulders. Had it not been show tunes that they were singing, I might have thought we had stumbled into an Irish pub in Boston on St. Patrick's Day. We spent the next few songs marveling at the fun of it all, joining in when we knew the words. Jared soon signaled our exit, and we followed him down the stairs and out the door.

The night air had grown cooler, a sharp contrast to the heat of the packed piano bar. We made it to the comedy club in time to watch the bizarre woman in curlers open her show. The curlers were gone, and with them everything else that had made her interesting. It was apparent within a few moments that she was better at singing goofy songs to strangers in the street than making rooms full of paying customers laugh at her jokes.

"The dance club should be open now, you guys want to check it out again?" Jared asked.

"Yes! Let's go, this lady isn't funny, and I wanna get my groove on!" Ella made for the door.

Back at the dance club, the bass was thumping and lights were flashing. A mass of bodies gyrated to the beat. A man walked past us with a tray of drinks held high in the air. He wore nothing but black boots and a pair of white underpants. I stayed close to Jared, and as a silent signal to her that I was deep in the throes of unease placed my hands around Ella's waist while following her into the fray.

The first few minutes on a dance floor had always been uncomfortable for me. Finding my feet and matching them to the beat seemed an impossible task. My hips tended to grind away like a fan unbalanced by a broken blade, my arms growing ever more cumbersome, ignoring my commands to be suave. Even my head felt lopsided and void of rhythm. Ella and Jared had never suffered the same dance floor afflictions, and that night in Ogunquit was no different. I looked on with envy as their bodies merged effortlessly with the thundering baseline.

Lights flashed, fog filled the room, and bubbles filtered down from above. People were writhing and jumping to the music. It seemed that everyone around me was finding his or her own groove. I stood like a pillar of anti-rhythm in the center of the pulsating crush. I was a white-heterosexual-married-male in his mid-thirties standing on the dance floor of a gay nightclub.

And then it happened.

190

The hands on my ass could not have been my wife's; Ella was in front of me, dancing like a diva. They weren't Jared's, because he too was in front of me, and my own brother, no matter how gay, would not have grabbed my butt in such a suggestive manner. This realization took but a fractured moment. I spun around to see whose hands had not only grabbed, but squeezed my cheeks.

A black man with a very muscular (and shirtless) build stood behind me, his hands only just removed from my butt, and a bright smile on his face. He winked at me before turning away, presumably to dance, but the thought occurred to me that perhaps he expected me to return the handy favor.

I didn't. Circling back to face Ella and Jared seemed to take several minutes. My dear wife was shaking what the good Lord had given her, but she stopped when she saw the look on my face.

"What?" She shouted, her hands gesturing confusion.

I leaned over to shout in her ear, and the words felt funny crossing my tongue. "I just got goosed by a very large, half-naked black man!"

"No way! Where is he?" Her squeal of delight lightened the situation, and I started to notice just how funny the situation actually was. I pointed across the floor at my suitor.

"Wow! He's good looking! You should be happy!" Ella laughed and grabbed Jared, pulling him out of his dance trance to include him in the fun.

"Nice one, Matthew! He's not my type, but he is hot!" Jared laughed, chasing the awkward away for good.

"What can I say? When you've got it, you've got it!" I shouted over the music. It struck me as a strange thing to say given my current location, but I was suddenly feeling sure of myself. I was an attractive heterosexual male, standing beside his beautiful wife on the dance floor of a gay night club. I was one of a kind!

My ego boost complete, I watched as Jared once again moved his body to the beat. Ella pulled me in and gave me a kiss. Her lips were salty with sweat, but the sweetness of the act was all I could taste. I put my hands on her hips and we began to move. I found my feet. My arms obeyed, following the rhythm as I commanded. I threw my head back and closed my eyes, and the blinking lights above painted my eyelids in colorful fireworks. It was a good night to be alive.

I had found my groove.

Chapter 63: October 2009

We drove into Flagstaff just before dark, and checked into a hotel that had a life-sized statue of a pony standing out front. We showered off the road fatigue before heading out to grab dinner.

After filling up on fast food, we picked up some snacks at a local convenience store.

"Could I get a pack of those menthols, please?" I asked the clerk, pointing at Connor's favorite brand of cancer sticks.

"May I see your identification, please?" The man asked.

I looked at Connor and smirked as I unfolded my wallet and held it up for the clerk to see, like a federal agent about to question a suspect. "Still looking young," I said.

"Yeah, that's it," Connor replied.

I paid with cash, dropped the change into the penny jar next to the register, and stuffed the pack of cigarettes into my shirt pocket. Connor shook his head and laughed, then grabbed the bag of snacks and followed me out to the car.

Back at the hotel we watched television, ate junk food, and drank chocolate milk. After an hour or so, I went out into the hallway and called Ella to let her know we had made it to Flagstaff.

"Hey, it's me, how're you guys doing?" I asked.

"Oh, we're good, I'm just trying to get everyone to clean up the house a bit before bath time," Ella answered.

"Fun for you," I said, imagining the chaos.

"Where are you tonight?"

"We made it to Flagstaff a few hours ago. Today was incredible; I have decided that the Painted Desert is my new favorite place on Earth. We'll have to bring the kids out here on a road trip someday," I suggested, the thrill of all that we had witnessed still coursing through my veins.

"So, how are you doing?" Ella asked, taking a soft turn in the conversation.

"I'm alright, we're having fun," I replied truthfully.

"That's good, I'm glad."

"Tomorrow's going to be tough," I said.

"I know it is."

"I wish you were here." The words scratched against my throat.

"I know, but you are with the people you need to be with. This is about you, Jared, and Connor," Ella reminded me, love in her voice.

A long pause allowed her words to settle over me. I heard the kids on the other end of the line, their happy voices chattering away. The thought of them made me smile.

"So, what are you guys doing tomorrow?" I asked Ella.

"We'll probably watch movies all afternoon, and then we're going to have cake and ice cream for Jared's birthday," she said happily.

"That's a good idea, they'll love that."

"I'm sorry, I want to talk more, but I have to go; we haven't had dinner yet, and it's getting late," Ella apologized.

"It's okay, kiss and hug them for me would you?"

"I will. I love you, and I'll be thinking about you guys all day tomorrow," Ella said, emotions rippling her voice.

"I love you too. I'll call you tomorrow night." I hung up and pocketed my phone, then stood alone in the hallway for a minute before going back into our room.

I walked through the door and saw Connor upside down in mid-air, his body flying across the room. He landed on his back atop my bed, and then rolled to his feet using a combination of kinetic energy and the bounce of the mattress springs.

194

"Sweet! Do that again, I'll get the camera," I laughed, heading over to the nightstand.

"Ready?" Connor asked, poised for a leap a few moments later, after I had moved back into the doorway.

"When you are," I replied, the camera already recording.

"What? You want me to flip to the other bed? Matthew, I don't think I'm supposed to do that," Connor said, grinning for the camera.

"Yeah, you're not supposed to do that, but do it anyway," I said, following my brother's lead.

Connor leapt from his bed and into a somersault towards mine. He flew over the gap and hit my bed with a bounce that sent him to his feet. He yelped in surprise as his forward motion propelled him into the wall.

Recovering quickly, he turned to adjust the mattress.

"I moved the mattress a little," Connor explained for the camera before leaping from my bed back to his.

After several jumps, Connor settled down beneath the mess he had made of his blankets, the fatigue from another long day finally overtaking him. I made Jared as comfortable as I could before climbing into bed without brushing my teeth. I drifted off to sleep with the television on to keep my thoughts at bay.

Chapter 64: Fall 2007

"I'm going blind in one eye, and I hope it's a brain tumor." Jared took a bite of his sandwich as if he had just told me he had stubbed his toe.

"Wait, what? I'm not sure which part of that sentence is more disturbing. Oh, wait, the part where you hope it's a brain tumor. Let's start with that; what do you mean you hope it's a brain tumor?" I frowned across the table at my little brother.

"I mean that I hope it's a brain tumor. If it's a brain tumor, I'm not going to get treatment so I can finally die without having to kill myself," Jared replied evenly.

"Why do you want to die?" I couldn't believe my own voice. This was not a question I had ever imagined asking anyone that hadn't been bitten by a zombie.

"Just because. Life isn't so great, and I hate all the fuss over money and possessions. I don't like having bills and I don't like that I have to work just to pay for things I need to stay alive." Jared took a sip of his soda before taking another bite of his sandwich.

"Well, I understand that part of your argument. It sucks that we spend so much time doing something we'd rather not, just in order to have somewhere to sleep, store all our junk, and take a dump. I wouldn't work if I didn't have to either, but what can I tell you, that's life," I argued, somewhat lamely.

"Exactly! That's life, and life sucks. I just don't want to do it anymore. So if this is a brain tumor, I'm not going to do anything about it. I am just going to let it kill me." There was no anger in Jared's tone. He had made his decision and was stating it as fact.

There was little more that I could offer up in argument against his plan. He had no kids, no partner, and no prospects. His life consisted of sleep, work, and a little bit of diversion on the computer or television.

"Well, I would miss you, Ella would be devastated, and the kids would be crushed if you died. We love having you around," I offered anyway.

"I know, and I will miss you too, I think..."

"You think? Nice, I thought we were worth more to you than that!" I laughed at his reply to my expression of love.

"No, no, no, that's not what I meant! I meant that if there is anything after death, I will miss you. I just don't think there is anything after this. We die, and that's it."

"I know what you meant, I was just kidding," I lied.

"Oh, man, I feel like you don't believe me now. I'll miss you guys, I'm serious! Ok, let me say it right; Matthew, I will miss you, and I will miss Ella, and I will miss your kids when I die." Jared's eyes were wide with worry.

"Ok, I believe you. And just for the record, there is something after this life, and I will see you there after we die, a long time from now," I reassured him, fully aware that he still doubted the existence of the afterlife. It was the long-time-from-now part of my reply that I wanted him to believe.

Ella walked in through the front door and came into the kitchen. She smiled at Jared, and then distracted me with a quick kiss as she picked up my sandwich to steal a bite.

"Jared is going blind in one eye and hopes that it is a brain tumor so that he can die," I tattled. If Jared feared falling from anyone's grace, it was Ella's.

"What? Oh no, no, no. There will be no dying!" She already had him in her sights.

"But what if it is a brain tumor? I will have to spend a ton of money that I don't have to fight it, and it will probably kill me anyway. That, or I will be so sick from chemo and drugs that I'll wish I were dead," Jared argued.

197

"Money isn't important, you are," Ella countered without hesitation.

"I'm with Jared on the chemo. That stuff is nasty. I don't know if I could take it," I shuddered. The topic of needles, chemicals and tumors had always made me feel a little weak.

"Matthew, if you get cancer and the doctors say you need chemo, then you will get chemo!" Ella commanded.

Jared laughed, putting a hand to his mouth.

"You too, Jared! No dying!" Ella waved a threatening finger in his face.

"You can't stop me," he laughed.

"Maybe not, but if you do, you'd better find a good hiding place in heaven, because she will hunt you down and kick your butt." I knew just how capable my wife could be when driven.

"He's right!" Ella sat down at the table and took a drink from my soda.

"Only if there is an afterlife," Jared countered.

"Trust me, there is an afterlife, but even if there weren't I wouldn't let that stop me. I'd find you," Ella threatened, smiling at Jared with a menacing sweetness.

"When we die, we want our ashes to be mixed together. The kids will have to spend some of their inheritance money scattering our ashes on trips around the world to destinations we choose in our will," I said.

"If we ever write a will, or save any money for them to inherit," Ella reminded me.

"True," I agreed.

"I want a party instead of a funeral. If anyone shows up crying, they have to leave. I won't be sad, so why should they be?" Jared explained.

Ella nodded in agreement. "A party would be nice. So many funerals are sad, but if someone lived a long and happy life they should be celebrated. The Laotian family around the corner had a weeklong celebration when their grandfather died. So many people came and went during the week, and on the last day they had a huge gathering. That is the way it should be done. I would want everyone that loved me to gather together to share stories, show photos, sing, laugh, cry, whatever makes them feel closer to me."

"Ella, I love you, and I will miss you, but I am not singing to feel closer to you. If anything, that will chase your ghost away from me," I said, earning the punch in the arm she gave me in reply.

Jared laughed, and our conversation about death ended on a happy note. Ella disappeared upstairs, leaving Jared and I alone in the kitchen.

"I'm going to take a nap on the couch, if that's ok." Jared stood and stretched.

"Sure, go ahead. The kids won't be home for a while," I replied.

I sat at the kitchen table and watched Jared walk over to the living room, lie down on the couch, and pull a blanket over his head.

Chapter 65: October 2009

We ate a big breakfast at the hotel to kick off Jared's birthday. The morning was chilly, so after finishing waffles, cereal, toast, and an egg scramble, I took a hot chocolate to go. Connor took a cigarette.

After dropping my suitcase into the trunk, I got Jared settled into the back seat. "Today's the big day, are you ready for the Grand Canyon?" I asked, not expecting a reply.

On our way out of the hotel parking lot I stopped the car and parked near the small patch of lawn out front.

"Picture time," I said, getting out and walking over to the pony statue.

Connor followed with the camera. "Can you get on his back?"

I knocked my knuckles against the horse's flank. It felt thin and sounded hollow. "No way, this thing would probably split underneath me if I jumped up onto its back. I think it's made of thin fiberglass," I replied.

"Too bad, that would be a great picture," Connor said, holding up the camera.

I nodded my head in agreement while wrapping my arms around the pony's neck. I leaned in and put my cheek against its head. The cold hard skin of the statue shocked my skin upon contact. "Damn, that's cold!"

I closed my eyes and smiled. Connor clicked off a photo.

"Hold on, let's get one with me in it." Connor leaned his head against the other side of the pony's head. I smiled as he held the camera in front of us and snapped a shot. He checked it on the little screen and grinned his approval.

We drove to a local grocery store to buy snacks and drinks for the morning's drive.

"I also need some tape," I told Connor without explaining why. He followed me to the odds and ends aisle, where I picked out a small roll of packing tape.

"Oh, I almost forgot, I need something else," Connor said on our way to the checkout.

It was my turn to follow. Connor looked up and read each of the aisle markers until making a turn into the household cleaners.

"How about this?" Connor picked a can of air freshener off the shelf and sprayed it into the air for my approval.

"Strawberry? Smells fine to me. Check the label, some of them claim to kill cigarette odor."

Connor read the label and nodded. "We can spray it in the car every time we get out. That should hide the smell for when we have to return the car."

"I don't know if that alone will do it, but I'm not sure what else we can do. Just remember, you're paying the cleaning fee if they catch it," I reminded him.

"Why don't I get one of these to put in the car? That would help, wouldn't it?" Connor was looking at a shelf lined with solid gel air fresheners.

"Oh, those things are nasty. Mom used to get them for the bathrooms when we were kids. I would play with them while taking a dump. I always poked my finger through the holes and touched the gel, and then it would smell like air freshener all day." My nose wrinkled at the memory.

Connor picked one up and gave it a sniff. "We'll open this up and keep it in the car, and we can use the spray every time we stop to get out," Connor suggested.

"Fine, so long as I'm not in the car when you spray it," I agreed.

We paid for our supplies, then left Flagstaff, heading north. Fifteen minutes later we turned onto Loop Road, which would take us up to the Sunset Crater Volcano.

"This road is cool, Ella and I drove it when we were out here in March," I explained. "Some guy in Sedona drew a map for us on a restaurant menu. It takes us over a volcano, through some more of the Painted Desert, and past a bunch of Native American ruins."

"Sounds good to me," Connor said, happy to let me navigate our way through the day.

Chapter 66: Spring 2008

I returned home from visiting clients one afternoon to find Ella waiting for me with a packed bag.

"Let's go, Jared's watching the kids. We are going to Portsmouth for some fun and lots of hotel sex," she informed me with a smile.

"What, seriously?" I looked across the room at my little brother.

Jared grinned. "Yep," he said.

"Let's go, Matthew. See you in the morning, Jared," Ella said, walking out the front door without so much as a backwards glance.

I wasn't about to argue with the offer of a fun night out, complete with hotel sex. I ran upstairs and kissed the kids goodbye before leaving the house with a smile and a thanks for Jared.

Ella and I had spent the better part of our marriage in pitched battle. We had both brought baggage into the relationship; my low self-esteem and self-loathing had not meshed well with her immaturity and selfishness.

Ella had never suffered from a lack of friends, attention, or self-worth, and so she couldn't hope to understand my insecurities. The chasm that existed between our personalities had made living together difficult during our best moments, and unbearable during our worst.

I had long felt inadequate and incapable of pleasing her. I believed myself destined to be an emotional, financial, and physical failure. This was in no way the case, but years of self-doubt had prepared me well for life as a loser. There had been short stretches of happiness during our time together, but the darkness always returned, brought on by the most minor of events.

With each return to darkness, all the progress we had made prior to it was erased, sending us back to the beginning. We would haul out the old arguments and insecurities, spending the next several days and nights in anger. We would sleep little, talk even less, and often shout or cry our way through the night. Ella and I had spent more nights of our marriage in passionate conflict than we had in passionate lovemaking. The sun had risen to the sound of our arguments more than a few times over the years. It was a depressing way to live.

Adding to the exhaustion was the fact that we chose to hide our troubles from family and friends. By all outward appearances, we were a sweet and loving young couple living the dream.

The great tragedy was that in many ways we were the happy young couple that people believed us to be. We loved each other and wanted to be together, even if we couldn't always remember why. We had refused to surrender, and were determined to overcome everything that plagued our marriage, but we were not sure how to make that happen. We had both said and done things that could not be taken back or fully repaired without the sincere regret and absolute forgiveness that eluded us.

We did our best to contain the fighting to the bedroom. We both knew from personal experience that kids suffer the most when their parents are unhappy. Sheltering our own kids from the stress of our relationship was one of the few things on which we agreed. Still, no matter how hard we worked to prevent it from escaping the confines of our bedroom, animosity bled through the walls. It began to corrupt our home and affect our children.

But each of our kids seemed to have come along at just the right moment, slowing the frightening freefall of our happiness. Noah, born during the difficult time in Seattle, had given us someone to love without conditions. His dependence upon the both of us served to distract us from our own selfish needs. Three years later, Isabel had burst from the womb like a firecracker. Full of an innocent determination that would not be denied, she had renewed our belief in an eventual end to our troubles.

With the birth of Samuel we had been given a fighting chance. A very happy baby, his arrival was like a shot of endorphins that sparked within us a focused search for happiness. Working together on the specifics of our relationship, we began to see marked progress. Before long we could see that the end to our misery was in sight.

Ella had planned the surprise night away in order to keep the happiness flowing. We checked into our suite and showered for dinner, but were soon delayed by the proximity of a bed void of both Lego bricks and a history of fighting. We made it to dinner eventually, and then walked around Portsmouth, holding hands and enjoying the time together. We took dessert back to the hotel suite, where we watched movies, made love, and fell asleep with smiles on our faces. It felt good to be happy for an entire evening.

We woke the next morning and had a late breakfast before heading home. Along the way we joked about the mental and physical state in which we might find Jared after a night with our brood. Images of my brother tied to a chair beneath a swinging light bulb came to mind.

Jared came out the front door of the house just as we parked the car. Samuel stepped out behind him, followed closely by Isabel.

"You guys look pretty tired," I said to Jared in particular.

"I went to bed around two o'clock. Isabel and Samuel were still awake, watching a movie. I am not even sure they went to bed," Jared confessed, shrugging his shoulders.

"I stayed up all night!" Isabel smiled, the pride of her accomplishment overpowering her fatigue.

We ushered Isabel and Samuel inside, then got a full report from Jared. The kids had been no real trouble at all, watching TV and playing video games through the night. Jared had been able to go without a cigarette for several hours, but he admitted to sneaking out to the backyard for a nicotine fix sometime after midnight.

We both thanked Jared several times, and as he said goodbye to the kids, they made it clear that they were sad to exchange their fun uncle for their boring parents. It was obvious to me that in spite of his exhaustion, Jared was thrilled to be adored. He endured their loud and happy goodbyes with smiles and laughter of his own, then drove off towards his apartment for a long nap.

Chapter 67: October 2009

We drove towards the volcano, marveling at the scars that remained from its eruption a thousand years ago. We parked the car at a marked viewpoint and stepped out for a look and some photos. To our right, a layer of dark ash so even and clean that it could have been mistaken for intentional landscaping carpeted the ground. A scattering of pines, aspens, and desert brush had pushed their way through the black, and tiny patches of wild flowers peppered the side of the road.

The view to our left, however, was a violent contradiction. A jagged, black reef of ancient lava stretched into the distance. Very little vegetation had managed to break through the hard, rugged, angry crust. I stared in wonder at the devastation, then looked back at the beauty on our right to remind myself that if given enough time, the Earth could mend even the ugliest of scars.

We drove higher up the mountain, and soon the black lava reef gave way to the same layer of ash and growth that had continued on our right. I pulled the car over on a straightaway, handed Connor the camera, and jumped out for a closer look at the ash. I bent down and scooped up a fistful, pouring it from one hand to the other and back again. It felt like cold, hard, burnt granola.

"I don't see any signs warning us to stay on the road, do you?" I asked Connor, dropping the handful of ash and wiping my hands on my pants.

"No," he replied, and stepped over the single wire barrier that ran along the side of the road.

We ran up the side of the mountain, burnt granola crunching beneath our feet. Connor stopped and turned on the camera. I picked up my pace, running past him and leaping over a fallen tree with a happy shout before the thin air of high altitude forced me to a halt.

"It crunches like a field of Grape Nut cereal!" I said, gasping for breath.

Connor approached me and held out the camera. I took it and switched it to video. He knelt down and started to fuss with his shoes.

"Putting on your shoepers?" I joked, the camera rolling.

Connor pulled the mashed-down heels of his shoes up over the heels of his feet. He bent over into a sprinter's starting position, and began to pump his legs like a cartoon cat about to run away from a cartoon dog. His feet dug trenches in the ash, and a cloud of dust formed around his shoepers as he crunched his way down several inches to the dirt below. Without warning, he took off running up the hill, kicking his heels so high behind him that they almost hit him in the butt.

"The smoker runs up the hill," I said for the rolling camera. I wondered how far he would make it up the slope; the air was thinner with each step, and sure to be a challenge for his smoker's lungs.

Connor made quick work of the first thirty yards before slowing down. I watched as he leaned to his left and began to run in a tightening circle, eventually dropping his left hand to the ground and running around it like a dog chasing its own tail.

"The smoker runs around the hill," I laughed, the absurdity of the moment striking me; Connor and I were running carefree across the ash field of a dormant volcano.

Back inside the car, we drove for a few hundred yards before noticing a tree that could have served as a character in a dark and terrible ghost story. It stood at least fifty feet tall, with a large fork branching off near the base. Dozens of dark, bare, gnarled limbs reached out like menacing fingers, waiting to pluck birds from the sky above, or perhaps children from the ground below.

"I want to check out that gnarly old tree," I explained as I parked on the side of the road.

We crossed the wire into the ash field, and crunched our way towards the tree. I stopped to take a photo of it with the backdrop of blue sky and white clouds above.

207

"Check out the bark," Connor whispered, as if speaking would awaken the evil tree and seal our fate.

I approached with the camera recording video. The tree looked dead, and most of its bark had been stripped away by the elements. What little bark remained hung loosely around the trunk, and was fractured into odd shapes that looked like the scales of a lizard's skin, only much bigger.

Connor reached out and prodded the bark. It crackled and snapped, splitting into even more scale-like sections.

"Here we have what is called 'treeous escalious,' from which you can make dragon shields." Connor's whisper took on the tone of an expert on ancient trees and the usefulness of their bark in fighting large, airborne lizards that ate virgins and belched fire.

He pulled at one of the scales. "We're not supposed to disturb this-" Connor stopped his sentence short as the piece of bark broke off in his hand.

Together we ran for the car, as if pulling the bark from the tree had stirred the evil spirit deep within and our souls were in danger of being devoured. I kept the camera rolling, pointing it in Connor's general direction as we vaulted over shrubs and fallen trees, panting, wheezing, and laughing as we made our escape.

I leapt over the wire fence right behind Connor and crossed the road without looking for oncoming traffic. We scrambled into the little black rental car and peeled away as fast as it would go. I looked in the rear view mirror and imagined the evil tree spirit thrashing about in great anger, unable to stray far enough from his roots to catch us.

We were on the run. It felt good to be free.

Chapter 68: Spring 2008

Jared's license was reinstated after a two-year suspension. I was proud of him for overcoming what I had thought to be an impossible hurdle. The rough road he had taken through life made mine feel like a straight stretch of smoothly graded, fresh-paved highway.

He had his license, but didn't have a car. Dad hoped that Jared would continue his routine of walking to work and forego owning a car, at least for a while. He expressed his reasons for this hope to me one afternoon as I was working to clean a virus from the computer in his office.

"I just worry that the freedom stemming from owning a car will provide temptation that he won't be able to overcome. He has had to depend on us for trips to the grocery store, to the mall, or anywhere else. The only store near his apartment that sells any alcohol is the gas station across the street, and he can't get anything in there that would be hard enough to get him good and drunk." Dad had clearly done some investigative work when looking for that apartment.

I was touched by the thought of Dad walking the aisles of a gas station mini-mart to check for hard liquor that might tempt his son to start drinking again. The fact that this concern had not waned, but rather carried over to concern about Jared owning a car was encouraging. Jared would most likely have to fight for his sobriety until the day he died, and Dad seemed ready to do what he could to reduce the pressures on his son.

While I worried about the risk of a drinking relapse, I was more concerned that were he to buy a car, Jared could literally drive right out of my life. Having a car would mean that he could make the hour-long trip down to Connor's apartment, and that meant that Connor was likely to steal Jared away from me.

In the end, Jared would not be denied a set of wheels. After much debate and even more negotiating, Dad agreed to co-sign with Jared on a used car. Jared asked me to go and check out the one he had chosen before signing the papers.

"Why do you want me to check it out? I don't know much about cars," I protested.

"You know more about cars than I do," Jared insisted.

"Not really. I just know that you shouldn't buy used cars from friends the way Dad always does. You get what you pay for, and Dad pays for crappy cars that people want to get off of their front lawn," I said.

"This car is at a dealership, so it has to be a good car, doesn't it?" Jared may have sobered up, but he remained as innocent and gullible as ever. He had never been able to grasp man's ability to lie, cheat, and steal.

"I'll look at it, but I won't be able to tell you anything other than what color it is and if the air conditioning works," I relented.

The color was gold, and the air conditioning did work. It was a tiny imitation SUV, and had probably been owned by a little old woman that could barely see over the steering wheel. It was the perfect car for Jared. He was so proud of it, and of the freedom it afforded him.

Jared spent the first few weekends of that freedom with Connor. I tried not to worry, reminding myself that Jared had changed, that I had changed, and that our relationship had changed.

I was able to keep my doubts at bay until one night while watching TV with Ella.

"I saw Jared at a stop light today. He looked like he'd been drinking," Ella announced without preface.

I felt a sudden hollowing in my gut. "Are you sure? Maybe he worked all night and stayed awake all day," I suggested, not wanting to imagine Jared drinking again.

"I know what drunk looks like, and he looked drunk. He turned away when he saw me, but I got a good look at him. He acted like he hadn't seen me, and kept his head turned as if he didn't want me to catch him."

The hollow in my gut filled with anger.

"I've told him that I will kick his ass if he starts drinking again. Maybe I should go pay Jared a visit at work right now." I was on my feet, adrenaline soaking my brain.

"Calm down, we have to be careful. If we accuse him, he's likely to get angry and disappear. Remember, this is not about us, it's about him." Ella's words were a reminder, not a rebuke.

"Ok, but what can we do? How do you casually ask a recovering alcoholic if he has been drinking?" I slumped back onto the couch beside her, confused and defeated.

We could not come to a reasonable solution that night. In the end we decided that the only thing we could do was to keep an eye on Jared as best we could, and watch for signs that he was in fact, drinking again.

But I didn't do a very good job of keeping an eye on him. The thought of Jared drunk made me feel sick, helpless, and betrayed. To confirm it would hurt even more, so I stayed away. I told myself that Jared was a grown man that did not need a babysitter to keep him sober.

After several days of arguing with myself, I drove to Jared's on the way home from work. I parked next to his golden car and climbed the stairs to his apartment. Knowing that he might be asleep, I knocked several times and waited a minute before knocking again. My mind considered the only two possible explanations; Jared was either asleep or drunk. I stuck my face to the window, but Ella had made a blackout curtain for it so that Jared could sleep in absolute darkness during the day.

I knocked again, and waited. At last the door opened. Jared stepped out fully dressed with a smile for a hello.

"Oh, I thought you might have been asleep, you took so long." My voice was a nervous flurry of syllables.

"I was in the bathroom making myself even hotter," Jared said with a laugh.

211

"Want a late lunch?" I recovered, relieved to see him sober. Maybe Ella had been wrong.

We walked down the single flight of stairs and across the parking lot to my car. I summoned my courage as we drove out onto the street.

"Hey, I told you that I will kick your ass if you start drinking again, right?"

"Yes you did," Jared replied.

"Okay, just checking."

"I know, Matthew. Don't worry. I'm fine."

"Okay, good. So if I tell you one more time that I'll kick your ass if you start drinking again you won't get mad?" I joked.

"Nope," Jared said.

"I'll kick your ass if you start drinking again," I threatened, and then added, "Because I love you, of course."

Chapter 69: October 2009

We followed the road down the backside of the volcano and into the foothills above the Painted Desert. The sky was the kind of blue that artists go mad trying to capture on canvas. A few wisps of cloud floated overhead, pushed by a cool and gentle breeze. The sun touched everything in sight, leaving the darkness nowhere to hide. All the landscape needed was a cowboy on horseback being chased by native warriors on war ponies.

Connor wasn't smoking, but I opened the windows to let the morning air rush over my skin and into my lungs.

"What a perfect day for driving to the Grand Canyon," I thought aloud over the happy noise of our latest play list.

I saw Connor's head nod in agreement. His dark hair was wrestling with the wind as his eyes scanned the beautiful, desolate world surrounding our little black rental car.

The road wound down through miles of curves and long straights before flattening out onto the plain. Several motorcycles passed us along the way, their riders decked out in black leathers and denim jackets. We sped up and passed a few RVs and slow moving pickup trucks, but the road was for the most part lonely and quiet.

After several miles I slowed the car and took a right turn onto the access road leading to the Wukoki Pueblo. Before long we could see it in the distance, a rusty red castle complete with lookout tower reaching high into the backdrop of blue. We pulled up and parked a couple of spaces away from the only other car in the tiny lot.

I ran up a marked trail and climbed the steps into the pueblo ruin.

"Turn around, I'll take a photo," Connor shouted.

I turned and rested my hands on my hips as he snapped a shot. Connor then made his way up the steps, joining me inside the ruin.

But ruin was hardly the right word to use when talking about the pueblo; the original owners had built their home to last. A formidable structure with straight edges, thick walls, and sharp corners, it had

213

been standing strong against the elements for nearly a thousand years. The tower stood three stories high from the base of the rock upon which it was built, affording the occupants plenty of time to prepare for welcome or war. I doubted that anyone had ever snuck up undetected, and was sure that any attackers had suffered a nasty assault from high above.

We ducked through a tiny opening and entered the tower. I stood on the uneven dirt floor and cocked my head back to look at the cobalt patch of sky overhead, framed by the high red walls.

"Beautiful," I marveled out loud. My voice bounced around inside the tower.

We took turns looking out through a hole that might have been a window. The walls were almost as thick as my arm was long. My imagination was hard at work as I looked out the window at the landscape. A band of enemy warriors was approaching, their lances held aloft. Connor and I rained arrows down on them from our fortress tower.

After repelling the attackers, I pulled my head back inside the pueblo and returned to reality. I turned to see Connor staring out through an even smaller square in the wall to my right. The camera cord hung out of his back pocket. I reached out and tugged the camera free without a sound.

Connor was lost in thought, as if he were searching for something or someone far away on the horizon. I snapped a photo of him from across the little room.

Leaving my brother to his daydreams, I crawled back through the little doorway and out into the sunlight. I looked out across the large open area that made up half of the pueblo. I could picture deerskins stretched and drying in the sun, baskets full of gathered foods, a fire pit ringed with stones, and children chasing a flea-ridden puppy in happy loud circles.

"That would have been a great place to stage battles with our Star Wars and G.I. Joe figures," Connor mused, interrupting my imagination with good memories.

214

I looked down from the pueblo to the rocks below us, where Connor was pointing. "Definitely, look at all the great places for waiting in ambush," I agreed.

As kids we had spent more of our playtime choosing our figures and vehicles, staging them on the battlefield, building their bases, and mapping out scenarios than we had in actual play. In fact, we took so much time to work out the details that we rarely played past the initial setup.

Connor and I stood in the ruins of an ancient Native American pueblo, reliving the best moments of our childhood. It was an unlikely moment in an even more unlikely setting.

And I hadn't forced it.

Chapter 70: Summer-Fall 2008

"Jared, have you been drinking?" Rather than juggle a hot potato, Ella dropped the burning question right in Jared's lap.

"What? No, not at all," Jared was quick to answer.

"I'm asking because I saw you in your car recently, and you looked drunk. I only ask because I care, I hope you know that," Ella explained.

"No, I'm not drinking anymore. I was sick for a few days, maybe you saw me then," Jared said.

Ella let it go at the time, but later confessed to me that she had not believed his story about being sick. I wanted to believe that Jared was sober, and so I brushed her suspicions aside, into the peripheral vision of my mind's eye where I could ignore them.

Before long we lost track of Jared altogether. We eased the pangs of conscience that we felt by telling each other that our little family came first. But this reasoning did little to calm the storm of guilt that raged inside of me whenever I thought of my little brother and all his troubles.

A visit from Jared and Connor on Thanksgiving helped to calm the storm, but not in a way that I would have expected or wanted. Ella and I hosted the holiday dinner at our house that year, and Mom had invited everyone that lived locally. She hadn't heard back from Jared or Connor, and I doubted that they would make an appearance.

We were seated in the family room, watching the parades and chattering away when Jared burst in through the front door without knocking. On his heels followed Connor, a big grin on his face.

I hadn't seen or talked to Connor in well over a year. I didn't know where he lived, didn't have his cell number, and wasn't sure if he even had an email address. To have him walk through my front door on Thanksgiving was for me an instant thrill, and the answer to a prayer that I had never uttered. I jumped to my feet and crossed the room to greet my little brothers.

216

"We aren't staying, we just came by to get the stuff I left in your basement," Connor explained quickly. The abrupt statement sliced across the muscles of my face, collapsing my smile without warning.

I didn't say anything; I was too hurt to formulate a reply.

"You still have my stuff downstairs, don't you? Connor asked, his tone conveying a subtle warning that I'd better not have thrown away the boxes he had left in my basement so long ago.

"Uh, I think so, it should all be down there," I managed.

Connor made for the basement stairs without another word. Jared followed close behind, and after casting a frustrated look back at the rest of the family, I did too.

"What are you guys doing today? Do you want to come by later when everyone else is gone?" I laced my words with a conspiratorial tone in order to suggest that I was just as eager to empty my house of the family members upstairs as my brothers were to avoid them.

It didn't work.

"We are moving Jared into a friend's house," Connor said, picking up a box of journals and comics.

"Oh yeah? I can come and help, we aren't going to eat for a while. Then we could come back later and get some food." I knew how desperate I sounded, but couldn't help myself. I missed my brothers, and the prospect of a day with Mom, Dad, and the rest of the family no longer seemed bearable.

"Maybe we'll come by later, when we are done. Plus, I am going to be living in the same town as you now, so we can hang out more," Jared offered.

It was a lie and we both knew it.

"Okay, sure, but call me if you need my help moving anything heavy, I'll be here all day," I reminded my brothers, watching as they left through the garage.

They didn't call, and I suffered through Thanksgiving with the new memory of them both bursting through my front door. I began to believe that they had conspired to hurt me, and anger replaced the guilt that I had felt over our strained relationships. I swore that I would never again make myself vulnerable to my brothers.

On that Thanksgiving I was only grateful for four people; all the love I would ever need could be found in Ella and the kids. I wanted everyone else to leave my house, and I wasn't sure that I wanted them to ever come back.

Chapter 71: October 2009

A few miles down the road from the pueblo, we parked outside the Wupatki Visitor Center. The map I had taken from the ranger's station indicated a larger pueblo ruin located directly behind the visitor center. During our trip earlier in the year, Ella and I had skipped the larger set of ruins in the interest of time. Connor and I were in no great rush, so I decided that we would check it out.

"I want to change into shorts and take a piss before checking out the big pueblo," I said, getting out of the car and popping the trunk.

I opened my suitcase and pulled out a pair of shorts. After a quick look around, I kicked off my shoes and unzipped my pants. Not wanting to get my socks dirty, I stood on top of my shoes as I yanked my pants off one leg at a time.

"Smile!" Connor held up the camera.

"Kid, knock it off," I laughed, throwing my pants in the trunk and turning away as if hiding my face from the paparazzi.

I tried to keep my balance while standing on top of my shoes and pulling on my shorts at the same time. The fact that I was bending down low to hide behind the car made the process even more difficult. Connor held the camera up to include himself in a photo of me dressing in the open air of the parking lot. We were still laughing as we walked over to the visitor center to use the bathroom.

Inside the bathroom we each assumed the position, a divider between us at the urinals. I pulled out my phone, turned it to camera mode, and then held it above Connor and snapped a photo. He grabbed the camera from his shirt pocket and tried to retaliate. I slid my phone into my pocket and held both my hands out over my private business to hide it from view.

"Mine's a two hander," I boasted.

"Shut-up," Connor groaned.

Back outside, we followed the path leading around the visitor's center and out to the ruins. From the path we had a full view of the entire site, a collection of red-earth buildings that must have housed dozens of people and all that they had needed to survive in the beautiful middle of nowhere.

Ahead of us was an older couple walking the path with a young woman that I assumed to be their daughter. She had shoulder length blonde hair and looked to be in her twenties. Connor nudged me with his elbow, and I nodded as he pulled out the camera.

I began to imagine Connor and his future fiancé telling their friends the story of how they met inside the ruins of an ancient pueblo in the Arizona desert.

"I'll go on ahead, so you can pretend to be taking photos of me with the ruins as a backdrop," I whispered.

Connor nodded, a grin on his face. I turned and started walking down the path towards the girl. As I approached her, I wondered if she thought false teeth were sexy.

The trail doubled back in a hairpin turn, and after passing her I was able to steal a glance in her direction. She was indeed good-looking, and very worthy of a photo. I missed Ella, and wished she were with us to take part in our reconnaissance.

I was behind the pueblo before Connor caught up with me.

"Did you get some good ones?" I asked, taking the camera.

"Not sure, I don't think so," he answered.

"Maybe she'll come around this way and we can take one of her passing," I suggested.

We walked along the backside of the pueblo together, entering the open rooms for closer inspection. In leaving the ruins so accessible, the parks department had placed an unfounded trust in the thousands of visitors that made their way into them each year. It was probably too much to ask of some people to respect the history found inside the beautiful red walls, and to refrain from stealing pieces of them to display on their coffee tables back home.

Connor proved me right by ducking into one of the rooms and lighting a cigarette.

"What the heck are you doing?" I protested, while pulling out the camera and taking a photo of him huddled in a corner with his shameful habit.

"The wind was blowing out the lighter," Connor explained, blowing smoke into the breeze.

"Now I have photographic evidence of you defiling a national treasure," I joked.

"I don't see any 'No Smoking' signs," Connor shrugged, taking the camera from me to check out the picture.

"Whatever," I said, disappearing into a room with high walls.

When I came out from exploring the room, Connor held up the camera as a signal for me to stop long enough for a picture. I stuck my hands in my pockets and looked up at the walls. The sun streamed down in shafts of light, as if filtered through a prism. It was beautiful, and I stood looking up for some time after Connor had taken what would turn out to be one of my favorite photos from the trip.

We walked further down the path, checking out several rooms along the way.

"Here she comes," Connor hissed, running past me through a doorway and into a room with high walls that we had just finished exploring.

"What do you plan on doing in here?" I asked, following him into his hiding place.

When she comes by I can get a good look at her when she passes this gap in the rocks," Connor explained. He handed me the camera before crouching down and sliding his body between two massive boulders that had been incorporated into the pueblo.

I stood at the mouth of the gap and stuck my arm, with camera in hand, deep into it. From my position I could not tell what was being captured by the lens, so I began snapping photos one after another on the off chance that I might catch a good shot of the girl as she strolled by.

After just a few shots I heard the gravelly sound of shoes scraping over dirt and rock. I looked down and there was Connor, suddenly pushing against my legs in an effort to escape the crack. I backed up, giving him room to pull himself into the room. I snapped a photo of him emerging with a look of surprised guilt on his face.

"I think she saw me," he said, his voice bounding up the walls and out into the sky above.

I laughed at the thought of Connor being caught staring out at a beautiful girl from the confines of a dark crevice in the wall of an ancient pueblo ruin.

I snuck over to the doorway and peeked around the corner. The girl was walking up the hill towards the visitor center, away from our hiding place.

"She's gone. Let's go this way, I think the ball court is at the end of this path," I said before sprinting off.

There was a quick right turn, followed by a sharp left. I leaned into each turn as I ran, extending my arms out wide as if I were flying. It just seemed like the right thing to do.

I had read about ancient ball courts back in elementary school, and had been fascinated by the "win or die" outcome that many historians claimed to be fact. As a child I was more often than not chosen last for team sports, due to my small frame and general lack of physical skills. This led me to believe that perhaps God did indeed love me, because he had spared me from living in an age when losers were killed, and their heads used as equipment for the next match.

I wasn't sure, but I doubted that the people of this particular pueblo had been so ruthless in their love of sport and hatred of losing. But imagination is a powerful thing, and standing in the center of the red-walled court, mine conjured up a losing team on their

222

knees, about to receive their silver medals in the form of decapitation.

"It's like the Cobra arena of sport!" Connor shouted from the doorway.

"Bring in the Joes! We'll watch them die at the hands of Cobra's elite!" I roared, shaking a fist in the air.

Cartoons had been a staple of our childhood. Every day after school (and before Dad came home) we watched a line-up of cartoons. Our favorite had been G.I. Joe, followed closely by Thundercats, He-Man, and M.A.S.K.

In more than one episode of G.I.Joe, captured Joes were made to battle the evil minions of Cobra Commander in the arena of sport. This feature had been included in many of our playtime imaginations, some with crossover scenarios in which the Joes would meet time and space traveling characters from Star Wars.

Connor and I wandered about the ball court for a while, our imaginations running hard and fast. We snapped photos of each other in combat poses and mid air jumps. My moves looked more like seizures than anything else, while Connor's looked cool, smooth, and natural.

We left the arena of sport and followed the final leg of the path to what is known as the Wupatki blowhole.

A sign nearby explained that the blowhole was an opening in the ground through which air passed either in or out, depending on the barometric pressure above ground. On our visit that day, the barometric pressure was high, and Mother Earth was sucking wind.

The parks service had built a small square of cemented stone about three feet across and one foot high around the blowhole. The center of the stone formation was an open space of about twelve inches square, with a metal grate inside that prevented people from dropping cameras, soda cans, and other items into the Earth.

We sat on the square and let the wind rush over our hands on its way into Mother Earth's lungs.

223

"Check this out," Connor said. I watched as he held a small stick of desert sage high above the grate and let it drop.

The stick was sucked down against the grate in an instant. I pulled out the camera and filmed as Connor repeated the action several more times.

"That is so cool!" I said, a childlike excitement in my voice.

Connor tossed the stick aside and lit a cigarette.

"I'll bet the shamans believed this was a portal to the afterlife. They probably built the pueblo here to be closer to the spirits of their ancestors," I speculated.

Connor nodded his agreement while blowing a lung full of smoke into the air above the grate.

We watched as it was stretched into a long white wisp before disappearing below.

Chapter 72: Winter 2008-2009

After Thanksgiving I retreated into my own life. My great experiment with unconditional love had failed, and I was tired of being sucker punched. I decided that my responsibility to Ella and the kids would forevermore trump anything my extended family asked of me. I dialed back the visits to Mom and Dad's house, minimized my contact with my siblings, and spent more time with the four people that mattered most.

Ella, although worried about Jared, was thrilled with the attention. For well over a decade I had paced the floor of our marriage, worrying about the state of my extended family. My preoccupation with bringing about peace had often taken priority over my own marital bliss. To have my heart and mind focused on our own little family made Ella happy, and her happiness was spurring me on in my efforts to be a better husband and father.

Jared made no attempt to see me or to speak with me. It was discouraging to know that although he lived in the same town, he never felt the need to stop by and visit. He had never given me his address, and since he was living with a friend whose name I didn't know, I couldn't easily find out where he lived. I could have visited him at work, but never did.

Whenever I felt guilty about not making an effort to see him, I would dredge up the memory of Jared and Connor bursting through my front door on Thanksgiving. The thought chased away the guilt and replaced it with pain, which was easily converted into anger. In time I had convinced myself that it was better for me to stay away from him in order to avoid being hurt again.

As hard as it sometimes was, I stayed away.

In February, Ella and I traveled to Sedona, Arizona. She had rented a little house resting on a hillside, complete with a pool and hot tub. We enjoyed a relaxing week together amid the red rocks. The weather was perfect, the sky blue by day and bright with stars at night.

Towards the end of our trip we spent a day driving up past Flagstaff, over the Sunset Crater Volcano and onto the plains to visit ancient the Native American ruins. Our drive ended at the Grand Canyon, which neither of us had ever seen before. Standing with Ella on the edge of such a beautiful wonder was humbling. A priceless work of art still in progress, time meant nothing to the elements that continued to shape her.

I left with a reverence for my life with Ella. The time that we had spent together measured as nothing more than a sliver on the great timeline of eternity. All of our struggles, anger, and pain were brief when put into perspective. This great epiphany didn't erase the past, but it reminded me that the more I moved forward, the further behind me the past would be.

Chapter 73: October 2009

We passed the next hour visiting the Citadel ruins. Built at the top of a hill and overlooking a massive limestone sinkhole to the south, the site provided a view for miles in every direction. We ran to the top, and then stood marveling at the scenery while sucking wind from the effort it had taken to get there.

After a few minutes of silence, I pulled out the camera and switched it to video. I stood on a flat rock at the center of the ruin and began to film. Turning in a slow and deliberate circle, I captured the flat brown plains, the blue and white sky, the distant grey mountains, the dark and menacing sinkhole, and finally, Connor standing with an exaggerated grin on his face, his hands held up in a double peace sign.

"Dork," I laughed.

In the distance I noticed a large grey cloud that seemed to billow from a dark line of earth on the northern horizon. It didn't look like it belonged there.

"Is that smoke?" I asked, pointing it out to Connor.

Connor looked and said, "I think so."

"A forest fire, maybe?" I wondered aloud.

"Maybe. What else could it be?" Connor asked.

"Smoke signals?" I joked.

"Matthew, don't be a racist," Connor warned in jest.

"Grandma was a Blackfoot, so it can't be racist. Maybe Grandma's spirit is trying to tell us something," I suggested, feigning serious.

Many times throughout my life, I wished that the blood of the Blackfoot Nation did in fact run through my veins.

But it didn't. Mom had been given up by her unwed birth mother, and adopted by a lanky cowboy-turned-rocket-scientist and his Native American wife. Growing up in the California sunshine with her dog Buddy at her side and her brother to look out for her, she seemed to have been spared a terrible upbringing. She adored her father, and would glow whenever she spoke of her childhood spent at his side. He had been a confident man of self-reliance and skill, a man whose word was worth more than any amount of signatures. My mother was his little pal, confidant, and shadow.

Her father had been her hero, but her mother had been someone to hide from. Obsessed with her own health, my grandmother had hovered over her daughter with enemas, diuretics, cure-alls, and doctor visits. In time, my mother learned to suffer through any hint of illness without a word for fear of whatever new methods of medicinal torture her mother might inflict upon her.

My mother's personal history had soured both Mother's Day and her own birthday forever. We were not allowed to celebrate either one, in spite of Dad's efforts over the years to remind Mom that we kids had the right to celebrate her as our mother. We eventually took to celebrating Cinco de Mayo, since it was close to her birthday. Piñatas became routine, which pleased the grandkids. They couldn't wish her a happy birthday, but helping her beat an effigy full of candy to pieces with a stick was a reasonable substitute in their eyes.

"Why can't we say happy birthday to Grandma?" At age six, our son Samuel could not understand why *birthday* was, at least for his grandmother, a four-letter word.

"Because Grandma doesn't like her birthday," I had answered, keeping it simple.

"Grandma doesn't like anything," Noah had said dryly.

Ella and I had stolen sideways glances at each other, choking back fits of laughter. The dark cloud that hung over my mother had not been imagined after all.

I had never been convinced that my mother wanted to be adored. Like a battered woman, she seemed to revel in suffering through the opposition in her life. She thrived on drama, and her ability to make any family situation all about her was remarkable. Nothing ever changed in my mother's miserable world; Dad was forever cold, and

228

her children permanently insensitive to the impact that their terrible choices had had on their mother. She had become someone that I pitied, and I hated feeling that way about my own mother.

But I had not always felt that way about her. As a little boy there had been no one more perfect in my life. She had taught me to throw a baseball, made the best Halloween costumes, and she had once painted my ceiling black when I went through an astronomy phase. Her cookies were legendary, in spite of the fact that she could burn water when cooking dinner. I had inherited her love of reading and her knack for storytelling.

Dad had been my idol, but Mom had been my muse.

"Let's bolt, I'm getting hungry," I announced to Connor, breaking myself free from my dark reverie.

We sped away from the ruins with music blaring and the windows open to the warm midday air. I glanced in the rear view mirror.

"Almost there, Jared," I whispered.

Our trip to Sedona turned out to be a happy and restful hush before the emotional storm brought on by Dad's phone call. Jared had been found near death on the floor of a shady motel in Independence, Missouri. That much we knew, and it should have been enough to send Mom and Dad running to the airport, but two days later there were still no signs of urgency or action on the part of my parents.

After another conference call with Becky and Sarah, in which I was able to convince them that Mom and Dad would soon see reason, I headed over to my parent's house for an update.

"I just talked to the Inn; Jared stopped showing up to work in January, so they fired him," Dad informed me when I walked into his office.

"Well, the pieces are falling together. He must have been drinking again," I suggested, ignoring the irritation in his tone.

"We also talked to Connor," Mom spoke up behind me.

"And?" I said, turning to face her. This was an interesting development; if anyone could shed more light on Jared's mental state, it would be Connor.

"Jared stopped by to see him last week on his way out of town. He gave Connor some of his things and said that he didn't need them anymore. He also hinted that he was going to go to the Grand Canyon and drive over the edge of it."

"What? Are you serious? He knew that his brother was going to drive to the Grand Canyon and kill himself, but he didn't bother to call anyone?" I pictured my hands closing around Connor's neck.

"Well, Jared didn't say it in so many words, but he hinted at it. Connor said that he had threatened to kill himself before, but had never done it, so he wasn't sure if Jared meant it or not," Mom explained, coming to Connor's defense.

230

"That's bullshit! His brother quits his job, starts giving away everything he owns, and then threatens to drive over the edge of the Grand Canyon, and he doesn't at the very least drop a dime? What's his problem? I admire loyalty, but give me a break! He has no excuse for not telling us!" Spit flew from my lips as I hissed out the last few words.

"We don't know exactly what happened, and we are basing this all on a single, brief phone call from Connor, who isn't all that talkative under normal circumstances. It sounds to me like he had heard it all before from Jared, and thought it was more of the same," Dad reasoned.

"I don't know, it sounds to me like Jared was making obvious cries for help. I find it hard to believe that Connor didn't know he was serious," I scoffed, discarding Dad's argument in my brother's defense.

"Well, there's nothing we can do about it now. Let's wait to hear what the doctors say tomorrow," Dad said, as if to stop me from suggesting that he and Mom get their butts on a plane.

I was about to make the suggestion anyway, when Mom spoke.

"Thelma and Louise," she said, the words followed by one of her signature dramatic sighs.

"What?" I swung around to face her, my mouth hanging open in unmistakable surprise.

"He was going to pull a Thelma and Louise; he wanted to drive his car over the edge of a cliff," Mom explained.

I stared at my mother.

"I knew that car would be trouble. Too much freedom, much too fast," Dad said.

I looked back at Dad. He turned to his computer and started reading his email, ending the conversation.

I glared at the back of Dad's head and ignored Mom, hoping that the long and awkward silence would unsettle them both as much as their words had unsettled me.

Chapter 75: October 2009

We stopped at the trading post in Cameron and wandered through the aisles of tourist mugs, tee shirts, native crafts, and jewelry. There was a little grocery store in the back corner, where I loaded up on chips, soda, candy, and gum. Connor grabbed a sandwich wrapped in plastic, chocolate milk, a bag of spicy fries, and a new lighter.

"A very healthy lunch for the two of us today," I explained to the girl at the counter. She smiled but said nothing in reply.

We returned to the car, and ate in silence as we followed the road that would lead us right to the Southern Rim of the Grand Canyon. Ella and I had made the same drive on a Sunday back in February, but the mood on that trip had been very different.

I had never believed in the phrase "everything happens for a reason." A cliché employed by people seeking purpose behind events that have fallen into place with too much coincidence, it ranked high on my list of intolerable idioms, alongside "God needed another angel in heaven" and "every time God closes a door he opens a window." People that repeated such unimaginative excuses for death and adversity always slipped a few rungs on my ladder of respect.

I often wondered why people would believe in God at all, if they held him to blame him for everything that took place in their lives. I believed in God and had felt his influence in my own life many times, but I wouldn't have dared credit him with everything that I experienced, whether good or bad. He had given me free will, and along with it the responsibility of accepting the results of my choices and actions. I had no doubt that he cared about results, but was confident that he had more interest in the decisions I had made to bring them about.

But looking back on the trip with Ella, I couldn't argue with the timing. It had been a relaxing adventure, a chance to breath deep, and rest from the world. That week in Sedona had proved to be a preparatory calm, and upon reflection it had seemed too coincidental.

233

I was beginning to believe that only the things that mattered happened for a reason. My problem was figuring out which things mattered, and the reasons for which they had happened.

Chapter 76: March 2009

"I'm going over there now, and I am going to tell them that they have to go tonight," I said with rehearsed conviction.

It was Sunday afternoon. Becky, Sarah, and I were once again in discussions about what to do. The news about Jared's suicide attempt had come four days ago, and Jared was still alone.

"Let us know what they say. If they don't go tonight, then Sarah and I are going to," Becky said.

"Ok, I'll call you tonight, hopefully with good news," I said before hanging up.

Nearing my breaking point, I was warming to Becky's plan; someone had to go to Jared, to let him know that we cared. I had assumed that it would be Mom and Dad, but they weren't proving to be the best choice after all. While Becky had been mean and nasty over the years, I didn't doubt that she had a heart. Perhaps seeing Jared in such a lowly state would break it to the point of change.

I pulled into Mom and Dad's driveway and parked the car. After a moment to gather my composure and utter a quick prayer for strength, I walked into my parent's house. I passed through the empty kitchen and into the family room. Mom was watching a movie. She paused it as I approached the couch.

"Hi, Mom, is Dad home?"

"Up here." I heard my father's voice above me before my mother could answer.

I looked up and saw Dad leaning over the railing of the walkway that led across the open ceiling of the family room and into his office.

"Could I talk to both of you in the kitchen?" I asked, knowing that if the request alone hadn't served as a warning that something was up, the scared tone of my voice had.

"Ok…" Dad's reply was loaded with caution, but he strode across the walkway and down the stairs, meeting Mom and me in the kitchen.

"Could you sit down? I need to talk to you both and I need to focus." I tried to mask the trembling in my voice, but failed.

"Oh, this must be serious, he wants our full attention," Dad quipped, his tone taking an obnoxious dive into condescension as he sat at the table next to Mom.

"I just wanted to say that I think you should go to Jared. He tried to kill himself; he is sad, lonely, and feeling worthless. He needs to know that people care about him. He needs to feel love. He needs his parents telling him that they love him. He needs you." The words came out in a calm rush until I spoke the final three, which were delivered through the onset of tears.

My parents sat in silence. I wiped my eyes and waited at the other end of the table that had served as the centerpiece for countless moments in our family history. We had gathered around it for happy dinners, arduous lectures, family meetings, and birthday celebrations. There wasn't a grandchild that hadn't slept for hours atop that table in a car seat, and most of them had probably had a diaper changed at least once on its surface. It had needed a few repairs over the years, but it had stood up against our abuse. The table had witnessed all of the good and the bad that our family had to offer.

"Well, it's not as simple as that," Dad said, breaking the silence with his all-too-familiar father-knows-best voice.

He could have stopped right there, at the end of that first sentence. I had heard that tone before, and I knew what was sure to follow.

"We don't even know that they would let us in to see him once we got there. He is in the mental health ward, and in my experience that is not a place where they allow many visitors. We could fly all the way there just to stand in the hallway," he explained, as if I were a child that had not considered such grown-up things.

"Then you stand in the hallway outside his room and shout through the door that you are there, and that you love him. You write notes to him, and give them to the nurses to give to him. He needs to hear that you love him. He needs his mother. He needs his father." My voice cracked, but I held the new threat of tears at arm's length.

"Look, we have to be realistic here. We can't do him any good if we aren't here to take or make phone calls relating to the situation. We don't know how long they are going to keep him there. It might be quite a while, and what are we going to do, live in a hotel until they release him? We can do more good from here than we can out there." Dad's reply was exactly what I had expected, but not what I had hoped for.

"The doctors are there with him. You can talk to them in person. You have a cell phone, you can make all the calls you need to from it." I tried not to layer condescension on top of exasperation, but it was hard not to when conveying such simple facts.

Mom sighed. I did my best not to glare in her direction as I waited for Dad's response.

"True, and there is also the issue of his car, or should I say my car, since it looks like I'll be making the payments on it now. I called the motel and they said it is still there in the parking lot, but I am not sure how much longer it will be safe there."

In my father's selfish words I saw a window of opportunity crack open. It wasn't a window that I could ever be proud of crawling through, and if the tactic worked it would forever cement my father in place as the most heartless bastard I had ever known.

"All the more reason to go now and get his car before something happens to it. After the car is secure, do what you can for Jared at the hospital." The words tasted bitter. I had just suggested that my father perform a wellness check on a motor vehicle before doing the same for his suicidal son.

"Well, I think the car will still be there tomorrow. Let's give it one more day and see where we stand," Dad said, refusing the bait.

From one angle I could see this as a good thing. Had he jumped up from the table and sped off to the airport at the suggestion that his financial investment was in danger, I might have decked him.

237

I drove home the long way, shouting a string of obscenities that made my throat ache. Once home I shared the news with Ella. Tears welled up in her eyes as I told her about my visit to Mom and Dad's. I paced the bedroom floor like a tiger in a tiny cage, his only wish to break free and do something terrible to his captors. It took me some time to calm down enough to call my sisters.

Becky and Sarah were furious. Once again I had to admit to myself that while I had detested Becky for many things over the years, I admired her motherly instinct. It was clear to me that she would have done anything for her children, and rushing to their side in their hour of need was not something she had to ponder. For her it was a natural reaction.

It was not proving to be an instinct that she had inherited from our parents.

Chapter 77: October 2009

Along the road that leads to the southern rim of the Grand Canyon, there is a poorly marked overlook. The view at this overlook is of the Little Colorado River Gorge. Although much smaller, very different, and almost unknown in comparison to the Grand Canyon, the gorge is a beautiful place. When Ella and I had stopped there in February, I had felt as though we had stumbled upon a closely guarded secret.

After parking the car in the gravel lot at the gorge, I gathered up the trash from lunch and dropped it into a large metal drum provided for the purpose. Connor did the same, and then together we walked to the edge of the gorge.

A metal railing painted bright blue kept visitors far enough away from the rim of the cliff to avert disaster, but allowed them to get close enough to experience the staggering depth of the gorge below.

"Wow, that is deep," Connor remarked at once.

"That's what she said," I muttered in reply.

"Why would she say that?" Connor asked.

"Ok, that's what *he* said," I countered with a laugh.

Together we looked into the abyss. I had read that the gorge was close to eight hundred feet deep at the overlook, and though I was terrible at judging distances, I found myself believing that to be accurate. I tried to picture a person standing at the bottom, but gave up after a few minutes of searching for a rock or bush that I could use for perspective. Anyone standing down there would appear to be very small.

I surveyed the walls. They were layered like the thick chapters in a history book. It was for me another powerful reminder that the passage of time was a matter of course.

I looked across at the flat, wide plain on the other side. The landscape conjured up more visions of warriors on ponies. This time they were taunting three young cowboys that had been forced to take shelter behind their own dead horses.

Looking up into the bright blue, I imagined a flock of buzzards making slow and lazy circles in the sky as they waited for the cowboys to die.

"So how much notice do you need?" Dad had once again bypassed not only the customary "hellos" exchanged at the start of a phone call, but any preface to his question, which might have hinted at what I would need notice for.

"Notice for what?" I asked, my tone conveying my annoyance, as well as his ranking on my shit list.

"To go and get your brother." My father's reply carried a message-delivering tone of its own. The obvious omission of Jared's name, and the absence of any warmth in his voice made it clear to me that he was tired of being a father to a handful of losers.

The message I received might not have been the one that he had consciously intended to deliver, but years of listening to the man speak in such disgusted tones about his own children had tuned my ears to the unspoken truths in his words and their delivery. I could not have been convinced that my father truly wanted to be a part of our lives, or that he was in any way proud of us. He seemed to tolerate us out of resented obligation and nothing more.

Over the years I had often imagined Dad arriving at the judgment seat of heaven after his death. He would file an objection with God's court, claiming that his children had stymied his success, and that an earthly life with seven millstones hung around his neck merited him a free pass into an eternal life filled with paradisiacal glory. How could he have possibly reached his full potential as a father when saddled with such undesirable children who had failed him at every turn? Had he been blessed with beautiful, strong, and successful offspring, he would have lived a very different life, one filled with the accolades and handshakes awarded to fellow members of some imaginary club made up of the amazing fathers of even more amazing children.

I was not alone in my imaginations. My siblings had each at different points in their lives confessed to feeling as though Dad resented us all. My sisters in particular despised the way he treated the daughters of family friends, upon whom he poured out affection and praise without a thought to how it pained his own girls.

My brothers had long ago given up their hopes for having deep relationships with Dad, but I had long suffered attacks of envy at the sight of his unmistakable adoration for handsome, successful, and confident young men that in his eyes had the world at their feet. Even as he worshipped these young men for everything he believed them to be, my father ignored his foot planted firmly upon the necks of his own sons as he complained about their uselessness.

"I don't need much notice, I can be gone in a couple of hours if need be," I answered, ignoring my own issues in the interest of Jared's.

"Well, there is no way I am taking your mother out there to get him. Can I assume from all that we have heard from you over the past few days that you'd be willing to go with me?"

I ignored the obvious dig and replied without reaction. "Yep."

"It may still be a couple of days, but be ready for the call."

"I've been ready," I said before hanging up.

His call had come just after lunch on Monday. Jared had been rushed to the hospital on Wednesday morning, and had spent every day since in the company of strangers. I was sure that the doctors and nurses in Independence meant well, but beyond caring for his physical and mental well being, there was nothing that they could do to assure Jared that he was loved. I wondered how hollow any declaration of love from any of us would sound in a few days time.

I spent the afternoon wandering through work without doing much of anything. Dad's insistence that Mom would not be going didn't surprise me. My parents were no longer capable of spending the night in the same room, so how could they be expected to spend a few days trapped in a car together? Add a chain-smoking suicidal son to the back seat, and a high-speed police chase across several state lines might have been the result.

The thought of Dad and Mom driving Jared home together set me to wondering about my own sanity should I make the trip. Jared was sure to be an emotional dirty bomb, likely to curse and rant all the way to New Hampshire. Dad would stare at the road ahead,

242

incapable of any outward display of emotion. I imagined my own mental and emotional state after fifteen hundred miles of highway paved with tension.

"I don't think I can do it," I worried, pacing the bedroom floor that afternoon.

Ella watched me from the bed. Her silence in moments of turmoil had angered me for the greater part of our marriage, but I had learned to appreciate it.

"I just can't spend that much time in the car with the two of them. Just me and Jared, maybe, but with Dad and Jared, no way, the tension would probably kill me." I looked at Ella, hoping for some sort of guilt-easing confirmation.

"Do you think you could go get him alone? It sounds to me like that is what you want to do."

"I've thought about that, but I am not sure how that would go down with Dad. I do know how it would go down with Becky and Sarah, but who cares? Why should it matter if I go and get him alone? What urgency has Dad shown since that first phone call from the hospital, and what claim does Becky have on Jared? She tossed him out of her life years ago. Sarah would be okay to go with, but she has the kids, and I doubt that Joshua can get the time off to watch them." My arguments for going alone convinced me that I should just jump on a plane and worry about their reactions after getting to Independence.

But I didn't.

Chapter 79: October 2009

Surrounding the edge of the gorge was a series of stone steps that led to other vantage points. Connor took a leap off of one, his mouth open in a wide shout of joy, his thumbs up and feet tucked up underneath his butt. I captured the moment from behind him and at a low angle so that in the photo it appeared as though he were jumping over the edge of the gorge itself.

"Damn," he shouted upon landing.

"You okay?"

"I hurt my foot when I landed," Connor answered, sitting on the ground to remove his shoes and rub his bare feet with his hands.

"Those shoepers have no support or cushion in them," I responded, pointing out the obvious.

"No kidding," Connor said, irritated.

"Can you move your toes?" I asked, repenting of my insensitivity.

"Yes."

I took a closer look at his foot. "No bruising, that's a good sign," I offered.

"It hurts inside though, like when you jump from the trampoline to the ground." Connor pulled his socks back on with care, then slipped his shoepers onto his feet.

"I know what you mean," I said, nodding in recollection of many unfortunate trampoline dismounts over the years.

"I'm just going to ignore it and hope it goes away," Connor said, wincing as he stood, putting weight on both feet.

Experience had taught me not to argue with Connor about pain management, so I just followed as he hobbled his way back up from where we came.

"Check out the lizard," he said, pointing over to his left.

244

I followed his finger and spied the little critter catching some sun between some brush. I pulled the camera out to capture the moment, but my sudden movement sent him scrambling to shelter.

We spent the next twenty minutes hoping to catch just one of the many lizards we saw wandering around in the brown brush that grew in small patches around the railing. They proved too fast for not only our hands, but also for the camera.

I wasn't sure if it was the distraction of lizard hunting or just his iron will, but Connor was soon walking without a limp. We wandered up towards the car, taking a long detour by browsing through the Native American merchant tables set out in rows along the edge of the parking lot.

Connor had no objections to this waste of time, and it occurred to me that I was doing my subconscious best to delay our arrival at the Grand Canyon.

"Dad asked me to be ready to jump on a plane the moment he calls," I told Becky and Sarah, my voice conveying the irony in Dad's request that I be ready at a moment's notice.

"I still can't believe that they didn't leave the moment the hospital called," Becky repeated.

I knew that she meant it, but her sudden attack of sincerity had done nothing for Jared. She could never wind back the time her little brother had suffered while living in her bigot empire.

"So Mom isn't going?" The question came from Sarah, whose relationship with our mother had seen its own trials. They had only recently come to a fragile peace over the war started by Mom's absence from Sarah's own wedding ceremony years before, a story as long and absurd as Becky's exclusion of Jared from her life.

"Nope. You know how Dad gets about Mom in these moments; they are his time to be a big man by stepping in front of the proverbial bullet to protect his wife from the terrible decisions made by her horrible children," I said callously.

A long silence thick with disbelief followed. I could almost hear the gears turning as my sisters plotted without speaking. It would not have surprised me to learn come morning that they were both in Independence.

"I'll tell you one thing, when this is all over, and Jared is well again, I am going to take him on a road trip to the Grand Canyon." The words left my mouth like an empty suit of armor astride a white horse.

Our family had forever thrived on dramatic moments, and always would. We loved to swoop in with hollow, conditional valor and save a brother, sister, daughter, or son from his or her own bad choices. My own history with my brothers was evidence enough for me to hide my head in shame, but the thought of Becky rushing dramatically to Jared's side after years of treating him as less than human would have been laughable were it not so pathetic.

Still, Becky was trying, and I couldn't say the same for Mom and Dad.

Chapter 81: October 2009

The smoke from Grandma's signal fire billowed high into the blue, allowing the wind to spread it into long white wisps across the sky.

"That has got to be a forest fire," I remarked.

"Isn't that where we are headed?"

"Pretty much. I hope they haven't closed the road up ahead," I worried.

We drove in silence for several miles. My mind wandered through time, as if taking its cues from the blend of quick curves and long straights in the road. So much history had led us to this final push, and every moment seemed to rush my mind's stage. Tears began to muddle my vision, and I reached up to wipe them with the back of my sleeve. The movement of my arm across my cheek brought the smell of fabric softener mixed with cigarette smoke to my nose. An invisible cloud of olfactory memories formed around my head.

Connor might have sensed my moment of difficulty, or perhaps was having one of his own. Whatever the reason, my little brother created a sudden and welcome distraction without saying a word.

I watched as he grabbed the roll of clear packing tape and secured the strawberry scented air freshener to the car's dash. He used an unreasonable amount of tape, pulling long strips of it from the roll and draping them over the air freshener and onto both the dash and the windshield.

The silent, determined manner in which he set about his work, and the absurdity of it made me laugh out loud. I forgot the tears drying in tight patterns on my cheeks.

"Nice! Now we are traveling in style. All we need is a hula-girl figurine and Jared's dashboard Jesus action figure," I suggested.

The next few miles were much lighter in spirit.

My mind wandered for hours into the night, allowing me very little sleep. I couldn't help wishing that I had left for Independence, and regretting that I had let slip my sudden and dramatic plan to take Jared to the Grand Canyon someday.

"Oh, that's a great idea, let us know when and we will be there," Becky had responded without hesitation.

I knew that unless she underwent personality surgery, I would never spend a moment of my life standing at the edge of the Grand Canyon with Becky. I could not imagine a scenario that involved us both in the same car for any more time than it took to drive her back to the airport to get rid of her. Even if by some miracle we were to survive the road trip, the temptation to push her into the void might have been too powerful to overcome.

I began to picture myself flying out alone to get Jared. Instead of heading for home we would drive west to the Grand Canyon. Jared would open up about all his fears, and I would listen without lecturing as we lay on the hood of his car, both of us staring up at the bright stars of the western sky. I would smoke my first (and last) cigarette, Jared would learn that he was loved, and all would be well. The trip would be worthy of a coffee house novel or an independent film full of adventure and self-discovery on the open road.

I spent the next morning ignoring my many responsibilities to clients, trying to find the courage to board a plane without telling anyone but Ella. I would worry about everyone's reactions after my life-altering odyssey with Jared. Or perhaps I wouldn't worry about their reactions at all.

After a morning of thorough reflection, I realized that to go to Independence without telling anyone would spark an emotional family fire that I would never be able to extinguish. I decided it best to call Dad and tell him that I was willing to go alone. With a little luck and a lot of acting, I might convince him that I would be doing him a favor, since both the drive and the company would be unbearable for anyone who made the trip.

I left work before noon and called Dad on the way home.

"Hello?"

"Hi Dad, it's Matthew."

"I haven't heard from the hospital yet," he said, assuming I had called for information.

"Oh, ok. I'm not calling about that. Well, I am, but not to find out if they called. I just thought I'd offer to go out and bring Jared back alone, in case that makes things easier. I know this is not an easy thing for you to deal with, and the last thing you probably want to do right now is spend three days in a car with Jared." I kept my tone light and easy, like a buddy calling up a friend and offering to help cut firewood or paint a shed.

Dad grunted through his nose in reply.

Dad's verbal responses to any expression of love or support tendered by one of his own children had never been a string of actual words, but rather a nasal grunt that almost sounded like a reply (although not in kind). I had always hated that sound, because to me it summed up my father's obligation to love me without expressing it.

I held the phone away from my face, and fought the urge to ask my father just what the hell the sound that he had been making for as long as I could remember really meant.

"Well, I thought I'd throw it out there. Think about it and let me know. I'm ready to go when you are." I hung up without a goodbye, threw my phone into the back seat, and shouted a few choice words out the open sunroof.

My decision was made. If Dad wouldn't let me go alone, I wouldn't go at all. Perhaps spending three days trapped in a car with his suicidal son for company would teach my father a few things about himself.

I ignored my thoughts on what it would probably teach Jared.

250

Chapter 83: October 2009

We had made it to the Grand Canyon around noon. I paid the entrance fee, and then drove to the first parking lot along the Southern Rim.

"Check it out, he saved us a spot," I said, pointing at the single crow standing in our chosen parking space.

The bird hopped out of the way of the car, but waited nearby like a tiny valet. I shut off the engine and settled into my seat. A desire to quiet my mind gave me pause; I wanted to absorb every moment at the Canyon.

Connor climbed out of the car without a word, and closed the door with a click. The crow hopped around the front of the car and out of my view, perhaps hoping for a long pull on the cigarette that Connor was no doubt lighting.

"It won't be long now, Jared," I said. My chest swelled, then collapsed behind a deep breath.

I knew Jared wouldn't offer a response, but I sat still and waited for one anyway.

Another deep breath filled my chest. I imagined the power of my lungs draining the car of oxygen. Another breath, and I had drained the parking lot. One more, and I had drained the Grand Canyon.

Chapter 84: March 2009

Dad called on Tuesday morning and asked if I was ready to go.

"I can't, there is a computer virus expected to infect millions of computers around the world tomorrow morning, I can't leave my clients to face it alone" I said evenly.

"Yeah, I read about that," Dad replied.

"So you are leaving today?" I asked.

"Yep, this afternoon. Well, I've got to pack," he said, hanging up.

He was obviously upset that I had found an excuse for not going, but I no longer cared about how he felt. I had listened to his excuses for the past week.

Sleep and I didn't spend a lot of time together that night. Visions of my father entering Jared's hospital room plagued my mind and kept me awake.

Dad was sure to stride in and say something awkward like "Better late than never!" rather than something warm, like, "Jared, I love you!" There would be no hug, just a weird moment of acknowledgment between them, and maybe a nasal grunt from Dad.

Jared would look over Dad's shoulder and into the hall, any hint of faith in his big brother crushed when I failed to appear in the doorway.

They would walk out past reception, and into the grey of the parking lot together, but Jared would feel more alone than he had before Dad's arrival. The realization that he was about to spend three days in a car with his father would melt his spirit.

The car door would slam shut with a hollow thud, trapping my little brother inside a metal cocoon filled the nerve gases of contempt and misunderstanding. Dad would stare due East for hours. When he did speak, his conversation wouldn't vary too far from the mundane, safe topics of road signs, their options for lunch, and the weather.

All the while, Jared would stare out the passenger side window, watching as the world blurred past, filled with people living their happy lives without a thought to his own misery.

Chapter 85: October 2009

I exhaled, refilling the car, the parking lot, and the Grand Canyon. I opened my door and stood tall beside the little black rental car, stretching silently. After a moment, Connor and I crossed the parking lot. The Southern Rim Watchtower stood high above the trees ahead.

"The view from the tower is incredible; Ella and I spent a long time at the top in February," I explained as we walked.

Connor didn't answer; he was distracted by a pretty young Asian woman standing at the side of the trail.

My spirits lifted, I smiled and ran ahead of Connor and his Asian interest. Standing seventy feet tall and faced in stone, the building would have looked every bit like an ancient watchtower had it not been for the tourists milling about, and the gift shop housed on the ground floor.

Connor caught up to me and we entered the tower together. We ignored the gift shop and made our way up the stairs to the top, a room with several large windows that provided a stunning view.

As I approached a window and looked down into the Canyon, my knees shuddered, threatening to give way. I put both hands on the glass to steady myself, and leaned forward to rest my head against the glass. My hands felt heavy, and I made no effort to impede their slide down the window and back to my sides. They hung useless beside me as air passed through my barely opened lips in a series of rapid shudders and bursts. Panic donned stiletto heels and danced across my chest.

I sensed Connor's approach on my left, and felt the proximity tingle of his arm beside mine. My body felt uneven, my left side alive and warm with Connor's presence, my right alone and cold.

Chapter 86: April 2009

"How was the trip?" I asked my father. He was at his computer, catching up on all the useless joke-filled and political emails that he had missed while gone to retrieve Jared.

"Well, let's see, three days with my chain-smoking son telling me what a crappy job I did at fathering him…" Dad's reply hung in the air like a dark cloud.

His words and the tone in which he delivered them told me that Dad had not learned a thing about himself during those three days with Jared. My guess was that the only thing he may have learned about Jared was which brand of cigarettes he smoked. I decided to leave the subject closed, the way my father kept his heart.

"So where is he now?" I asked.

"Connor's apartment," Dad answered.

"Really?"

"Believe me, it's the best place for him to be right now," Dad said.

"How so?" My confusion was quickly being replaced with incredulity.

"Well, he won't find it too comfortable to be around me for a while. Plus, Connor lives next to a mall. Jared can find a job and start over. I think that Connor should live with all the crap that we have been dealing with for the past couple of years when it comes to Jared." The loud click of Dad's keyboard warned me not to push the issue.

I decided that I didn't find it comfortable to be around my father either.

Within a week, Dad called to tell me that Connor had kicked Jared out of his apartment.

"He made Jared call me to come and get him. I guess his own life is more than he can handle, and to have Jared around was dragging him down." Dad's voice sounded tired, but somehow comical at the same time, as if he were trying to find humor in a situation that was far beyond his control.

"Is he at your house?" I asked, as if on a dare.

"He is back at his friend's house. Looks like you and Jared will be neighbors again, for as long as the guy can stand to have him there."

I ignored the acid that Dad had poured over the words "friend's house" and "the guy." Since the day Jared had told us he was gay, Dad seemed to suspect any male friend of Jared's to be a degenerate homosexual predator taking advantage of his son's temporary confusion over his sexuality.

I didn't bother to ask for Jared's new address. To know where he lived would have come with the obligation to visit him, and to visit him would have brought on the responsibility of fixing him, and I could not afford the cost.

The next few weeks passed without any word or discussion about Jared. Everyday life returned to its normal, drama-free pace, and I allowed it to do so. I packed up my soapbox and stayed away from my parents. Any remorse stemming from having abandoned Jared to a three-day road trip with Dad was replaced by a regret for having been involved at all. I had once again wedged myself into my family's drama and come out the other end holding nothing more than a bag of emotions that I didn't know what to do with. I steeled my heart against any further involvement.

If Jared wanted to reach out to me for help, I would be there to do what I could, but only so far as it didn't upset my own happiness. I settled back into the comfort of my own life and didn't wait for the phone to ring.

And then it did.

"Face it, I suck and your life will be better off without me." Jared's voice was loud and desperate, wrapped in panic.

"Jared?" My own voice sounded panicked, as my mind raced through the possible reasons for his call, none of them good.

256

"Why is my life so messed up? Everything I do is wrong, and I will never be what everyone wants me to be. I'm a loser, and everything I touch turns to shit! I can't even succeed at killing myself!" My ear filled with the sound of his sobbing, and my eyes with my own tears.

"Jared, listen to me, you are not a loser. You are one of my favorite people. Don't give up," I offered weakly.

"I want to believe you, but I can't, I am nothing but a loser and a milestone. You know it's true!" he bawled in reply.

"Jared, you are not a loser, and you certainly aren't a milestone." I steered clear of making light of his confusion between millstone and milestone. It was likely that the only time he had heard the term was in church, in regards to a wicked man finding it better to have a millstone placed around his neck and being cast into the sea than to face the wrath of God for his sins.

"Prove to me that I am not a loser, Matthew. You can't do it because I am one!" Jared roared.

I felt as though he were daring me to admit to his miserable status, adding fuel to his desire to leave this life.

"Jared, I can list of any number of reasons that you are not a loser, but in the end, you have to believe it for yourself," I said quietly.

A long silence followed my words.

"I'm waiting..." Jared spoke at last, reissuing his challenge.

"Ok, what about Noah, Isabel, and Samuel? They adore you. They see nothing but the good in you, and whenever you are here they can't leave you alone. Does that count for nothing?"

I waited for a response. When nothing but sniffling sounded in my ear, I continued.

"What about Ella? She loves you, probably even more than I do. You guys make me jealous sometimes, the connection that exists between you two," I confessed.

"Okay, but-" Jared began to protest.

257

"No buts! I am not done! You asked me to prove that you are not a loser, and I am going to do just that. I love you, and my family loves you. So do a lot of other people, in spite of what you think and in spite of what you do or say to hurt them and push them away. You are an amazing artist with more talent in the tip of your ear lobe than I carry around in my pasty-white-wonder-bread body! You are kind, sensitive, handsome, and funny. People lean towards you like plants to the sun, because you have something inside of you that makes them want to be around you. I was jealous of you all through high school because you were so likeable, and you had so many friends. Face it Jared, you are an amazing person!" I ended my speech, feeling confident that my string of praise would be a pivotal moment for my little brother. Decades after the conversation ended, we would still be talking about the day I changed his life.

"Matthew, I appreciate all those things you said, and I know that you guys love me," he started.

"But?" I said, knowing what was next.

"We both know that I am a loser."

"Jared, if you think like a loser, then you will always be a loser," I almost shouted. I felt stupid, repeating advice that I didn't quite believe myself.

I spent a long while on the phone with Jared, doing my best to help him crawl out of the sewer he had made of his life.

"One day, one hour, one minute, and one second at a time. Take your meds, get a job, pay your bills, and find hobbies that keep your mind occupied," I repeated near the one-hour mark in our conversation.

"Wait, I need to write this stuff down. I won't remember it in the morning, because I am drunk right now," Jared confessed.

Over the line, through the silence, I could hear the scratching of pen on paper. I pictured him drunk, his hand shaking as my little brother scribbled my life-changing counsel on the back of a liquor store receipt.

Chapter 87: October 2009

After having lived nearly forty years without seeing the Grand Canyon, this was the second time in an eight-month period that I had stared down into its beautiful depths.

"Wow. What more can be said?"

"Hmmm..." Connor hummed his agreement.

We spent a good amount of time in the tower's top floor before heading down to visit the gift shop.

We browsed the post cards, key chains, mugs, and other tourist knickknacks, marveling at the things that people would spend their money on in order to remember something so unforgettable. Connor made his way over to the far side of the shop while I checked out the selection of books.

I slid my forefinger across the spine of a title that stood out from the others. The title suggested that the book recounted the harrowing stories of the many unhappy souls that had leapt willingly to their deaths from the edge of the natural wonder.

My breath sounded loud in my ears, and panic's sharp heels returned to dance across my chest. I looked around and saw that Connor was occupied with something on the other side of the shop. I pulled the book from the shelf and held it in both hands, hefting its weight and checking the number of pages. It was far too thick a volume when taking into account its miserable contents, and I wanted to buy it just so that I could burn it that night by the side of the road, somewhere on the drive back to Flagstaff.

Instead, I flipped through it, allowing terrible images to fill my head. Not all of the stories were of suicides. Many of them detailed plane crashes, accidents, lost hikers, and even murder, all at the Grand Canyon. It was a depressing but fascinating piece of work. The thought occurred to me that had I seen the book during my visit with Ella in February, I might have bought and read through it in a matter of days with gruesome interest.

I replaced the book, a shudder in my shoulders as I did. I caught up with Connor on the other side of the shop and together we exited into the sunlight. I could sense that both of us were wondering how to best complete our journey, giving it an ending moment worthy of the love and emotions that had triggered it.

We followed a path to the rim and stood beside each other in silence, watching a single crow circling overhead.

Chapter 88: April 2009

"Dad, where does Jared live?"

Shame warmed my ears as Dad gave me directions to Jared's house; my little brother had been living on a street that I passed every day.

"Are you going over there now?" Dad asked.

"Yeah, I am in the car, I'll be there in a minute. When are you coming over?"

"I'll be there in about an hour. I have to run to the post office and the bank first," he answered.

"I hope he is packed, ready, and eager to go," I said.

"He'd better be, he agreed to this!" Dad protested.

"Yes, but he was drunk last night, and he might not even remember calling you, let alone agreeing to commit himself to the psyche ward," I warned, as I pulled onto Jared's street.

"Well, as far as I am concerned, this is his last shot, he's run out of options," Dad said.

"But he has to want the help for the help to work," I countered.

"If he gets arrested again for DUI he'll sober up whether he wants to or not," Dad threatened.

"See you in an hour," I said, then hung up without a goodbye, unable to stomach any more of my father's voice.

Jared had drunk-dialed Mom and Dad the night before, angry, depressed, confused, and wanting to kill himself. He had cried, cursed, and shouted, resisting their desperate pleas that he get help, but in the end he had agreed to commit himself to the local mental health unit. Dad and I had planned on meeting at Jared's house that morning in order to take him there.

Jared came to the door, a cigarette on the go. He was barefoot, wearing jeans and a tee shirt that would have fit me in the ninth grade.

"So, how're you doing?" I asked carefully.

"Well, I've been drinking, so I feel really good!" my little brother responded.

My stomach soured and my chest tightened. Jared laughed at my obvious discomfort, the cigarette bouncing between his lips. A small part of me wanted to tear it from his mouth and grab him by the throat, the violence of my reaction shocking him into reality.

I ignored the impulse, choosing to instead follow him through the breezeway and out to the back porch. A comfortable silence fell upon us, as if we had already finished the conversation we were about to have. I watched him staring out across the back yard, sour smoke billowing around his head like a physical manifestation of the heavy thoughts wafting through his mind. I marveled that in spite of the cigarettes, booze, and depression, my little brother retained a measure of his status as a beautiful creature. I had always felt fat and ugly in comparison to Jared.

Two cigarettes into our comfortable silence, Jared spoke.

"Are you going to make me go to the hospital?"

I cleared my throat and leaned forward, resting my forearms on the porch railing. The weathered wood was hot and threatened splinters.

"No one can make you do anything you don't want to do," I admitted.

"What will you do if I don't go?" Jared asked, a hint of challenge in his voice.

I sighed heavily, instantly regretting the direct imitation of our mother. I waited a moment before speaking, in order to let the sound scatter skyward with the smoke from Jared's third cigarette. "Jared, you have to want their help for it to work. To go just because other people will be disappointed in you if you don't is worthless. No one can do this for you, no one can wish or take away your sadness, and no one else can force you to be happy."

Silence followed the words of wisdom that I wanted desperately to apply in my own life but had only just begun to understand.

I had lost count of how many cigarettes Jared smoked by the time Dad arrived. To his credit, Dad didn't demand that Jared immediately jump in the car. The three of us stood on the back porch discussing Jared's limited options for some time. Dad had been on the phone with the hospital that morning, and they had suggested that Jared come in of his own free will, and sign himself into their program for at least a few days.

After what must have been an entire pack of menthols, Jared agreed to give the program a chance. Dad waited in the kitchen while I followed Jared into his bedroom to help him pack a bag. The room was functional to the point of depressing. Devoid of the comics, artwork, action figures, and hobbies that he had pawned for money to buy booze, it seemed more like a metaphor for Jared's life than his living space.

There was a card table in one corner of the room, and on it sat a partially assembled model, the only hint of the Jared I used to know. I picked up the box and looked at the cover. The finished product would be a replica of a Boba Fett's space ship from "Star Wars: The Empire Strikes Back."

"I haven't built a model since I was in high school," I remarked.

"I'm building it to keep my hands and mind busy. When I concentrate on it, I don't think about booze," Jared explained.

I put the box down on the table, next to a juice glass that was more than half full of the brown, gut-rotting liquid.

"Does it work?"

"Maybe you can help me with the next piece, I can't figure out how it fits," Jared suggested, ignoring my question and handing me the instructions.

263

He showed me which step he was having trouble with, handed me the problem piece, and turned to start packing his bag for the hospital.

I reviewed the instructions, then picked up the model, turning it and the piece in my hand, trying to make sense of how they were supposed to fit together. After a couple minutes I shrugged and put them back on the card table.

"That is weird, there is no way for that piece to go where the instructions say it does, and I don't think you're going to be able to finish the model without it," I admitted.

"I need one last drink," Jared said, looking to me for the okay.

"Whatever," I replied, withholding approval and condemnation at the same time.

Jared scooped up the glass and emptied it faster than I could drink the same amount of water. He set the empty glass down on the nightstand, and walked across the room to his closet. I watched as he pulled some clothes off their hangers, then threw them on the bed beside his backpack. I picked up a shirt and folded it.

Jared stopped rummaging in the closet and turned to face me. A sudden quiet fell over us both, filling the room. Jared started shaking as if he were cold, and his eyes widened with fright. After a long moment something inside him gave way, and he collapsed against me, his arms reaching around me for support.

"I am so scared..." he cried, his voice like that of a little boy afraid of the monsters under his bed.

I held him in my arms, his slender frame trembling against my chest.

"I know you are, I know you are," I whispered into his hair.

"I love you, Matthew."

I hugged him tighter, as if my strength could somehow cross over from my body into his.

"I love you too, Jared."

Chapter 89: October 2009

The crow continued to circle overhead. I watched it glide on invisible currents, making subtle adjustments with its wings to stay on course. I tried not to wax poetic, but I couldn't help it, I was jealous. To swoop, climb, and glide on the wind, ignorant of schedules, wireless signals, and emotions was to me, in that moment, the most appealing thing in the world. I wanted to leap into the air and stay there, circling high above the Earth.

Jealousy took a sudden, sharp turn into anger. *Why was such a gift wasted on a shiny black bird that lived on a diet of garbage and carrion? Did it even notice the beauty below it?*

Chapter 90: April 2009

The long, frightened hug from Jared overwhelmed me. My heart had felt a crushing weight at the sight, sound, and feel of my little brother so overtaken by panic and fear. I had caught a glimpse of his hours alone in that sleazy motel, during what he thought were to be his final moments on Earth.

And yet, moments later, I had abandoned him. The ride to the hospital was sure to be filled with tension, fear, and panic, but I had bowed out, leaving Jared to take it alone with Dad.

"I will check in on you as soon as I can. Be strong and get better. I love you, Jared," I had said after another long hug beside Dad's car.

Jared nodded, then climbed into the passenger seat and closed the door. Dad started the car, and I waved as the mini-van left the driveway.

My little brother was once again someone else's responsibility.

I went home, hoping that Ella would be there, but she had already left for lunch with some girlfriends. I stood alone in the kitchen with Jared's nearly empty bottle of booze in one hand, my car keys in the other. The memory of Jared's collapse sent me to my knees, and soon I was curled into a ball on the kitchen floor. I stayed there for the better part of an hour, the bottle in my hand, my body shaking with sobs brought on by a heavy mix of sadness and guilt.

After a heavy dose of self-loathing, I calmed down, sat up, and called Ella.

She picked up on the first ring. The sobs returned at the sound of her sweet voice.

"I'm so sad," I cried into her ear. The bottle sat on the floor between my legs.

"What happened? Matthew, talk to me, what happened?" An unexpected, uncontrollable thrill passed through me at the panic in Ella's voice.

267

This must be what Jared wants, to know that someone cares enough to panic at the thought of his misfortune..."Jared..." I managed to whimper.

"Oh..."

"He is so scared, and I am so scared for him."

"Me too." There were tears in Ella's reply.

"No matter how long he lives, he will always have to fight this overpowering sadness. He is so lonely and afraid. What kind of life is that?"

"It's not a life, it's a prison," Ella said.

Chapter 91: October 2009

I barely noticed when Connor took the camera from my hand and walked away.

As if being sucked down by some invisible whirlpool of wind, the bird circled both tighter and lower with each complete revolution. I watched as its conical decent brought it down even with the rim. It leveled out and began to widen its gliding circles, coming ever closer to the edge where I stood.

What do you want? The question that both Connor and I had asked earlier remained.

I looked around and began to feel stupid. There were other crows, and dozens of people all around. Why should this single, circling crow be anything other than a hungry bird waiting for me to drop the remnants of a hot dog on the ground?

I don't know what to make of you. Am I missing the obvious, or am I making something out of nothing?

I looked skyward, my thoughts on the verge of becoming a prayer. I felt silly and dramatic. Had I actually expected an answer?

Chapter 92: May 2009

Jared was released after spending just four days inside the mental health unit, in spite of Mom and Dad's hope that they would keep him longer. After years of listening to my parents dismiss depression as weakness, therapy as useless, and medication as a crutch, it was strange to see them angry at the hospital's refusal to provide more help for Jared. The irony was not lost on me.

No matter their personal fallacies, Mom and Dad meant well in their pleas that Jared be allowed to stay longer. They wanted him to sober up and get into the habit of taking his meds before being released. They believed that left to his own devices, Jared would most likely relapse within a few days, if not hours. I pointed out that if he lived with them, they could better monitor his behavior, but they resisted that idea.

After his release, Jared went back to living at his friend's house nearby. Although I drove past his street every day, I limited my contact with Jared to the occasional phone call. Our conversations did much to push aside the guilt I felt for avoiding him. I was encouraging, expressing my belief that he could fight off the sadness so long as he kept himself busy.

"Get a job, make new friends, and keep busy when you are at home. Find a hobby that will keep your mind preoccupied." I dispensed the advice with confidence, as if I had long ago put it to the test in my own life and come out a believer.

It wasn't that I didn't believe in my own advice, it was that I didn't believe that it would work for Jared. I had tried for years to push away self-doubt, regret, and sadness with preoccupations and distractions, and had only enjoyed limited success. Making good friends was difficult when you hated yourself, and I had learned that true happiness would not come from a job, or from filling your time with hobbies.

Jared suffered the same self-loathing that I had started to overcome, but being a gay alcoholic in a self-righteous family had exponentially decreased Jared's chances of winning the day.

270

At the end of every conversation, I added the obligatory offer to come running to Jared's aide, any time of the day or night.

All he had to do was call.

Chapter 93: October 2009

I turned away from the circling crow. Connor had returned to my side. He looked as lost as I felt.

"Are you ready?" I asked.

"No, but let's do it," Connor sighed.

Together we walked back to the parking lot.

"I thought we'd just drive the road, looking for a good spot," I suggested.

"Whatever..."

As we approached the car, I looked around.

"What?" Connor wondered aloud.

"No crow," I answered.

"Hmmm," Connor nodded.

We drove out of the parking lot, taking a right turn onto the Southern Rim Road.

Connor put on some music. I looked across the sky at the tall white cloud of smoke and wondered just how far away the forest fire raging beneath it was.

Jared got a job at a pet store, which I took as a sign that he was getting better. He expressed an affection for his co-workers, not because they were nice, or because they were new best friend material, but because they were weird like him. He claimed that each one of them was like a character in a sad, but funny book about life as a crazy person.

Every time we spoke on the phone, I told Jared that I would stop by and take him out to lunch sometime soon. A few weeks passed, and I had still not made good on my promise. There were too many reasons to drive past his street and head for home. I was living the dream with my beautiful wife and our three children, and the thought of Jared's personal mess disrupting all that I had at last achieved scared me.

One day, however, I was in an exceptional mood, having finished work by mid-morning. I decided it was time to check in on Jared, and see if he wanted to go to an early lunch. As I approached the house, Jared stepped out onto the screened-in breezeway.

"Hey," Jared said. He lit up a cigarette and waved for me to follow him.

We walked out to the back porch, where Jared turned and nodded his head upwards towards the roof. I looked up to see a shirtless Connor sitting on a blanket. A cigarette hung from his lips, and he was flipping me off with both his middle fingers.

I hadn't seen Connor in six months. During that time I had barely given him a few moments of thought, all of them dark and menacing. I had written my youngest brother off as lost; he had proved himself to be a selfish individual that held little regard for the feelings of others. I had hardened my heart in preparation for the day when I might see him again.

Connor smiled, and then laughed. It wasn't a mean and insulting laugh, but a silly laugh. I looked at Jared, and he shrugged his shoulders.

"Don't ask me, the kid is weird."

273

I looked back at Connor. He had pulled on his shirt and was climbing down to the porch. I had yet to say a word. My body, heart, and mind were still processing Connor's presence, readying for fight or flight, whichever proved to be the most prudent.

He crossed the distance between us in a couple of steps, and surprised me with a brief but solid hug. My arms went around him in an automatic response. The embrace ended quickly, and I watched as Connor picked up a guitar from a deck chair, then left the porch for a hammock strung between two tree stumps in the yard. In another move that surprised me, he sat down in the hammock and began to strum some chords, all of them making musical sense.

"What the hell? When did you learn to play the guitar?" I asked, finding my voice.

"I taught myself over the past year or so. It's easy Matthew, you should try it," he replied, his words carrying a happy encouragement that I had not expected.

"Yeah right, I took lessons, and I sucked. How did you teach yourself?" I walked over to watch him play.

"It's easy. I have learned a lot from watching online videos of people playing covers. I just copied their hand movements. It's easy." He finished the song and lit another cigarette.

"Maybe someday. Isabel is taking lessons now, and has both my guitars in her room," I said, dismissing the possibility that I could learn to play guitar.

"I'll be right back," Jared called out from the porch, before disappearing inside.

I turned back to Connor in the hammock. "Is he drunk?"

"No."

"Are you living here now?"

"Just visiting. My manager made me use some vacation time. I have been here for a few days, and might go home tomorrow. I can't take being around him for too long. It gets to be annoying after a while, you know?"

I nodded in understanding, relieved that even Connor had a threshold when it came to time spent with Jared. I felt a tad less guilty for living so close but staying so far away.

Jared came back out, a fresh cigarette hanging from his lips.

"You guys hungry? Lunch is on me," I offered.

Chapter 95: October 2009

I pulled over at the next parking lot and we climbed out of the car for a look. There were people everywhere, sitting, standing, climbing on rocks, and taking photos of each other with the Canyon as a backdrop. I wondered how many of the photos would be sent out as Christmas cards at the end of the year.

Connor walked ahead of me, camera in hand. He looked as alone and defeated as I felt.

We walked out to the edge and sat down, our feet dangling hundreds of feet above the ground.

"This spot would be good, but there are too many people. Let's keep looking," I said eventually.

Connor agreed, and we made our way back to the car.

Chapter 96: May 2009

"The anus is the new vagina."

I took a bite of my cheeseburger and raised an eyebrow at Connor's announcement.

"It's true; most girls think that guys won't like them unless they are willing to do anything and everything. It's so stupid." Connor took a bite of his chicken.

"Um, okay." I looked at Jared for an explanation. He offered me nothing but a shrug.

Connor had a lot to say about women, and all of it demonstrated to me that he wanted nothing more than true and happy love, but didn't know how to find it. The biggest issue I could see with Connor ever finding a soul mate was that the woman he wanted didn't exist and never would. His perfect woman was an impossible blend of personality traits and never-aging looks that couldn't be hoped for, even with years of genetic experimentation that would embarrass a Nazi scientist.

During Connor's rant, Jared ate much more than I did, and I found that encouraging. Had he been drinking heavily, he would have merely picked at his food.

We finished our meal and made our way out to my car. I drove us back to Jared's and parked in the driveway.

"You leaving?" Jared asked.

"No, I can stick around for a while." I was not about to put an end to what had already proved to be the most pleasant time the three of us had spent together in years.

We pulled some chairs out of the garage and sat in a circle of three on the driveway. Jared and Connor lit up their after-lunch cigarettes. I sipped at my soda refill.

The conversation from lunch shifted into a deeper discussion about Connor's girl troubles. Jared made no secret of his disdain for

Connor's latest ex-girlfriend, a fellow employee that had dropped a large pile of excrement all over Connor's affections. The fallout had been so bad that Connor's manager had demanded that he take some time off to decompress. It was touching to witness Jared's protective anger when talking about his little brother, and the fact that Connor had run to Jared in search of support was for me a bittersweet reminder of the bond they would share forever.

I felt for Connor and his troubles. It didn't matter that a healthy portion of them could be blamed on so many poor decisions he had made over the years. I knew what it was to take a risk, allow yourself to become vulnerable, only to have your heart broken. Connor came off as cocky and self-confident, but under the display hid a lonely boy who wanted to love, and to be loved.

A comfortable silence wrapped up the topic of Connor's woes. Smoke wandered overhead, while caffeine and nicotine raced through our systems. I was afraid to break the silence and risk ruining the peaceful moment, but I had something that I had to say.

"Jared, I am sorry for not coming to get you," I said. A bird chirped in a nearby tree, giving me an excuse to look away and hide my shame.

"I know you are," Jared replied.

"No, I mean it, I am really sorry. I know that riding alone with Dad must have been terrible, and I should have been there for you. I am so sorry." I looked at Jared, knowing that my apology meant nothing if I could not look him in the eye while giving it.

"It did suck," he acknowledged.

"I wanted to go get you by myself, but I chickened out and didn't. When Dad finally called and asked if I was ready to go with him, the thought of spending three days in the car with him scared the hell out of me, so I told him that I couldn't because of work," I explained, feeling unforgiveable.

"Matthew, it's okay. I understand. Hell, I would have done the same thing. I forgive you," Jared offered.

"I'm also sorry for being a dick to both of you for so long," I said, looking from Jared to Connor.

"You have been a dick," Connor agreed.

"I know, and I am sorry," I repeated, my head dropping in shame.

"Why were you such a dick?" Jared asked.

"Because I wanted you to be the brothers that I hoped you'd be. You weren't living the lives that I had always thought you would, and that didn't fit with my vision of our perfect, eternal family," I answered.

"Sounds like you wanted to be Dad," Connor suggested, half a joke to his tone.

"You're right, I was like Dad, and I am sorry," I said, looking up at my brothers.

"Matthew, you hung out with Dad all the time when we were kids, of course you were going to be like him," Jared offered, concern in his voice.

"I know. I sometimes wonder why I spent so much time in his shadow. I think I was hoping he would suddenly tell me that he loved me, and that I was awesome," I admitted.

"Yeah right. That's never going to happen." Jared flicked his cigarette onto the lawn.

"Since we are talking about what a dick you are I have to ask you something..." Connor paused, as if expecting me to bolt.

"Go ahead, this is very therapeutic for me, I can take it," I said, believing every word.

"Why did you go with Dad and the other crazy Mormons to protest gay marriage at the statehouse?" The look on Connor's face seemed to extend a challenge my way.

"To be honest, I am glad that I did," I choked back my emotions with a long pull on my soda before continuing. "I went because I

279

didn't know how I felt about it. Ella and I decided it was a good idea for me to go and see what it was all about," I explained.

"I was so surprised when I heard that you went. It really hurt," Jared said.

My little brother's words encouraged me. As poorly as I had treated him over the years, he had still thought it unlike me to demonstrate against who he was.

"Well, like I said, I am glad I went, because I learned a lot from the experience. I was embarrassed to see how men that I respected acted that day, especially Dad. When two gay guys walked past us, he pulled his legs up underneath him and moved back into his seat so they wouldn't brush against him. He muttered that he didn't want to 'get it on him.'" I shook my head at the memory of my father's bigotry.

"What the hell? Did he really do that?" Connor leapt from his chair in anger.

Jared said nothing. He just stared glass-eyed at the ground, as if defeated.

"He did. But that wasn't all. One of the men from church jumped up and booed at one of the gay men while he was speaking. I got up and left after that. I had seen enough," I said quietly.

"If you have seen enough, why do you still go to church?" Connor continued his bitter line of questioning.

I took a deep breath and held it for a moment.

"To be honest, there have been times that I wanted to run from the building and never come back," I admitted.

Jared closed his eyes and nodded.

"Not to sound corny, but I love the gospel. And I don't mean man's interpretation of it, but the raw, unfiltered teachings of Jesus. I would never have changed my attitude without his example of loving everyone unconditionally," I said with feeling.

"But what about people like Mom and Dad, and Becky? They go to church, but they don't seem to love unconditionally, and they don't seem to be very happy," Jared countered.

"What can I say? They read the same scriptures, go to the same church, and believe in the same God that I do, but I don't feel the way they do, not anymore. They'll figure it out one day. As for being happy, I don't know, Mom and Dad have every truth that they will ever need to live a happy life together, but most of the time it's like they don't want to," I replied, doing my best to answer without sounding self-righteous.

"And Becky?" Connor asked.

"I have no idea who Becky is or what she is thinking, and I've given up trying to figure her out. But it's like you told me, Jared; she's my sister. I still love her, even though it's hard to like her," I said.

Jared opened his eyes and leaned forward in his chair, as if to emphasize what he was about to say. "All I know is that there are a lot of Mormons that judged me, and they are all hypocrites like Dad and Mom, because they are far from perfect themselves."

"You're right, and I was one of them. But my life got a whole lot easier to live once I decided to try leaving the judging up to God. I look at it this way; the gospel is perfect, but the people trying to live it are not. That's not an excuse; everyone will have to account for his or her own actions. I'm just glad I'm not the one that has to sort it all out in the end," I admitted, my proclamation coming to a close.

In spite of their own misgivings, Jared and Connor seemed to accept my sincere explanation. It felt good to be heard.

I imagined that in that moment, they were both feeling the same way.

Chapter 97: October 2009

"We need to avoid the parking lots, there are too many people and cameras," Connor suggested after several failed attempts at finding the perfect spot to end our journey.

"Yeah, you're right. We need to just pull over and walk into the trees until we find a secluded spot along the edge," I agreed.

We drove the rim road, looking for a place to park the car without arousing suspicion.

As difficult as our search for the perfect spot was proving to be, finding it would be the easy part.

Chapter 98: May 2009

"So, how are you doing, Jared?" The three of us seemed to be whipping up an emotional three-egg omelet, and we had yet to break any of Jared's eggs. My question was a calculated risk.

"Well, the meds make it hard to be sad, and that sucks," he joked.

"But you want to be happy, don't you?" I asked.

"Yes, but I want to be happy because I am happy, not because of some pills," Jared argued.

"The pills are there so that you can get to a point where you are able to find that happiness," I replied, as if I knew anything about anti-depressants. I couldn't dispute Jared's desire to be genuinely happy, but felt that the meds were a starting point.

He agreed with a shrug and said, "I just want to find someone that loves me no matter what. Someone that loves doing something, anything, other than sit around or nap after work before going to bed early," Jared repeated his need-for-love mantra.

Connor nodded in agreement and the voiced his own desires for love. "I want someone who wants to be with me more than anyone else. I just want to know that there is someone that I can reach out and touch at any time."

Jared lit another cigarette. I watched his first puff of smoke fill the air above his head and remembered that he had once told me that the first drag often felt to him like the rippling sensations of an orgasm.

"I want what you have," Jared said, pointing at me with his cigarette.

"Me too," Connor agreed, pulling a cigarette from Jared's pack.

Jared's eyes locked in on mine as he continued. "You have a hot wife that loves you no matter how stupid you are, the coolest kids I know, a nice house, a business of your own, a good car…"

"It's true, Matthew. I would love to have everything that you have," Connor said, blowing a cloud of smoke out the corner of his mouth.

A long silence followed. I looked away from my little brothers, searching the trees for that noisy bird.

After a moment of thought gathering, I turned back to face them.

"It took me a long time to figure out that what I have is special. Ella and I made a terrible mess at the start of our life together, and we took it out on each other for years. Well, I mostly took it out on her. I hate now who I was then. I wasted so much time being angry and treating her like shit." I leaned forward in my chair and picked up my soda, taking a sip. The ice had melted, watering down the flavor.

I continued my confession. "I spent years being angry about a past that I couldn't change. I said and did terrible things. I felt so worthless and miserable, and I searched for ways to pull Ella down to my own level of self-loathing. I was biting and cold, cynical and bitter, and I betrayed her so many times I get sick inside thinking about it."

"Why did you stay together if you hated each other?" Jared asked.

"There were times we came close to splitting, but we didn't want to give up on what we knew we could become. We knew that we loved each other, and that if we could just make it through the bad, we would be alright one day," I answered.

"How bad did it get?" Connor asked.

"Pretty bad," I admitted. "She threw a plate of food at my head once, and I punched a hole in a closet door one night because I wanted to hit her so much. I spent a lot of nights driving around with the windows open, shouting and pounding my fist against the seats while she cried alone in bed. We once went a full week without talking to each other." I sat back in my chair, winded at the revelation of so many bad memories.

"Wow," Connor exclaimed, his eyes wide with wonder at the truth about my marriage.

"Yep, we were pretty pathetic. Having Noah helped. Things calmed down for a while after each one of the kids was born, but the bad times always came back. We would fight after the kids went to bed,

284

usually until two or three in the morning, sometimes until the sun came up. We even fought on vacations, when we were trying to get away and forget all our problems. It was so much work, being so unhappy."

"Damn! So, do you guys still fight now?" Jared was captivated by my truths, and eager for a happy ending to the sad story.

"No, not really. We have moments like any couple will have, but we never fight like we used to. We looked at our marriage and saw that we were just like Mom and Dad. That was a scary awakening, and we had a 'do or die' moment. If we didn't make some major changes we were going to be unhappy for the rest of our lives," I said.

"What did you have to change?" Jared asked.

"I had to start letting go of things beyond my control. I had to live in the present, and stop being so cynical and biting with my comments. I made a practice of complimenting Ella, and expressing the good things that I felt about her. It was all in there, it always had been, but I had buried it under resentment and self-loathing. I realized that I was becoming Dad; my kids were afraid of me, and my treatment of them put them in danger of having the same low self-esteem that I had. I didn't want that for them," I answered.

"And Ella, did she have to change?" Connor asked.

"Oh yes, she was not perfect either. She admitted that she didn't respect me, and that she had not only taken me for granted, but had dismissed my feelings and insecurities, and had even mocked me for having them. She didn't value me, and acted as if she were better than me. She believed that I wouldn't dare leave her because I would never find anyone as good as her," I said, feeling both regret and liberation as the truth poured out of me.

"And everyone thought you guys were so happy and perfect," Jared said, a hint of relief in his words.

"Yep, we hid it well. I told Dad and Mom a few things in the beginning, but they scoffed, as if we couldn't possibly have anything to complain about. Ella has never shared a close enough bond with her own parents to talk to about heavy things like that, so they knew nothing about it. We had to fix it on our own."

"Well, you still have everything we both want, even if it took a long time for it to be perfect," Connor confirmed, flicking his cigarette butt into the grass.

"It was worth it. And I wouldn't say perfect, not yet. I still have to figure out how to let go of everything I hate about Mom, Dad, and Becky," I admitted.

"Good luck with that," Jared said.

"If you figure it out, let us know," Connor added.

"Well, I have to take a nap before work," Jared said through a yawn.

"Yeah, I have to get going. I told Ella five hours ago that I was just taking you to lunch." I stood, stretching my arms into the air with a groan.

Jared did the same, and then hugged me goodbye.

I felt closer to him than I had in years.

"Hey, when you are feeling better, let's take a road trip out to the Grand Canyon," I suggested.

"That would be cool, let's do it." He turned and walked into the house.

Connor and I watched him go.

"This was good. I am glad I stopped by," I said.

"Me too," Connor agreed, standing to say goodbye.

We hugged, and it felt good. I climbed in my car and headed for home.

My happy home.

Chapter 99: October 2009

There were no parked cars or people in sight, and no parking lot or marked viewpoints to attract them. I pulled the little black rental car over onto the dirt, parking it far enough from the road that I could open my door without fear of it getting ripped off by a passing vehicle.

Connor and I got out and walked into the trees. There was no trail to follow, nothing to indicate that park rangers or tourists frequented the area. We pushed through a thick line of bush and trees like explorers heading into uncharted territory. After a few minutes of careful wandering, we stepped out of the forest.

Canyon and sky filled our view. Above us hung a solid expanse of unblemished blue, while below stretched a rugged landscape of earthly browns and rocky reds, much of it spotted by the green of vegetation. I held my breath and listened to nothing; the corner we had discovered was quiet and still. We could stand there for days and not once be disturbed.

My heart began to kick against my chest as I approached the rim. I walked out onto a large, pointed rock that jutted over the edge like a diving platform. I looked down over the point and into the rocky abyss below. Had the beauty of it not been so distracting, I would have found the spot terrifying.

I looked at Connor and saw the quiet agreement in his eyes.

It was the perfect site.

Chapter 100: June 2009

Jared went missing a week later.

Mom had gone to see him at work, to give him an artist pad and some pencils in the hopes that he would start drawing again. The manager of the pet store told her that Jared had failed to show up for work several times, and that he had been fired.

She tried to reach Dad, but could only leave a voicemail on his cell phone. By the time she called our house Mom was panicked.

"Ok, I will go over and check in on him," I offered, expecting to find my brother either passed out drunk in the hammock, or still awake, working his way to the bottom of a bottle.

Jared's car was not in the driveway, and no one answered my knock on the front door. I looked in the bay window of the living room. The TV was off and the furniture was empty. He wasn't passed out on the floor either.

I entered the breezeway and pounded on the side door, then listened for footsteps while looking through the kitchen window. Turning around, I noticed Jared's car through the windowed door of the garage. The skin on my arms and legs pimpled and my neck broke out in a sweat.

I crossed the breezeway, my feet moving through the thick mud of dread. My hand was heavy and slow as I reached for the doorknob. It felt cold against my skin, in spite of the summer heat. My pulse quickened as time slowed around me, and terrible images entered my head. I pushed the door open and looked inside.

The garage was too dark to see inside Jared's car. I stood in the doorway for a full minute, allowing my eyes time to adjust to the darkness, and my mind to the possibilities of what I might find.

"Don't be stupid, he's not in there," I said aloud to no one but myself.

I stepped into the garage and opened the driver side door. The car was empty. Jared was still missing, but at least he wasn't sitting dead inside his car. I walked out and checked the porch and the hammock in the back yard.

Growing desperate, I walked around to Jared's bedroom window and rapped on the glass. The curtains hung quiet and still, with enough of a gap between them to see his bed and the floor beside it. The bed was made, and the floor clear but for a laceless pair of shoes, the same pair he had worn to the mental health unit. They were a grim reminder of Jared's fragile mind and broken heart.

I walked back behind the house and over to the barn that stood in the middle of the back yard. I circled around to the big open doors and looked inside, the terrible thought that I might find Jared hanging from a rope filling my head. But the barn was empty, and in it I found no evidence of my brother or where he might have gone.

I made my way back to a collection of junk rusting at the edge of the back yard, close to the woods. Included in the hoard was a tiny old camper resting on cracked and crumbling tires. It was covered in moss and mildew, and the windows were dark with grime. I approached the camper, my body wet and warm with anxious sweat. The door was locked. I hesitated for a moment before sticking my face to one of the windows, my hands cupped over my eyes to look inside. To my great relief, the tiny space was empty.

I stood at the edge of the yard and stared into the woods for a minute before shouting my brother's name.

"Jared!"

He didn't answer, and I felt silly.

Back at my car, I called Jared's cell phone and got his voicemail.

"Jared, this is Matthew. I am at your house and you aren't here but your car is. Could you call me? Just want to make sure you are okay. Love you, bye."

I headed for home, calling Ella on the way. She was at Isabel's softball game with the boys.

"Okay, I am calling the police right now," she said after listening to my report.

"Don't you think that is a bit much? He might just be with a friend," I suggested, unwilling to admit that Jared might actually be missing.

"No, I don't. He has tried to kill himself once already, it won't hurt to call the police and find out what they recommend. Plus, they can at least keep an eye out for him while they are driving around," Ella said, her reasoning valid.

"Alright, let me know what they say. I love you," I signed off.

I called Mom to bring her up to speed. She said she would keep trying to reach Dad.

A moment after I hung up from Mom, Ella called back and told me the police were on their way to Jared's house. I got back in my car and drove over to find a police cruiser in Jared's driveway. I could see the officer standing at the side door, talking to someone inside the kitchen. Hope welled up within me; maybe Jared had been out with a friend after all, and had been dropped off moments after I left his house.

It wasn't Jared, but rather his roommate, who introduced himself as John. I shook his clammy hand, and wondered at the look of nervous surprise in his eyes. The officer's last name was Taylor. He was young, strong, and serious. I introduced myself to the two men as Jared's brother and thanked them for any help they could offer in finding him. The three of us discussed the possibilities.

John had no idea where Jared was, or why we were so concerned. He worked a second job as a bartender, so he wasn't home all that much, and wouldn't have missed Jared for some days had we not come by to search for him.

"He has been gone for days at a time before, but he always comes back," John said without concern.

"Well, since he already tried to kill himself once, we are not taking any chances," I said.

The look on John's face turned from nervous to shocked.

"Wait, what?" he stammered.

"He didn't tell you about Independence? The hospital in Portsmouth last month?" I shook my head. How could Jared have kept so much of his life a secret from a friend and roommate?

After a quick search of his room, and a second search of the property by Officer Taylor, it was clear that only Jared knew where Jared was. He hadn't returned any calls or left any hints as to where he was headed.

Or what his intentions were when he got there.

Chapter 101: October 2009

We made our way through the trees and back to the car. I popped the trunk and handed the keys to Connor. I heard the flick of his lighter, and a moment later felt the car settle as he sat in the passenger seat. I stepped out from behind the car to fill my lungs with his secondhand smoke as it drifted past me.

Back at the trunk, I opened my suitcase and pulled Jared's remote control truck out from beneath my clothes. The truck had seen better days. The plastic body was complete, but was no longer attached to the undercarriage. The faded blue paint was heavily scarred, and many of the stickers were torn. The tires were old and dry, on the verge of crumbling.

I thought back more than twenty years, to a Christmas that ranked among my top five. Dad had spent more than he could afford to buy remote control cars for Jared, Connor, and me. They weren't the cheap, pre-assembled remote control cars found on the shelves in a toy store at the mall. They were the real deal, bought from a hobby shop, assembly required.

Powerful, fast, and durable, the three cars had survived all of the jumps, crashes, rain, snow, mud, and puddles that we threw at them. They had remained in the number one slot on my list of greatest Christmas presents ever received.

Twenty years later, I held Jared's play-worn truck in my hand, and thought back to the hours spent building our remote control cars with Dad. He had been as much of a kid as we were at the time, and the fun of building them had brought us together in fits of laughter and big smiles. Not once had our father poked fun at our lack of skills when it came to tools and paintbrushes.

I closed the trunk and carried the truck around to the passenger side of the little black rental car. Connor had left his door open, one foot resting on the ground outside the car. I knelt in the shade of his open door, and placed Jared's truck gently on the ground.

Connor dialed up a song on my Ipod.

"Pass me the tape, would you?" I asked.

293

Connor handed me the roll, then settled into his seat.

The first notes of my brother's song choice sounded in my ears as I began to wrap Jared's truck with tape, joining the body to the undercarriage. My throat made a strange sound, and my vision blurred. Lyrics joined the music, and a flood of memories rushed my head.

My tape job soon complete, I set the truck down in the dirt and surveyed my work. It wasn't perfect, but it would do. I walked around to the driver's side of the car and climbed in beside Connor. I leaned back against the headrest and closed my eyes, listening as the song ended.

Chapter 102: June 2009

Come Saturday morning, Jared was still missing. Officer Taylor had checked his cell records, and found that the last call Jared had made was to his voicemail on Wednesday afternoon, a full day before Mom had gone to see him at the pet store. Jared had been at or at least near his house when he made the call, and his phone had not been active since.

His bank records showed no sign of recent withdrawals or debit card activity, and he didn't have a credit card, so there was no money trail to follow. Officer Taylor had talked to all of the local bus and taxi services, but none of them had seen Jared.

A call to Connor at work confirmed that Jared had not been down to see him, nor had he told Connor where he was going. I told Connor that I would keep him up to date on any news, and he promised to let me know if Jared showed up or reached out to him.

I was not yet convinced that this wasn't all a big mistake. My theory was that Jared just walked away from his life and all the problems surrounding it. It wasn't impossible; Ella's oldest brother, a recovering alcoholic and heavy drug user, had in the past vanished for months at a time, leaving his family to wonder where he was or if he were even alive.

On Saturday afternoon, a full forty-eight hours after Mom had called me in a panic, most of the family had gathered at Mom and Dad's house. The kids swam in the pool and played in the garden, their laughter keeping our spirits from tumbling into complete despair.

I was sitting on the front porch with Sarah when Officer Taylor called my cell.

"I had a State Trooper come to your brother's house with his search-and-rescue dog today. We spent three hours out in the woods and found nothing," he told me.

"I guess that is good news," I replied, not sure that it was in fact good.

"Well, maybe. Sometimes dogs get confused or distracted and the handler doesn't even know it. Of course, if Jared is out there, we would probably need a cadaver dog, rather than a search-and-rescue dog to find him in all the brush and undergrowth..." he paused, and the line grew thick with the severity of what he had just said, and his regret at having to say it.

"Okay, so what do we do next? How soon can we get one of those dogs out there?" I asked.

"Well, I would like to search his room again. Maybe he left a clue that we have missed. We didn't really dig around too much on Thursday. Can you meet me over there now?"

"I can be there in five minutes," I answered, already off the porch and half way to my car.

Sarah ran to catch up, and together we made the quick drive over to Jared's.

Officer Taylor was already there, waiting for us in the driveway. John let us in, and we made our way back to Jared's bedroom. Sarah and I searched through Jared's possessions under the watchful direction of Officer Taylor. There was nothing to indicate that Jared had packed a bag, left a note, or taken anything with him other than his wallet, cell phone, and keys.

Sarah sat on Jared's bed, her face a vacant grey mask. Officer Taylor stood in the center of the room, asking us questions he had already asked, and walking us through the past several days, hoping to spark some memory or detail that we had missed. Looking around for something new to search through, I noticed a small garbage can beside Jared's nightstand. I knelt down and dumped the contents onto the floor.

I peeled open a dozen scraps of paper, one after another. Most of them were random thoughts and reminders Jared had scribbled to himself. I read each of them to myself, scanning them for some hint of a note, address, or anything else that might serve as a clue. Nothing stood out or made sense of Jared's disappearance. Not until I opened the last piece of paper in the pile.

The date and time stamp on the drug store receipt were for Wednesday afternoon, the day before our search had begun. My eyes blurred as I read aloud the items purchased.

Sarah sat on Jared's bed and cried.

Chapter 103: October 2009

Connor's song ended. I sat forward and picked up the Ipod.

"This one is corny, but I don't care," I managed between tearful gasps.

"It's not corny," Connor said, his own voice strained and wet.

It was a song that I rarely listened to. The lyrics were a series of flowing, beautiful descriptions of Van Gogh's artwork, intertwined with the sad story of his wandering through a world that would never understand him. A world not meant for someone so beautiful.

I closed my eyes and let the lyrics punish me. I had failed to understand and support Jared's frantic search for happiness. In my selfishness, I had dismissed and ignored his desperate attempts to convey the overwhelming sadness that plagued his heart. I had abandoned him.

My chest heaved and my shoulders shook. I felt my hands trembling and my back twitching. Regret pulsed through me like venom, my frame shuddering from its effects. The song faded to its end. My chest continued to heave.

"Now it's Jared's turn," I heard Connor say, his voice a weak and quivering sound.

Chapter 104: June 2009

It was a quiet drive back to Mom and Dad's house. The kids had been fed, ice-creamed, and banished to watching a movie in the living room. The adults gathered around the table to eat, and to discuss what Sarah and I had learned while over at Jared's.

"We found a receipt in Jared's bedroom," I began.

Sarah began to tremble.

"It was dated Wednesday afternoon, and the only thing he bought were two bottles of sleeping pills." I stared down at my plate, tears falling into the food I hadn't touched. Ella grabbed hold of my hand.

"It seems a foregone conclusion that we will not find Jared alive," I said softly.

My mother and sisters began to cry. The sound was soft but terrible. I looked up at my father, and saw the hollow darkness of defeat in his eyes. My heart broke, and I crushed Ella's hand with the force of my grief.

The sweet and happy sounds of the children's laughter bounded in from the living room, invading the terrible moment. I got up from the table and stepped outside to call Connor.

Chapter 105: October 2009

The cascading notes of "Final Cliff Jump" thundered through the tiny speakers of the little black rental car. I closed my eyes and pictured Jared sitting at his computer, composing a song in tribute to his wish for death at the Grand Canyon. My little brother had forgotten how to hope, believing his life ruined beyond repair and unworthy of living. Even at my lowest I had never lost complete faith in my potential; I knew that I was at the very least, worth the life that I had been given.

The song ended. Connor and I sat quiet for several minutes, giving our emotions time to settle down, if only just a little bit.

"Let's do this," I sighed at last.

Connor nodded, lighting a cigarette.

I closed the windows and pulled the key out of the ignition. A good stretch was in order after the long and emotional sit down. I reached for the sky, clenched my fists, and spread my feet. Connor climbed out and did the same, a cigarette dangling from his lips. His flat white belly made a brief appearance as he touched the blue above him.

I picked Jared up from the back seat, and kicked the rear door closed. Connor scooped up Jared's remote control truck and followed me into the trees.

Back at our chosen spot, I walked out onto the rock balcony. Connor set the truck down and stood beside me.

"We could not have found a more perfect place," I whispered.

Chapter 106: June 2009

Connor was silent on the other end of the line. I had just finished telling him about the receipt for the sleeping pills, and that Jared was most likely already gone. I waited through a long silence before speaking again.

"Connor, no matter what happens, I want you to know that I love you. The five hours we shared last week was amazing, I am so glad that I got to apologize to you for being such a dick. Let's not allow anything to ruin our relationship again," I said.

"I love you too, Matthew. Don't worry; you and I are good. Nothing will change that, no matter what happens," he assured me.

I hung up after promising to call him with any news, no matter how grim.

I returned to the kitchen to find that the movie had ended, sending the kids swarming into the kitchen. Their happy, innocent faces lightened the mood and provided a welcome distraction. We sat and ate cookies as a family until it was time for bed.

The hugs goodbye lasted a little longer that night.

Ella and I headed for home. After putting the kids to bed, I wandered into our bedroom in search of a hot shower. The weight of my family's new reality overwhelmed me, and I collapsed into a heap on the floor. Ella rushed to my side, and wrapped her arms around me.

"He's out there all alone," I sobbed, my face buried in the carpet of our bedroom floor.

"I know, I know, I know," she cried softly, her body trembling against mine.

"How can we sleep? He's out there, and he's alone. We have to do something right now, we have to go out there and find him. We have to bring him home," I whimpered.

"We will, but we can't go out there now, we'll never find him in the dark. Please, Matty, please don't go out there tonight," Ella begged.

She held me until I promised that I wouldn't sneak out in the middle of the night to look for Jared. We climbed onto the bed and fell asleep in our clothes.

Morning church services were a blur. I sat through the meetings without hearing a word, images of Jared alone in the woods or wandering a dirt road in the middle of nowhere running through my head.

That afternoon I told Ella that I was done sitting around waiting for news from the police, and that I was going to search the abandoned railroad tracks that passed through the woods a half-mile from Jared's house.

We left the kids at home alone, putting Noah in charge and letting him know that we had our phones and that we would be just a few minutes away.

We drove to Jared's house and walked the tracks together. Every few minutes we would shout his name and listen for a reply that never came.

"I don't think he would go this far from the house, he would want to be found quickly," Ella repeated several times throughout our search.

Although I agreed with her, I didn't move our search any nearer to the house. I missed the denial that had ended so abruptly during our search of Jared's room the night before.

I wanted to bring Jared home, but didn't want to be the one to find him.

Chapter 107: October 2009

I held Jared tight.

"I'm so sorry that I abandoned you. I thought my life was so bad, and that I had so much to deal with that I couldn't help you. I'm sorry that you hurt so bad for so long, and that I didn't do enough for you. I should have spent more time being your brother and loving you, but I didn't. I spent too many years telling you what was wrong with your life, I wish now that I had just loved you. All you wanted was love, and it took me too long to give you mine. I was selfish, hypocritical, and wrong. Jared, I miss you so much, and I will until the day I see you again..." I paused, my breath outpaced by my emotions.

Connor reached out and grabbed my hand. I felt a surge of warm strength course through me.

"And I know that I will see you. This is not the end; we will be together again, and we will laugh, and you will be happy, and you will never be sad again. I know this." I said firmly.

I looked up at the sky and continued. "God, you'd better be listening. Please take care of my little brother Jared. He is sad, and he is lonely, and he needs love. We failed to give him enough of it here, so you need to do right by him. He is so beautiful, but he is broken. Please take care of him," I begged heaven.

Connor and I stood holding hands.

It was a comfortable silence.

Chapter 108: June 2009

Ella and I sent the kids off to school on Monday morning, then rushed to the local hardware store to buy garden gloves, bug spray, and orange marking tape. We planned to search all day if we had to, and we weren't coming out of the woods behind Jared's house until we had found him.

Driving back through town, we saw Officer Taylor waving cars through some construction. We pulled over to get an update on his search for Jared. Being a good policeman, he clued in on the fact that we were wearing long pants, long sleeves, and hiking boots on a hot and humid summer day.

"I can't tell you not to go out and look for him, but I wish you wouldn't," he said.

"Well, we have to do something; my parents need their son to come home," I said.

"I understand, I would want to bring an end to my parent's suffering too," he replied.

"We know that you are doing everything you can, we just want to do something to help our family. We are all going crazy with waiting," I told him.

"If you find anything, if you find him, please call us immediately, okay?" Officer Taylor reminded as I shook his hand and turned to go.

"We promise," I said, walking back to our car.

We made the short drive over to Jared's. I pulled into the driveway but left the car running and the air conditioning on high.

"Would you say a little prayer?" I asked Ella.

"Of course," she agreed, taking my hand in hers.

We bowed our heads, and she began to pray.

"Dear Father in Heaven, we need thy help this morning. Jared is missing, and we need to find him and bring him home. We love him and we miss him, and we want him to find the peace he so desperately needs. Please take care of him, and help him to never be lonely again. And please bless our family. We are hurting and sad, and we need thy spirit to be with us. We pray for these things in the name of Jesus Christ, Amen."

"Amen," I said, and squeezed her hand in thanks.

"Ready?" My sweet wife asked.

I wondered how I had ever been so terrible to such a loving creature.

"Yep. Let's do it."

Chapter 109: October 2009

"My life was getting better, and yours was getting darker. I was making new friends, and you saw that I was moving on without you. I'm sorry that I didn't bring you with me..." Connor paused, his voice tripping over a sob.

I squeezed his hand, and hoped that I was returning the strength that he had passed to me earlier.

"I-" he sputtered.

"I was with friends the night you texted me, and I was having a good time. I didn't want to deal with your problems. I should have talked to you, but I didn't. I'm so sorry, Jared. I wasn't there for you. You were always there for me, and I failed you. I love you, and I miss you," Connor cried.

A warm wind blew up from below, billowing softly around us.

Chapter 110: June 2009

"Matty, come here!" There is alarm in Ella's voice.

I sprint across the few hundred feet of woods that separate us, jumping logs, dodging branches, stumbling over rocks.

"What? What do you see?"

"I don't know, it looks like clothes, but I am not looking again." Ella has turned to face me. She is pointing back over her shoulder.

"Ok, ok, I'll look," I say, passing her in a hesitant rush.

Stopping, I scan the forest floor. I take in the brown of dead leaves, the green of clustered ferns, and the clear water of a small stream. At the far edge of the water, I spot something large and blue lying on the ground. It does not belong in the woods. The whole of its shape does not make any sense, and before my mind can work out what it is, I jerk my head up and seek out the blue sky peeking through cracks in the canopy of green above us. My breathing is faster now, and I close my eyes for just a moment.

Mosquitoes buzz in my ears. Beads of sweat slide down my back. I lower my head and open my eyes. My vision clouds. I am looking at something just thirty feet away, but I cannot tell what it is. There is a break in the circuits connecting my eyes to my mind. I feel as though an auto-protection sequence has been initiated inside my head.

"Is it him?" Ella's tone is soft and pleading.

"I don't know, my eyes won't focus." I take a step forward, and try to zoom in on the blue blur that doesn't belong, but my mind is thick and sluggish, slow to react to my commands.

I take another step forward.

"Don't go any closer," Ella warns. In the corner of my muddled vision, I see her arm reach out to stop me.

"I won't, I just can't-" My vision snaps into focus without warning, and I know that I am looking at a blue blanket. One corner is folded up over something.

307

Shoes. They are shoes, sticking out from under the folded corner of the blue blanket. The feet are crossed at the ankles, the corner of the blanket lying over them, creating the odd form that made no visual sense. My mind works cautiously as my eyes scan upwards. The puzzle's picture takes form with each new piece that snaps into place.

More blue, but not the blanket.

Jeans. I move up the legs, then stop and focus at the waist.

A black belt, two rows of silver grommets running around its length.

I know that belt.

I pause to summon strength I don't have. All the strength in the world will never be enough. My eyes dart across the green striped shirt and up to his face.

"No!" I am shouting long and loud. I feel weak, and reach out, grabbing hold of a nearby tree.

"It's him. It's him. It's him." No longer shouting, I whisper, stuck in slow motion.

"Oh, no," Ella begins to weep. She reaches for me as I take a faltering step closer to him.

"Don't go over there," she pleads. Her fingers grip my sleeve.

I turn to her. I am looking for help, for answers, for clarity. My mouth is open, and I begin to wail.

"Oh, Jared, why? Why? Why?" I am shouting, sobbing, gasping. A great shift has befallen me, sending me to my knees. My face hits dirt. I have no strength, no control. I look up and stare across the forest floor at the blue blanket.

At the belt.

There is a tightness in my chest with each anxious, life-giving breath. Strange, feral, sorrowful sounds are coming from my throat. I look down at the ground, away from him. Through blurry eyes, I see long strands of spit dripping from my lips, and as I watch them coat the dirt beneath me, I marvel that I don't care.

My mind leaps across time. From one memory to another, a rapid, fitful slide show of the past thirty-six years flashes before me. I am trembling, weak, and defeated.

Something warm glides across my shoulder, a reminder that I am not alone. Ella is with me, and I thank God that she is here with me in this terrible moment.

I can hear her whimpers, and feel her body shaking. She kneels beside me, her hand sliding up and down my back. She has put it there to connect with me, to comfort me, but also to hold me in place. She knows me. She knows that I want to run over there, to scoop him into my arms. To hold him. To fix him. I lift my head up, and my knees press harder into soil from the effort. My arms are limp and useless, my chest is heaving. I look over at him once more, and another growl escapes my throat.

Ella has her pink phone against her ear. I can hear her speaking, but her words make no sense.

I fall forward, and my forehead touches the earth again. A deep breath, and I begin to wail. I am surrounded by darkness as the whine of a distant siren blends with mine.

My brother Jared lies dead on a blue blanket in the woods.

Chapter 111: October 2009

I kneel beside Jared's remote control truck. Connor is beside me. He watches as I tape the bottle of Jared's ashes to the truck bed.

I pick up the truck. Connor pulls the cork from the mouth of the bottle.

"I love you Jared!" Connor and I shout together as I heave the truck into the air.

Jared and his truck climb into the blue for just a moment, then drop into the Canyon below. An updraft lifts a long trail of Jared's ashes into the sky above us.

"Jared!" I gasp in sudden reaction to the beautiful sight.

We watch as Jared swirls overhead before disappearing on the wind. After a moment, Connor and I lie down on our bellies and look into Jared's corner of the Grand Canyon below. We can't stop crying.

Connor reaches out and takes my hand in his.

We stay there on the rock for a long time before standing to leave.

I hug my brother. "I love you Connor, and I always will," I tell him.

"I love you too, Matthew."

I pull out the camera and take a photo of the spot. Later that evening I will attach it to an email addressed to Ella. The subject line will read "Jared's Corner of the Grand Canyon." In the body I will write, "Please know this: I love you above all else."

And I do. Thank-you, Jared.

75273595R00172

Made in the USA
Middletown, DE
04 June 2018